D1566333

The Relevance of Higher Education

The Relevance of Higher Education

Exploring a Contested Notion

Edited by Timothy L. Simpson

LEXINGTON BOOKS
Lanham • Boulder • New York • Toronto • Plymouth, UK

Published by Lexington Books
A wholly owned subsidiary of The Rowman & Littlefield Publishing Group, Inc.
4501 Forbes Boulevard, Suite 200, Lanham, Maryland 20706
www.rowman.com

10 Thornbury Road, Plymouth PL6 7PP, United Kingdom

British Library Cataloguing in Publication Information Available

Library of Congress Cataloging-in-Publication Data

The relevance of higher education : exploring a contested notion / edited by Timothy Simpson.
pages cm
Includes bibliographical references and index.
ISBN 978-0-7391-8252-9 (cloth : alk. paper) -- ISBN 978-0-7391-8253-6 (electronic)
1. Education, Higher--Aims and objectives. 2. Education, Higher--Philosophy. I. Simpson, Timothy
(Timothy L.), editor of compilation.
LB2322.2.R448 2013
378.01--dc23
2013024262

∞™ The paper used in this publication meets the minimum requirements of American
National Standard for Information Sciences Permanence of Paper for Printed Library
Materials, ANSI/NISO Z39.48-1992.

Printed in the United States of America

Contents

Acknowledgments

This volume grew out of a deep concern with the direction of higher education in the United States, particularly an assumption that it should be relevant. It appeared that a "new" idea leading higher education policy was not "new" at all in one sense and yet "radically new" another sense. We wanted to investigate from different vantage points the relevance of higher education, understand its current meaning, examine alternative meanings, and search for what it should mean for higher education. Our hope was to provide a beginning point for renewed scholarly attention to the root assumptions guiding higher education.

If this volume is successful, it is due to the generous support of others. The Adron Doran Endowment, the Presidential Lecture Series sponsored by Morehead State University President Wayne Andrews, Dean Cathy Gunn of the College of Education, Associate Dean Stephen Lange of the School of Public Affairs and Business, Dean Scott McBride of the Caudill College of Arts, Humanities and Social Sciences as well as the Buckner and Sally S. Hinkle Endowment, and Chair David Barnett of the Department of Foundational and Graduate Studies in Education generously funded a speaker series and symposium on relevance and higher education in 2011–2012 at Morehead State University. I am grateful to the chapter authors for participating in that series and symposium with enthusiasm and a collegial spirit of inquiry and debate. I am thankful to Steve Wrinn for invaluable advice on producing an edited volume. Lexington Books and my editor, Eric Wrona, offered tremendous support for this volume for which I am much obliged. I am appreciative of Megan McKnight, my undergrad research fellow, working tirelessly for the series and symposium, and Jennifer Downey, a graduate assistant, for her superb organization and editing skills. I am especially grateful to my family, who make life a joy, for their patience as I complete this volume. Thank you Marsha, Maddy, and Ian.

Introduction

The Relevance of Higher Education

Most statements today about higher education begin with the assumption that it should be relevant. That it should be relevant, however, does not settle the matter. For relevance, to borrow from the Freudian lexicon, is an anaclitic term. That is, its significance, real may it be, depends on the power of something else that is more fundamental. As Jacques Barzun states, capturing both the significance and ambiguity of the concept, "relevance is indeed a true standard of judgment, but it does not stand by itself; it expresses a relation to something else—relevance to what? for whom? at what point?"[1] Assuming higher education should be relevant, the question emerges, relevant to what? Why? How? At what costs? And, relevant in what sense? These are some of the central questions animating this study.

There exist two sharply distinct views regarding the relevance of higher education. The first view holds as its standard the "formation of a human being possessing intellectual and moral virtue."[2] Relevant studies are "liberal and philosophical in nature" and should be "required for everyone regardless of the life he has in view."[3] The relevance of higher education on this view is not to produce useful workers, but excellent human beings.

The second view holds as its standard to prepare the student for the tasks of work life and acquaint him with the responsibilities of civic life. This view tends to oppose the former view as unnecessary and unrelated to the demands of real life and as preparation for a social order that no longer exists. Relevant studies on this latter view focus on practicality in the sense of responding to the immediate needs of the economic environment and solving social problems. The relevance of higher education on this view assumes that the student needs to be equipped for adjustment to the current environment.

Underlying these different views of the relevance of higher education, at a deeper level, there appear to be two diverse views about the relationship between higher education and society. According to the latter view, higher education is "simply an adjunct of the world and that the closer the two can be brought together, the better for both."[4] Under this conception higher education does not establish a mission incongruent with social standards, expectations and needs: instead, it establishes its mission based upon current social standards, expectations and needs and attempts to familiarize the student with them. This attitude explains the emphasis upon classes designed to promote twenty-first century skills and knowledge, create real-world problem solvers, and abandonment of traditional liberal arts (or at least their redesign of them for the twenty-first century).

The former view holds that higher education is "not simply part of the world, but a part set aside and reserved for progress in new areas of knowledge, for the attaining and demonstrating of higher standards, not simply accepting current social standards, and in general for the cultivation of excellence."[5] This view welcomes and encourages rather than deplores a certain distance between higher education and society. It believes that both higher education and society fare best by giving higher education a certain independence as well as sanctuary to carry on its work of learning free of the necessities of everyday living. This view supports the development of skills and knowledge applicable to any era. Based on these deeper views, the question arises, what should be the relationship between higher education and society? This is another central question animating this study.

If we assume that these views represent the two ends of a continuum regarding the relevance of higher education and its relationship to society, then we possess a useful lens through which to read the history of higher education in the United States. Throughout its history, higher education institutions defined themselves based on a conception of relevance and an understanding of their relationship to society. In their classic work, *Higher Education in Transition: A History of American Colleges and Universities*, John Brubacher and Willis Rudy show that the college of the colonial era defined a relevant education as satisfying local needs.[6] For example, in 1636 English colonists founded Harvard College to advance Puritan Christianity.[7] Soon after, the colonists established eight other colleges to fulfill pastoral and missionary demands, arising from a variety of Christian denominations. After the American Revolution, colonial college mandates were modified to include training of religious and civic leaders for a new nation. As an example, consider the founding of the University of Virginia by Thomas Jefferson.

After the Civil War, societal demands on higher education created new missions for institutions of higher learning. As Carol Gruber demonstrates in *Mars and Minerva*, institutional differentiation occurred during the nineteenth century as state, land-grant and research universities were founded.[8]

Their different institutional missions reflect varying, sometimes conflicting, conceptions of the notion of relevance and the relationship between higher education and society. The desire for practical, scientific knowledge led to the founding of land-grant universities after the historic 1862 Morrill Land-Grant Act, including the University of Illinois, University of California, Iowa State University, and seventy-three others. In *The Uses of the University*, Clark Kerr skillfully shows how this Act irrevocably tied state institutions of higher education to society.[9] After this Act, Kerr explains, the United States government viewed higher education as a critical resource for applied science, and the mission of higher education shifted toward solving public problems such as health, infrastructure, agricultural economy, and other emerging problems.

By the middle of the nineteenth century, curiously enough, the nation witnessed the founding of a very different type of institution of higher education, namely, the research university. The desire for pure scientific inquiry, particularly espoused by the German research university, encouraged early efforts to launch research oriented institutions of higher education, such as Johns Hopkins University, Stanford University and the University of Chicago. In the research university, relevant education did not mean immediately applicable knowledge to social problems. Rather, research was for research's sake. The drive to advance scientific knowledge defined the relevance of higher education for research universities. To achieve this goal, research universities desired a distance from the practical demands of society and argued for the freedom to pursue knowledge. In this case, as opposed to the land-grant universities, higher education and society grew apart.

The history of higher education in the twentieth century illustrates the tremendous influence of both national public policy as well as economic goals on postsecondary education. Within this century, we see higher education and society growing closer and the relevance of higher education is increasingly determined by economic goals. Both The Servicemen's Readjustment Act of 1944—commonly known as the G.I. Bill of Rights—as well as the 1947 report of President Harry S. Truman's commission on higher education, *Higher Education for American Democracy*, encouraged the education and training of all citizens and the growth of community colleges.[10] The Higher Education Act of 1965 (HEA) signified the growing federalism of higher education and led to mass higher education.[11] By the late twentieth century, a strong link between higher education and economic success began to form as a result of the 1980 Bayh-Dole Act which "allowed universities to keep patent rights to inventions resulting from federally funded research at their institutions."[12] In short, then, higher education in the twentieth century began to function increasingly as an industry with fluctuating, predominately economic goals and market oriented values.

In the history of higher education in the United States, a small, yet constant and significant, alternative to applied and pure science persisted. Laurence Veysey, in *The Emergence of the American University,* identifies this conception as "culture" but it is similar to what we today term "general" or "liberal" education.[13] The relevance of higher education, according to this view, is the cultivation of humanity. As opposed to the sciences, proponents of this view, like Martha Nussbaum in her latest study *Not For Profit: Why Democracy Needs the Humanities,* tout relevant studies such as the humanities for their capacity to create thoughtful human beings.[14] In contrast to learning to "make a living," these proponents propose learning to "live well." This kind of college is represented today by the liberal arts colleges, such as St. John's College, Hillsdale College, and Carthage College, to name a few.

While relevance remains a useful lens through which to read higher education, in contemporary higher education policy there is a growing consensus that "relevance" itself should be advanced explicitly as defining the mission of higher education. What relevance means for higher education and its relationship to society in our contemporary era becomes clear through a brief review of those advocating that relevance be the mission of higher education.

In October 1998, UNESCO hosted a World Conference on Higher Education. At that meeting, Michael Gibbons, Secretary General of the Association of Commonwealth Universities, delivered an address entitled, "Higher Education Relevance in the 21st Century."[15] In that address, Gibbons declared that for higher education to be relevant it must adapt to a new distributed knowledge production system. That is, higher education must not simply produce knowledge, which has always been a basic function of higher education, but also connect that knowledge to the people who can use it and need it. This service, argues Gibbons, requires that higher education create a "cadre of knowledge workers."[16] At the conclusion of this conference, UNESCO published a plan entitled *World Declaration on Higher Education for the Twenty-First Century: Vision and Action.*[17] In that plan UNESCO stated as one of its central tenets that higher education should take a "long-term orientation based on relevance."[18] By relevance it meant "basing long-term orientations on societal aims and needs," with specific concern for "targeted career-specific education."[19]

In a relatively short time this meaning of relevance began to influence higher education policy in the United States. By 2001, the Kellogg Commission on the Future of State and Land-Grant Universities published *Returning to Our Roots,* a report that called for an "engaged institution" that addressed the immediate needs of society, and primarily the economic needs of a changing economy.[20] In 2002, the American Association of State Colleges and Universities published *Stepping Forward as Stewards of Place,* which also called for the "engaged institution" and provided a "practical and strategic guide" for higher education to transform itself to better connect to the technology-driven economy. [21]

By 2006, the Alliance for Regional Stewardship, the American Association of State Colleges and Universities, and the National Center for Higher Education Management Systems published *Making Place Matter: Tools and Insights for Universities called to Regional Stewardship* (*MPM*). This report stated that the traditional university was no longer able to respond to the changing economy. [22] According to *MPM*, American colleges and universities have been charged with delivering greater efficiency, less duplication and more accountability. For decades, and especially since the early 1990s, argues *MPM*, universities have been pressured to "run-more-like-businesses." [23] In the late 1990s, according to the report, universities were called to be more "engaged" in "regional and state economic development efforts, producing partnerships between universities and businesses." [24] For proponents of the proposition that colleges and universities become relevant, however, these changes were not radical enough. The report states that,

> [E]ven though these efforts sought to change the university, they still remain within the traditional university model, one where the university serves the community/region/state but remains separated from these and other stakeholders in the many crucial respects. It is becoming increasingly clear that the time has come for a *new model*, not a tune-up. It is not clear that the traditional university has the mission, the culture, or the might to play the role that it must play today in the regional economy, that of being more attuned to local challenges and more responsible for community success. [25]

By the report's own admission, then, the call to relevance is a radical departure from the traditional university model. "In an age where the economy is driven by ideas," argues *MPM*, "more is required from colleges and universities than merely creating and disseminating the ideas. Such an economy requires academic institutions to *redefine the university model* so that they are permanently engaged as a full partner in the viability and vitality of the regions to which they are connected." [26]

According to *MPM*, the new "governing principle [of the university] must be *relevance* to the publics' [*sic*] they serve." [27] In fact, proponents of relevance claim that the "new standard" for colleges and universities in the twenty-first century is the ability to respond to immediate needs of society. By adopting this new standard, the university would signal to administrators, faculty and students that it has adopted a new model and role for higher education. In addition, it signals to outsiders that higher education is "current, connected and striving to be relevant." [28] Taking this step, argue its proponents, will allow colleges and universities "to gain new respect and cash in on new opportunities." [29] The contemporary call for relevance in higher education, then, is in fact a call to *redefine* the nature and role of the university model and its relationship with society.

This redefinition may be under way. In September 2006, then–Secretary of Education, Margaret Spellings, produced *A Test of Leadership: Charting the Future of U.S. Higher Education*, which called on higher education institutions to more closely connect their mission to the immediate needs of society, and primarily the economic needs of a growing and changing global economy.[30] In January 2013, North Carolina Governor Pat McCrory stated, "I'm looking at legislation right now . . . which would could change the basic formula in how education money is given out to our universities and our community colleges. It's not based on butts in seats but on how many of those butts can get jobs."[31] Governor McCrory bemoaned a "major disconnect between the education establishment and commerce." As a result, he planned to "adjust [North Carolina's] education curriculum to what business and commerce needs to get our kids jobs."[32] North Carolina Rep. Linda Johnson, co-chairwoman of the House Education Committee, added, "[W]e need to change what we're doing. I'm not thinking the degrees would change, but the content of the courses."[33] The problem outlined by Governor McCrory, Rep. Johnson stated, "is a national issue of matching graduate skills to business needs."[34] Underlying these policymakers' statements is a fundamental assumption that higher education should be relevant. More specifically, higher education should be relevant by preparing graduates with skills immediately applicable to the tasks of work life and thus bind itself to the practical, narrowly defined economic interests and needs of society.

It is clear, then, that relevance is not only a useful lens, but that in fact a powerful conception of its meaning may be fast redefining both the mission and content of American higher education. Fortunately there exists much good scholarship that discusses matters related to the strengthening relationship between higher education and society, specifically the economy. For example, studies such as *Academic Capitalism: Politics, Policies and the Entrepreneurial University* and *Universities in the Marketplace: The Commercialization of Higher Education* offer excellent explanations of the movement of faculty and higher education into the marketplace.[35] *Ivy and Industry: Business and the Making of the American University, 1880-1980* is equally insightful and provides a unique description of how both business and the humanities compete as dual missions for higher education.[36] Two further studies, *Education's End* and *What is College For?: The Public Purpose of Higher Education*, recognize the impact of the growing commercialization of higher education and lament the loss of focus on the question of the meaning of life and the civic purpose within higher education.[37] Yet, as useful and important as are these contributions, they ignore the underlying assumption of relevance. For it is a conception of relevance that explains the growing relationship between higher education and the economy and the exclusion of higher education ends not central to that relationship.

Too often today the central issues of higher education scholarship are of secondary importance. Studies such as *Academically Adrift*, *Our Under-achieving Colleges*, *The Innovative University*, *Higher Education?*, *Why Do Colleges Cost So Much?*, and *The States and Public Higher Education Policy*, which dominate recent discussions of higher education, offer valuable insight on issues such as access, cost and affordability, financial aid, learning, transparency and accountability and innovation.[38] In addition, issues such as technology, including the explosive idea of MOOCs ("massive open online courses"), and the higher education bubble, are also a primary focus of higher education scholarship.[39] As important as these issues are, they are arguably of lesser importance than the mission of higher education itself. For example, why does access matter if you are uncertain regarding the mission you are accessing? How can you accurately tally cost and affordability without first understanding the quality of the mission? How can you properly evaluate the quality of learning without grasping the kind of learning prescribed by the mission? In short, the question of mission is of primary importance. It must be addressed before assessing access, cost, learning, etc. It behooves us, then, to examine that which is primary. That examination better prepares us for comprehending and evaluating the other critical issues facing higher education.

What we need, then, is a critical and engaged examination of the concept and meaning of relevance as it defines the mission of higher education and shapes the relationship between higher education and society. Such an examination needs to be broad and deep to capture the many ways its meaning penetrates higher education. Due to its historical and contemporary impact on higher education, relevance is a subject that clearly warrants a critical engagement. This volume addresses relevance in higher education by situating it within a historical and contemporary context.

The purpose of the present study is to examine the relevance of higher education by bringing together the work of historians, political scientists, and educational philosophers. It seeks to probe the meaning of relevance in its many guises. It intends to provide an historical and philosophical account of the roots of this concept and its impact on the institution of higher education. It aims at providing a critical evaluation of the impact of relevance on our understanding of the political and economic relationship between higher education and society. It suggests views of relevance that could guide the future of higher education. Its goal is a penetrating analysis of relevance and its underlying assumptions, potential implications and long-lasting effects on higher education and society. In the end, it should be possible to develop a rich framework for understanding relevance and its impact on higher education and society.

Two contemporary phenomena create an urgent demand for this kind of reflective inquiry on the relevance of higher education. The first of these is the increase in enrollment in higher education. According to the National Center for Educational Statistics, in the Fall of 2012 "a record 21.6 million students" were expected to attend American Colleges and Universities, "constituting an increase of about 6.2 million since Fall 2000."[40] The causes for the vastly expanded enrollment are legion and include globalization, online opportunities, and financial support. The point is that higher education, in its many forms, has never before played such a dominant role in the life of young adults and our society. The transition to post-secondary education has become a rite of passage. Therefore, because higher education institutions occupy such a significant role in our culture, we ought to become clearer regarding their purpose and impact. This study attempts to address that need. The second of these is accountability. Currently there is a preoccupation with accountability, primarily in K-12 state assessment systems. As Governor McCrory's comments suggest, however, federal and state governments want to know if the investment in higher education is defensible. Studies such as *Academically Adrift* and *Our Underachieving Colleges* raise significant questions regarding the performance of higher education. Therefore, if higher education will be held accountable, then we should know our purpose and communicate it clearly to those who invest in higher education, so that we are held accountable for that purpose and not something unrelated or of minor importance to it. This study attempts to be part of that conversation by exposing a conception and meaning of relevance driving contemporary higher education.

The present study is organized thematically to provide a diverse array of perspectives and insights on the meaning of relevance within higher education. Part I explores philosophical dimensions of relevance and the prospects for it to guide higher education. Lee Trepanier examines what would make higher education relevant and argues its primary mission should be to cultivate the character and practice of Aristotelian prudence. Through a brief review of the early literature on relevance and higher education, Jon Fennell clarifies the meaning of relevance and offers a proposal to reconcile the need to be relevant and still maintain an allegiance to liberal education. Bryan Warnick acknowledges that the university needs to be relevant but suggests that we err by looking only at immediate needs rather than attending to questions of meaning that haunt human life.

Part II provides some historical perspective on relevance in higher education. Michael Schwarz examines Thomas Jefferson's thinking on education as a response to the revolutionary and republican currents of his day and concludes that modern higher education policy inverts the Jeffersonian order, thus fundamentally misunderstanding America's republican experiment. Wayne Willis outlines elements of Robert Maynard Hutchins's *The Higher*

Learning in America, offers some ideas for its reconceptualization and argues that with slight modification Hutchins's proposal is more relevant in today's relevance-focused academic environment than it was when it was written. By means of John Dewey and the early origins of the American Association of University Professors, James Scott Johnston claims that only by being clear ourselves about higher education and our discipline's contribution to society can a robust and effective case for higher education's relevance to the public be made.

Part III probes the political dimensions of the relevance of higher education. Bradley C. S. Watson maintains that civic learning is relevant to the lives of students and suggests some ways in which the American university can begin to re-engage the theme of civic education in a coherent, scholarly way. Michael Hail examines the crisis of Western civilization through contemporary higher education curriculum and recommends the core function of higher education to be understood as the conservancy of the highest knowledge. Jason Jividen investigates the seeming tension between liberal education and American democracy and its effects upon American ideas, habits and the institutions of higher education. Mark Jonas assesses whether Friedrich Nietzsche's educational and political theory is incompatible with the public good and argues that it is not, and that it offers us, perhaps surprisingly, an alternative conception of relevance more attractive to democratic flourishing than the one currently in fashion.

Part IV examines the socio-economic dimensions of the relevance of higher education. Stephen Clements maintains that by culture and practice most American academics have long placed their work beyond the pursuit of relevance, but he asserts that higher education institutions are already entwined deeply within the socio-economic system of the nation—and are therefore already more relevant than many faculty members realize. Wilfred McClay presents a careful and learned study of David Riesman, the distinguished American sociologist and eminent scholar of American higher education, to argue that a firm insistence on the preservation of institutional diversity can be seen as the single most valuable contribution to relevance that American education can make.

Despite this study's best intentions to provide considerable insight on the concept and meaning of relevance in higher education, there is still much to be done. As Richard Weaver asserted some time ago, ideas have consequences. The ideas we deem as worthy shape our culture, our institutions and our lives. The current meaning of relevance is such an idea and it presents significant consequences to both higher education and society. We should, therefore, strive for a proper and informed understanding of this idea to determine its limitations and its possibilities for the vital institution of higher education. Perhaps in the end if this book can spark or maintain a conversation regarding the relevance of higher education, then it will have fulfilled its purpose.

NOTES

I want to thank *Philosophical Studies in Education* for granting me and Lexington Books the right to republish portions of this introduction in this volume.

1. Jacques Barzun, "Of What Use the Classics Today?," in *BEGIN HERE: The Forgotten Conditions of Teaching and Learning*, ed. Morris Philpson (Chicago: The University of Chicago Press, 1992), 144.
2. Allan Bloom, "The Democratization of the University," in *Giants and Dwarfs: Essays 1960–1990* (New York: Simon and Schuster, 1990), 369.
3. Richard Weaver, "Education: Reflections On," in *In Defense of Tradition: Collected Shorter Writings of Richard M. Weaver, 1929–1963*, ed. Ted J. Smith, III (Indianapolis: Liberty Fund, 2000), 167.
4. Weaver, "Education: Reflections On," 168.
5. Ibid.
6. John S. Brubacher and Willis Rudy, *Higher Education in Transition: A History of the American Colleges and Universities, 1636–1976*, 3rd ed., rev. and enl. (New York: Harper and Row Publishers, 1976).
7. See Lawrence A. Cremin, *American Education: The Colonial Experience, 1607–1783* (New York: Harper and Row, 1970).
8. Carol Gruber, *Mars and Minerva: World War I and the uses of the higher learning in America* (Baton Rouge: Louisiana State University Press, 1975).
9. Clark Kerr, *The Uses of the University* (Cambridge, MA: Harvard University Press, 1964), see especially chapter 2.
10. The Servicemen's Readjustment Act, http://www.ourdocuments.gov/doc.php?doc=76, accessed April 21, 2013; President's Commission on Higher Education, *Higher Education for American Democracy* (New York: Harper and Bros., 1948).
11. Higher Education Act of 1965, http://www.nrcyd.ou.edu/publication-db/documents/higher-education-act-1965.pdf, accessed April 10, 2013.
12. Arden L. Bement Jr. and Angela Phillips Diaz, "U.S. Public Research Universities: A Historical Perspective," Global Policy Research Institute, Purdue University, June 2011, http://www.purdue.edu/research/gpri/publications/documents/revisedcolombiapaper_final.pdf, accessed April 10, 2013.
13. Laurence Veysey, *The Emergence of the American University* (Chicago: University of Chicago Press, 1965).
14. Martha C. Nussbaum, *Not For Profit: Why Democracy Needs the Humanities* (Princeton: Princeton University Press, 2010).
15. Michael Gibbons, "Higher Education Relevance in the 21st Century," http://siteresources.worldbank.org/EDUCATION/Resources/278200-1099079877269/547664-1099079956815/Higher_ed_relevance_in_21st_century_En98.pdf, accessed August 21, 2012.
16. Gibbons, "Higher Education Relevance in the 21st Century," i.
17. UNESCO, *World Declaration on Higher Education for the Twenty-First Century: Vision and Action*, http://www.unesco.org/education/educprog/wche/declaration_eng.htm, accessed August 21, 2012.
18. UNESCO, *World Declaration*, Article Six.
19. Ibid.
20. Kellogg Commission on the Future of State and Land-Grant Universities, *Returning To Our Roots*, http://www.aplu.org/NetCommunity/Document.Doc?id=187, accessed August 21, 2012.

21. American Association of State Colleges and Universities, *Stepping Forward as Stewards of Place*, http://aascu.org/WorkArea/DownloadAsset.aspx?id=5458, accessed August 21, 2012.

22. Alliance for Regional Stewardship, American Association of State Colleges and Universities, National Center for Higher Education Management Systems, *Making Place Matter: Tools and Insights for Universities Called to Regional Stewardship*, http://aascu.org/publications/regionalstewardship/, accessed August 21, 2012.

23. Ibid., 19.

24. Ibid., 20.

25. Ibid., 6 (italics added).

26. Ibid., (italics added).

27. Ibid., 31 (italics added).

28. Ibid., 22.

29. Ibid., 24

30. Margaret Spellings, Secretary of Education, *A Test of Leadership: Chartering the Future of U.S. Higher Education*, http://www2.ed.gov/about/bdscomm/list/hiedfuture/reports/final-report.pdf, accessed August 21, 2012.

31. Mark Binker and Julia Sims, "McCrory: Fund higher education based on results," WRAL.com, January 29, 2013, accessed March 22, 2013, http://www.wral.com/mccrory-fund-higher-education-based-on-results/12037347.

32. Ibid.

33. Ibid.

34. Ibid.

35. Shelia Slaughter and Larry L. Leslie, *Academic Capitalism: Politics, Policies and the Entrepreneurial University* (Baltimore: Johns Hopkins Press, 1997) and Derek Bok, *Universities in the Marketplace: The Commercialization of Higher Education* (Princeton: Princeton University Press, 2003).

36. Christopher Newfield, *Ivy and Industry: Business and the Making of the American University, 1880–1980* (Durham: Duke University Press, 2003).

37. Anthony T. Kronman, *Education's End: Why Our Colleges and Universities Have Given Up on the Meaning of Life* (New Haven: Yale University Press, 2007) and Ellen Condliffe Lagemann and Harry Lewis, editors, *What is College For?: The Public Purpose of Higher Education* (New York: Teachers College Press, 2012).

38. Richard Arum and Josipa Roksa, *Academically Adrift: Limited Learning on College Campuses* (Chicago: University of Chicago Press, 2011); Derek Bok, *Our Underachieving Colleges: A Candid Look at how much students learn and why they should be learning more* (Princeton, N.J.: Princeton University Press, 2006); Clayton M. Christensen and Henry J. Eyring, *The Innovative University: Changing the DNA of Higher Education from the Inside Out* (San Francisco: Jossey-Bass, 2011); Andrew Hacker and Claudia Dreifus, *Higher Education?: How Colleges are Wasting Our Money and Failing Our Kids—and What We Can Do About It* (New York: St. Martin's Press, 2011); Robert Archibald and Henry Feldman, *Why Do Colleges Cost So Much?* (New York: Oxford University Press, 2011); Donald Heller, *The States and Public Higher Education Policy: Affordability, Access and Accountability* (Baltimore: Johns Hopkins Press, 2001).

39. See, for example, Cathy N. Davidson and David Theo Goldberg, *The Future of Learning Institutions in a Digital Age.* (Cambridge, MA: MIT Press, 2009) and Glenn H. Reynolds, *The Higher Education Bubble* (New York: Encounter Books, 2012).

40. National Center for Educational Statistics, *Fast Facts*, accessed April 10, 2013, http://nces.ed.gov/fastfacts/display.asp?id=372.

BIBLIOGRAPHY

Alliance for Regional Stewardship, American Association of State Colleges and Universities, National Center for Higher Education Management Systems. *Making Place Matter: Tools* and *Insights for Universities Called to Regional Stewardship.* Accessed August 21, 2012. http://aascu.org/publications/regionalstewardship/.

American Association of State Colleges and Universities. *Stepping Forward as Stewards of Place.* Accessed August 21, 2012. http://aascu.org/WorkArea/DownloadAsset.aspx?id= 5458.

Archibald, Robert and Henry Feldman. *Why Do Colleges Cost So Much?* New York: Oxford University Press, 2011.

Arum, Richard and Josipa Roksa. *Academically Adrift: Limited Learning on College Campuses.* Chicago: University of Chicago Press, 2011.

Barzun, Jacques. "Of What Use the Classics Today?" In *BEGIN HERE: The Forgotten Conditions of Teaching and Learning,* edited by Morris Philpson, 133–147. Chicago: The University of Chicago Press, 1992.

Bement Jr., Arden L. and Angela Phillips Diaz. "U.S. Public Research Universities: A Historical Perspective." Global Policy Research Institute, Purdue University, June 2011. Accessed April 10, 2013. http://www.purdue.edu/research/gpri/publications/documents/revisedcolombiapaper_final.pdf.

Binker, Mark and Julia Sims. "McCrory: Fund higher education based on results." WRAL.com, January 29, 2013. Accessed March 22, 2013. http://www.wral.com/mccrory-fund-higher-education-based-on-results/12037347.

Bloom, Allan. "The Democratization of the University." In *Giants and Dwarfs: Essays 1960–1990,* 365–387. New York: Simon and Schuster, 1990.

Bok, Derek. *Universities in the Marketplace: The Commercialization of Higher Education.* Princeton: Princeton University Press, 2003.

——. *Our Underachieving Colleges: A Candid Look at how much students learn and why they should be learning more.* Princeton, NJ: Princeton University Press, 2006.

Brubacher, John S. and Willis Rudy. *Higher Education in Transition: A History of the American Colleges and Universities, 1636–1976,* 3rd ed., rev. and enl. New York: Harper and Row Publishers, 1976.

Cremin, Lawrence A. *American Education: The Colonial Experience, 1607–1783.* New York: Harper and Row, 1970.

Christensen, Clayton M. and Henry J. Eyring. *The Innovative University: Changing the DNA of Higher Education from the Inside Out.* San Francisco: Jossey-Bass, 2011.

Davidson, Cathy N. and David Theo Goldberg. *The Future of Learning Institutions in a Digital Age.* Cambridge, MA: MIT Press, 2009.

Gibbons, Michael. "Higher Education Relevance in the 21st Century." Accessed August 21, 2012. http://siteresources.worldbank.org/EDUCATION/Resources/278200-1099079877269 /547664-1099079956815/Higher_ed_relevance_in_21st_century_En98.pdf.

Gruber, Carol. *Mars and Minerva: World War I and the uses of the higher learning in America.* Baton Rouge: Louisiana State University Press, 1975.

Hacker, Andrew and Claudia Dreifus. *Higher Education?: How Colleges are Wasting Our Money and Failing Our Kids—and What We Can Do About It.* New York: St. Martin's Press, 2011.

Heller, Donald. *The States and Public Higher Education Policy: Affordability, Access and Accountability.* Baltimore: Johns Hopkins Press, 2001.

Higher Education Act of 1965. Accessed April 10, 2013. http://www.nrcyd.ou.edu/publication-db/documents/higher-education-act-1965.pdf.

Kellogg Commission on the Future of State and Land-Grant Universities. *Returning To Our Roots.* Accessed August 21, 2012. http://www.aplu.org/NetCommunity/Document.Doc?id= 187.

Kerr, Clark. *The Uses of the University.* Cambridge, MA: Harvard University Press, 1964.

Kronman, Anthony T. *Education's End: Why Our Colleges and Universities Have Given Up on the Meaning of Life.* New Haven: Yale University Press, 2007.

Lagemann, Ellen Condliffe and Harry Lewis, editors. *What is College For?: The Public Purpose of Higher Education.* New York: Teachers College Press, 2012.

National Center for Educational Statistics. *Fast Facts.* Accessed April 10, 2013. http://nces.ed.gov/fastfacts/display.asp?id=372.

Newfield, Christopher. *Ivy and Industry: Business and the Making of the American University, 1880–1980*. Durham: Duke University Press, 2003.

Nussbaum, Martha C. *Not For Profit: Why Democracy Needs the Humanities*. Princeton: Princeton University Press, 2010.

President's Commission on Higher Education. *Higher Education for American Democracy*. New York: Harper and Bros., 1948.

Reynolds, Glenn H. *The Higher Education Bubble*. New York: Encounter Books, 2012.

Servicemen's Readjustment Act. Accessed April 21, 2013.http://www.ourdocuments.gov/doc.php?doc=76.

Slaughter, Shelia and Larry L. Leslie. *Academic Capitalism: Politics, Policies and the Entrepreneurial University*. Baltimore: Johns Hopkins Press, 1997.

Spellings, Margaret. *A Test of Leadership: Chartering the Future of U.S. Higher Education*. Accessed August 21, 2012. http://www2.ed.gov/about/bdscomm/list/hiedfuture/reports/final-report.pdf.

UNESCO. *World Declaration on Higher Education for the Twenty-First Century: Vision and Action*. Accessed August 21, 2012. http://www.unesco.org/education/educprog/wche/declaration_eng.htm.

Veysey, Laurence. *The Emergence of the American University*. Chicago: University of Chicago Press, 1965.

Weaver, Richard. "Education: Reflections On." In *In Defense of Tradition: Collected Shorter Writings of Richard M. Weaver, 1929–1963*, edited by Ted J. Smith, III, 167–175. Indianapolis: Liberty Fund, 2000.

I

Philosophical Dimensions of Relevance

Chapter One

A Philosophy of Prudence and the Purpose of Higher Education Today

Lee Trepanier

In the past decade there have emerged several studies that have spoken about the crisis in American higher education. However, what this crisis is and how institutions should best address it remains uncertain. For example, some critics have followed the concerns laid out in the Spellings Commission's 2006 Report, *A Test of Leadership*, that find the American workforce is increasingly ill-prepared for a globalized "knowledge economy" because of the marginalization of undergraduate learning in American colleges and universities.[1] Studies such as *Academically Adrift: Limited Learning on College Campuses* and *We're Losing Our Minds: Rethinking American Higher Education* confirm these fears that American higher education is not providing the requisite skills for a twentieth-first century workforce: faculty indulge their passion for specialized research, students are preoccupied with their social lives, and administrators and staff support every perceived need and interest of both faculty and students but have no coherent idea about the essential mission of higher education.[2] Adopting an economic utilitarian approach to American higher education—the purpose and relevancy of colleges and universities is to prepare students to become economically productive actors—these critics see the crisis confronting higher education institutions as their inability to deliver the requisite skills for the United States to remain competitive in a globalized economy.

Another and entirely different set of concerns about American higher education is the erosion of the liberal education curriculum. Studies like *Not for Profit: Why Democracy Needs the Humanities*, *Why Choose the Liberal Arts*, and *Education's End: Why Our Colleges and Universities Have Given up on the Meaning of Life* defend the need of liberal education in a world that is increasingly being defined by economic utility.[3] Although these authors differ in their reasons as to why liberal education is essential to American higher education—preparing students for democratic citizenship, instilling a morality of secular humanism, or giving young people the critical skills needed for an ever-changing workforce—they all agree that liberal education, particularly the humanities, should return to the center of college's and universities' curriculum—a similar argument that was made a quarter century ago in Allan Bloom's *Closing the American Mind*.[4]

Besides these two groups, there also have emerged another set of critics that have focused on the organizational and administrative issues of American higher education institutions. Mark Taylor, for instance, sees faculty specialization in arcane scholarship as the source of the marginalization of undergraduate teaching in colleges and universities. His solution is to end tenure, restructure departments for interdisciplinary studies, and embrace technology to connect students worldwide.[5] Naomi Schaefer Riley is also of the same mind with Taylor in ending tenure as a way for faculty to return back to teaching as their primary mission.[6] Motivated by the recognition of their peers in publications rather than how well they teach their students, faculty give priority to scholarship and pay little attention to teaching. Andrew Hacker and Claudia Dreifu agree with Riley and Taylor that teaching is marginalized but they believe that the cause of this problem is the lack of student access to higher education and the present inequalities in resources that exist among institutions.[7] Their answer is to look at those institutions that exhibit what they deem to be best practices as potential models for other colleges and universities to emulate.

It is clear from these critics that a crisis exists in American higher education, but there is no agreement about the nature of this crisis and how to address it. Perhaps another way to approach this problem is to ask how American colleges and universities are relevant to society, as this appears to be the underlying concern among these authors. What should be the role, mission, or relevance of American higher education institutions for society: should it be to make our students economically productive actors, democratic citizens, or morally informed people? And once this mission is determined, how should it be implemented? Are certain institutions, such as research universities or small liberal art colleges, better prepared for this mission than other types of institutions?

I propose that the primary mission of American higher education should be to cultivate the character and practice of Aristotelian prudence. Among the various functions that higher education institutions can serve, the cultivation of prudence is uniquely suited for American colleges and universities. Prudence provides a bridge not only between theoretical and practical reasoning for students, but it also can combine the traditional activities of the university—teaching, research, and public service—into a coherent mission that makes colleges and universities relevant to society. In a certain sense, prudence has always played a critical role in the mission of American higher education since the inception of the republic. Although never explicitly artic- ulated, prudence is required not only for the development of democratic citizens, which was the primary concern of American colleges and univer- sities in the nineteenth century, but also for these institutions to fulfill their public service role as that became increasingly prominent in the twentieth.

AMERICAN HIGHER EDUCATION

Before delving into the details about prudence and its role in American higher education, a brief history is required in order to illuminate American higher education's evolving character and how prudence could play a role. Initially influenced by the European Enlightenment, the American founders desired an educated and self-governing citizenry in order to keep the new republic intact.[8] As Hellenbrand wrote, "many of Jefferson's contemporaries fervently believed that only education and a general reformation of manners could ensure America's political separation from Britain."[9] Education was to instill the republican values of liberty and self-government. There also was concern that American youth, as the future civic leaders, were being drawn to the great European universities. To remedy this situation, at least ten of the nation's founders were also founders of academic institutions with the most famous being Thomas Jefferson's University of Virginia, which was estab- lished in 1819 and opened in 1825. As a nondenominational place of higher learning, Jefferson "wish to establish in the upper & healthier country, & more central for the state an University on a plan so broad & liberal & modern, as to be worth patronizing with the public support."[10]

Although President Washington along with other prominent founders fa- vored the creation of a national university, a system of many state-supported institutions emerged instead.[11] Rev. Manasseh Cutler, an author of the North- west Ordinance of 1787, successfully negotiated with Congress for setting aside two square miles for a public university. Ohio University in Athens, founded in 1804, became the first state university west of the Appalachian Mountains. When new states entered the Union, they also received public land for the endowment of a university.[12] By the time the Morrill Act of 1862 was enacted, land grant colleges and universities extended to the west coast with twenty states already having state universities.[13]

Prior to the Civil War, the primary mission of colleges and universities was teaching undergraduates to become good democratic citizens and lead- ers.[14] These institutions offered a liberal arts curriculum because it was be- lieved that a well-rounded preparation for the individual was necessary for them to fulfill this role.[15] However, there also emerged institutions that emphasized technical education in agricultural and industrial sciences. The Morrill Acts of 1862 and 1890 provided land grants and federal funding that stimulated state legislatures to establish agricultural and mechanical colleges and universities. Influenced by the German research-oriented university, these types of universities started after the Civil War with some of them later becoming leading institutions in American higher education. [16]

In the late nineteenth and early twentieth century, American colleges and universities continued their mission of serving the nation of making good democratic citizens and leaders through liberal and technical education. But they also expanded opportunities to previously excluded groups as the concept of democracy itself widened to include equal treatment of students and equal access for all people, including the poor, women, and racial and ethnic minorities. [17] Adult education programs were established in such places like Chautauqua University (1883–1892) that pioneered summer sessions, correspondence courses, and extension services. These ideas would in turn influence other institutions, culminating into what would be known in 1904 as the "Wisconsin Idea." [18]

The democratization of American higher education continued throughout the twentieth century with the community college movement, the G.I. Bill, the California Plan, the Civil Rights Movement, and other federal funding programs. But it was the emergence and dominance of graduate institutions around 1900 that redefined the mission of American higher education as teaching, research, and public service. [19] Teaching was a legacy from the American Founding of creating good democratic citizens and leaders, while research was influenced by German-style universities and comported well in the practical culture of the United States in the belief that great research universities would advance basic knowledge and provide technical expertise required by a modern industrial society. [20] Public service came from the Progressive political ideology that sought to combine the teaching and research missions of colleges and universities to transmit higher knowledge to the public through external activities like applied research, off-campus courses, and service learning.

The "Wisconsin Idea" was the most famous articulation of this public service mission and became a model for subsequent schools. The "Wisconsin Idea" was the University of Wisconsin's commitment to serve the entire population of the state. Specifically, university faculty expertise was incorporated into state government planning and the university extension services were made available throughout the state. [21] Drawing national attention, the "Wisconsin Idea" influenced many other state universities to elevate public service with teaching and research as part of a university's core mission. [22]

Critics of this new mission argued that public service was in practice submission to business or state interests. Faculty also was concerned about business leaders involving themselves in higher education and universities patterning themselves after the bureaucratic structures of corporations and the state.[23] Since this time, this threat of institutional autonomy whether from government or commercial pressures has remained a constant concern among faculty, whether during the Vietnam War or in the current age of economic globalization.[24]

Most of this concern has centered on the source of funding. Prior to World War II, funding for expensive and specialized research came from philanthropic foundations or business corporations. During and after World II, the federal government became the dominant patron of major research universities, although private foundations continued to fund academic research in the social sciences. Most recently, starting in the 1970s there has been a shift from basic and military research to civilian and commercial in order to meet the needs of a global economy.[25] This latest shift from a theoretical model to an entrepreneurial one under the rubric of public service has raised questions about what actually constitutes public service and what should be its rationale.

Today the United States multifunctional university still clings to its three-fold mission of teaching, research, and public service. When looking back at the history of American higher education, these three activities have fulfilled critical functions in society: teaching democratic citizens and leaders, research for economic progress, and public service for the improvement of society. However, this mission has become increasingly questioned and criticized as to its relevancy. But what each of these three activities had implicitly promoted was an understanding of prudence whether in democratic politics, economic growth, or social stability. The cultivation of prudence therefore should be explicitly articulated as the central purpose of American higher education as opposed to the missions of economic utilitarianism, scientific research, liberal education, or civic formation. But before explaining why the cultivation of prudence is uniquely suited for institutions of American higher education, I want to present an understanding of Aristotelian prudence that differs from contemporary interpretations.

THE RECOVERY OF ARISTOTELIAN PRUDENCE

The recent interest in Aristotelian prudence is part of an overall attempt to recover the notion of judgment in political philosophy and pedagogy as a response to postmodern critics who have questioned the validity of theoretical reasoning and its fusion with practice.[26] Convinced of the existence of such a gap, some scholars have looked to political judgment as a way to replace theoretical and scientific reasoning in order to reinforce rather than undermine the politics.[27] In their task, these scholars have returned to Aristotle for guidance in the recovery of political judgment. For them, Aristotelian prudence (*phronesis*) is the model of political judgment that avoids the elitism of Plato's philosopher-kings as well as the rigidity of theoretical and scientific reasoning.

One of the problems with theoretical or scientific reasoning is its rigid, abstract, and moral disengaged character that is focused solely on universal solutions to particular problems.[28] This form of reasoning immobilizes judgment of any type and creates a politics of expertise and bureaucracy that is democratically unaccountable.[29] Furthermore, as a solitary activity rather than one of shared deliberation, theoretical and scientific reasoning is essentially a product of self-interest rather than deliberation about the common good.[30] Even if one were able to understand the common good, the person, as a scientific and detached observer, would lack the sympathy to promote and sustain it. The end result is an education that cultivates theoretical and scientific reason at the expense of the virtues of accountability, deliberation, and sympathy for the common good.

Unlike theory or science, *phronesis* is flexible, practical, and a product of a common understanding about particular, concrete action. However, this recent revival of the study of *phronesis* either downplays or steers clear of Aristotle's natural sciences and theoretical reason. For example, Barber, and Beiner claim that theoretical wisdom is not required for the cultivation of prudence, while Sullivan subordinates theory to serve practical ends, such as civic education, rather than the contemplation of the truth.[31] Other thinkers, such as Steinberger, have argued that *phronesis* is an alternative form of intellectual virtue, like theoretical reason, but applicable only to particular matters, such as politics.[32] In their attempt to supplant scientific reasoning with *phronesis*, these scholars have detached Aristotle's understanding of prudence from both his conceptions of science and theory.

I argue that Aristotle's conceptions of science and theory, particularly his understandings of nature and noetic intelligence, are critical to understanding Aristotle's *phronesis*.[33] Without these key elements, *phronesis* becomes either another type of theoretical reasoning preoccupied with particulars or a form of calculation concerned with power struggles. The Aristotelian conceptions of nature and theory therefore are critical components to the construction of *phronesis*. Without a proper understanding of these concepts first, thinkers make the error of engaging in a form of abstract reasoning themselves in their recover *phronesis*, a mistake that they accuse their non-Aristotelian colleagues of committing.

THE PARADOX OF NATURE

To understand Aristotle's understanding of *phronesis*, we must first look at conception of nature with particular attention to the paradox that he pointed out in the *Nicomachean Ethics* where the "right of nature" (*physei dikaion*) "everywhere has the same force and does not exist by people's thinking this or that . . . and yet it is changeable—all of it (*kineton mentoi pan*)."[34] Aristotle's statements are perplexing: *physei dikaion* is everywhere the same, with such acts like murder, theft, and adultery as always being bad, but all of it is also changeable (*NE* 1107a12–14). How can *physei dikaion* be both universal and contingent at the same time? And how is it related to *phronesis*?[35]

On the one hand, Aristotle argued that *physei dikaion* was universal: it had the same force everywhere in the forbidding of such acts like murder, theft, and adultery. On the other hand, *physei dikaion* was changeable in the sense that universal principles can have diverse actualizations according to time, object, aim, and method: "the right time, with reference to the right object, toward the right people, with the right aim, and in the right way" (*NE* 1106b20–23). The criteria of time, object, aim, and method allowed Aristotle to make the distinction between murder and killing. If certain acts fell short or exceed this criteria (the mean), then they were considered bad, for as Aristotle wrote: "There is neither a mean of excess and deficiency, nor excess and deficiency of a mean" (*NE* 1106a25–1107a26).

For instance, murder is distinct from killing. When done at the right time, with respect to the right persons, and with the right aim and method, killing is naturally right. When overshooting or falling short of their mark, this action is murder. The act of murder did not break some abstract rule but it missed the mean in concrete action. Although the criteria of time, object, aim, and method may appear vague, for example, "do not kill at the wrong time, involving the wrong object, with the wrong purpose and method," for Aristotle it was appropriate to a reality that did not yield a permanent, detailed standard. Moral and ethical acts were not governed "by any art of set of precepts" but rather "according to right reason" because what was right was "not one, nor the same for all" (*NE* 1103b31–1104a9, 1106a32). Each situation must be evaluated on a case-by-case basis with the underlying universal substance of ethics—the one way of being good—driving all of the means.[36]

The paradox of *physei dikaion*, being simultaneously universal and changeable in action, is personified in the excellent person (*phronimos*) who could choose the mean in practical situations (*NE* 1107a1). This *phronimos* was probably also the serious person (*spoudaios*) who saw "the truth in each class of things, being as it were the norm and measure of them," and the "man called without qualification good" who possessed not just *phronesis* but all the virtues, for "with the presence of the one quality, *phronesis*, will be given all the excellences" (*NE* 1113a30–35, 1144b30–1145a1). The *phronimos* or *spoudaios* therefore was guided primarily by *phronesis* but also included other intellectual virtues, such as noetic intelligence, in his decisions.

THE PARADOX OF PRUDENCE

Like *physei dikaion, phronesis* also appears to be contradictory. Aristotle defined it as the "ability to deliberate well about what sorts of things conduce to the good life in general" but could produce "no demonstration" of its first principles, even though its particular actions were true in practice" (*NE* 1140a24–1140b30; 1142a11–30; 1146b35–1146a7). In other words, *phronesis* could not become a science (*episteme*), which was concerned with first principles that of necessity were always the same. Because its attention was on the particulars and the contingents of the world, *phronesis* could not start from universal premises or produce universal conclusions. But if there were so, how could *phronesis* deliberate about the good in general, especially as it could not demonstrate such a deliberation? How could *phronesis* have a theoretical capacity when its objects were particular?

This paradox about *phronesis* can be clarified by looking at Aristotle's concept of *nous* (intellect) as something both divine and human and the source of theoretical reasoning, like noetic intelligence. *Nous* was "something divine" and superior to "our composite nature," but it was also "more than anything else is man." By following *nous*, humans could make themselves immortal and "strain every nerve to live in accordance with the best thing in us" (*NE* 1177b27–1178a8). Aristotle discovered that human beings possessed something within themselves that was different from them and yet paradoxically that was the best thing of them. This thing could be discovered by the cognitive faculty that Aristotle termed *nous*.

Humans possessed a divinity that was superior to but connected to them. Aristotle wrote that there were "things much more divine in nature even than man," which included not only the heavenly bodies but also the creator god as a physical force (*NE* 1141b1–2; *Metaphysics*, 98b–984a). In the *Metaphysics* Aristotle stated that "first philosophy" studies ontology, eternal causes, and the "first mover" god who was "in a better state" than humans (*Metaphysics*, 1003a–1005a, 1026a, 1072b). Although this "first mover" was not a creator god, it was the one who set things in motion as a final cause. It accomplished this not by the act of creation but as the object of desire and thought that attracts all desiring and thinking things. Thus, when Aristotle spoke of *nous* present in nature as the cause and order of the world, he conceived of the world as being preserved by the rational and love-inspiring attraction of the prime mover (*Metaphysics*, 1072a20–1072b4; 984b15–20).

Nature (*physis*) therefore was reality moving toward the prime mover. Defining nature as a member of "the class of causes that acts for the sake of something," Aristotle declared that "the form" of any reality and the "mover" of any nature "often coincide, for the what and that-for-the-sake-of-which are one, while the primary source of motion is the same in species as these" (*Physics*, 198a20–198b10). *Physis* was reality in its immediate form that moves toward its own final cause while simultaneously existing in a state of tension toward the prime mover as the ultimate final cause. The different "natures" that exist are only diversely experienced aspects of the prime mover's rational and love-attracting permeation of the cosmos.

The evidence of the claim that *physis* was both natural and divine was the "experience of *nous*" itself. In *Eudemian Ethics*, Aristotle asserted that "the object of our search is this—what is the commencement of movement in the soul? The answer is evident: as in the universe, so in the soul, it is God. For in a sense the divine element in us moves everything" (1248a25–27). Aristotle's prime mover was a transcendent entity that still existed in the cosmos and generated a two-in-one motion that gave *physis*, including humans, a dual and yet single final cause (*telos*). This double-single movement of the soul toward the prime mover was what Aristotle called *physis*: it was both everywhere valid and changeable at the same time.

For humans, the path to unity with the prime mover was through *nous*: humans were to follow a single ethical direction with various adjustments made to remain on this path. Virtue was not the obedience of abstract rules but following *phronesis* as led by the primer mover's pull. *Phronesis* consequently was the motion between the prime mover and humans that occurred within the *nous* of the *phronimos*. It was the motion of the divine-human *nous* of the *phronimos* to choose action in daily life (*NE* 1151a15–20). The *phronimos* looked to universals insofar as he was attuned to the prime mover, but these universals varied because the correctives were dictated by fluid needs. It was the *phronimos'* judgment and action that became the standard of virtue because his attraction to the *nous* enabled him to find the right intermediates that testified to his goodness.

THE PROOF OF PRUDENCE

The universal-variable principles of *phronesis* were simultaneously one, eternal equilibrium between humans and the prime mover and the many pragmatic paths to it. Because of the changeability of these ruling, first principles (*archai*) precluded syllogistic proofs and dialectical inferences (*NE* 1140a30–40b2, 1151a15–20). The *archai* simply had to be recognized in a world of fluid situations: their universality in relation to the prime mover was known as soon as they were perceived, so they could immediately serve as the grounds of means-ends calculation that was prudential rather than scientific or rule-bound. Given its variable character, Aristotle denied *phronesis* the status of science (*episteme*) by categorizing it as a deliberate intellectual virtue. Although the variable character of *phronesis* prevented logical and consistent proof, its universal objective remained unchanged. This allowed the *phronimos* to make his decisions based neither on moral relativism nor deontological thinking but on something in between: *physei dikaion.*

But if *physei dikaion* cannot be studied at the level of *episteme*, how can it be demonstrated or taught? The impossibility of studying it at the level of *episteme* certainly restricts the types of demonstration of its existence. Such an account of *physei dikaion* cannot be verified by the positivism that theoretical or scientific reasoning demands. Deductive and logical reasoning are also avenues that are blocked, since *physei dikaion* has no axioms from which one can reason to conclusions or first principles. It is only the reliance upon habituation in the moral virtues and the experiences of the mature person that the proofs of *physei dikaion* and *phronesis* become possible.

This demonstration requires not only introspection of one's own experiences but also an appeal to others'. Agreement among virtuous people can constitute the grounds for confidence about the existence of *physei dikaion* and *phronesis*. Of course, this presupposes a degree of common sense among people. For example, most people would state that they know that genocide was wrong rather than opine about it. These people have experienced something inside themselves that would not tolerate such crimes, although they do not possess the scientific certainty about its wrongness. Such a case could show the existence of some universal principles.[37]

This intuitive recognition of first principles is not circular reasoning, that is, people believe their views that genocide is wrong because they believe it is true. This criticism confuses first principles when people try to give validation what they immediately apprehend. Of course, people can work themselves in a state of doubt about the wrongness of genocide, but Aristotle would tell them that they are being foolish because these kinds of facts are starting points: it is fallacious to try to deduce everything from something higher as if it were an infinite regress (*NE* 1095b6).

This inability of people to distinguish and defend first principles is to acknowledge they are incomplete beings when compared to the paradigmatic *phronimos*, the one who is fully conscious of the presence of *nous* within him and therefore who has a noetic understanding of the principles of actions. But the people's incompleteness raises a broader question of whether a measure of *phronesis* is possible without a *phronimos*. For example, how could Aristotle have speculated that the many as a whole, with their inclination toward mediocrity, be better than the few individually (*Politics* 1283b30–35)? Or that perverse regimes still operated on some principles of partial wisdom (*Politics* 1253a37–39)?

The answer for Aristotle was in the actions of the political communities. People may think like animals when they make conscious choices, but they cannot consistently live like animals without destroying themselves first. They consequently educate their young to pre-rational training in the virtues necessary for social stability and continuity. Aristotle observed that such habituation "teaches right opinion about the first principle" (*NE* 1151a15–20). The pre-rational discipline that states were forced to impose on their children opened their souls to the attraction of *phronesis*, such that they can acquire a quasi-noetic attunement to the means between excess and defect. So even when society lacked a *phronimos*, a pre-rational version of the virtue can still persist; otherwise, the society would annihilate itself. This incomplete *phronesis* was referred to as "common sense," which was a lesser degree of practical wisdom but can still sustain imperfect and even perverse regimes.[38]

Phronesis therefore requires both Aristotle's understanding of nature (*physei dikaion*) and theoretical reason (*nous*). Both *physei dikaion* and *nous* enable *phronesis* to be flexible in its pursuit of moral virtue without collapsing into cynical calculation or abstract thinking. Because *physis* is both natural and divine, its two-in-one motion character allows reality to seek its own particular, contingent *telos* as well as the universal and eternal one of the prime mover. In humans, this divine component is *nous*, a type of theoretical reason that can direct *phronesis* toward its ultimate ends while it is focuses on intermediaries. Without these key elements, Aristotle's *phronesis* becomes unmoored and runs into the difficulties that contemporary scholars have discovered.

THE PROBLEM OF CURRENT PARADIGMS

With this understanding of Aristotelian *phronesis* as a type of reasoning that is both theoretical and practical, how does it fit into the mission of American higher education? Why should the cultivation of *phronesis* be the essential core of colleges and universities when compared to other missions like economic utilitarianism or civic education? How does *phronesis* provide coherence to the traditional three-fold mission of teaching, research, and public service? And, finally, how would one implement a mission of *phronesis* in colleges and universities today?

I do not pretend to be able to provide adequate answers to all these questions here. However, I do want to propose a paradigm that might enable us to think past the variety of crises of American higher education that critics so loudly proclaim today. But before I discuss the incorporation of *phronesis* into American higher education, I want to point out some of the problems that I see in the current missions of American higher education when compared to the paradigm of *phronesis*. Specifically, missions like economic utilitarianism, liberal education, or civic formation can be done better at institutions that are not educational ones. Although American higher education can accomplish these tasks, the results are ultimately inferior in their delivery when compared to these other social institutions.

One primary mission of American higher education, and of concern because it is not delivering results, is economic utilitarianism: the purpose of colleges and universities is to make economically productive actors. This mission is particularly attractive to the state and the public which see economic growth and increased productivity as justifiable goals to support public colleges and universities. However, as studies such as *Academically Adrift* and *We're Losing Our Minds* have demonstrated, American higher education institutions fare poorly in preparing students for the workforce. Students are not learning the requisite skills to become economically productive. The conclusion is that students, their parents, the state, and the public have wasted resources on institutions that do not deliver results.

But I would argue that even if colleges and universities were able to prepare students with the requisite skills to become economically productive, these institutions would still be inferior in their delivery of these services when compared to non-educational institutions. Although empirical studies are required to verify this hypothesis, I would venture that students who specialize in particular disciplines could be better served if they were to do an apprenticeship with their employer rather than spend time at a college or university. This hypothesis applies specifically to students who study pre-professional degrees, including those in education and business. The fact that these non-educational institutions usually incorporate some type of new employee training that can range from a few weeks to many months testifies that higher education does not prepare students for immediate, economically productive employment. These students could be taught more efficiently and effectively—and increase their likelihood of becoming employed and economically productive—if they spent their time learning their craft with their potential employers rather than spending it in college or university.

Related to economic utilitarianism is the mission of scientific research for universities. Although these institutions can be sites where research occurs, it is not the only institution that can engage in this activity: businesses and government agencies also can conduct scientific research. Furthermore, the rules and regulations imposed on universities for research are not as cumbersome as those in these non-educational institutions because the purpose is explicit to serve either commercial or public interests. Again, empirical evidence is required, but I suspect when compared to public research universities, these non-educational institutions can deliver similar scientific results without the weighty rules and regulations and conflict-of-interest statements that characterized research universities.

These problems that plague public research universities can be partially attributed to the Bayh-Dole Act, which reversed the presumption of title, that is, universities can elect to pursue ownership of their research in preference to the government. As in the early twentieth century, concerns that public research universities are serving business rather than the public interests have recently resurfaced.[39] These concerns would be alleviated if American higher education either removed scientific research from its mission or repealed the Bayh-Dole Act. Although politically popular and publicly digestible, the mission of scientific research brings a new set of problems, such as conflict-of-interest and corruption of university policies and practices, which would not be an issue if research was conducted elsewhere.

Critics of economic utilitarianism and scientific research often push forward the ideas of liberal education or civic formation as the genuine mission of American higher education.[40] Although I am personally sympathetic to the idea and ideals of liberal education, I believe a defense of it, at least for public colleges and universities, would be difficult, especially in these times of economic retrenchment when the argument of economic utilitarianism becomes more attractive. But more problematic about the mission of liberal education is the question whether it ever truly existed or is merely part of myth and selective memory. Perhaps for a few, American higher education was a place where students spent time pursuing questions for their own sake with their professor's detailed attention, but for the many, college and university is the experience of searching for employable skills in an over-crowded, underfunded institution. For the typical student, a liberal education curriculum is merely a series of hoops to jump through in order to gain a certificate that attest to his or her skill set.

So if liberal education does exist in American higher education, it would appear that it can only transpire when both students and professors are truly committed to studying things for their own sake; and this setting is either in tutorials or in a small group. This type of education would not be a problem for private colleges and universities, which can be selective in their admissions and tuition policies, but for public institution, a defense of liberal education would impossible, especially in democratic regimes. In an attempt to overcome this problem, public institutions rationalize their liberal arts curriculum as teaching students transferable skills such as "critical thinking" or "quantitative reasoning." However, the assessment of these skills requires quantitative measures that are antithetical to the original purpose of liberal education.[41] Public institutions would find themselves at the mercy of various quantitative metrics that lack any mooring other than themselves.

Finally, there is the mission of civic formation: to make students responsible and active democratic citizens and leaders. The recent growth in the scholarship and actual programs in civic formation, for example, leadership, statesman, or service learning, in American higher education reveals the attractiveness of this mission.[42] Often included with civic formation are the objectives of teaching students the importance of diversity, multiculturalism, and cosmopolitanism.[43] Although these goals are relevant and publicly defensible, as well as continue the original mission of American higher education to form good democratic citizens and leaders, the implementation of such a vision has encountered some obstacles.

First, there is the question about the content of such a curriculum. Critics of diversity, multiculturalism, and cosmopolitanism claim that instead of strengthening democratic citizenship, some civic formation curriculum actually undermines it by teaching cultural relativism or blatant anti-Americanism.[44] Second, and more importantly, the implementation of these programs either tends to too theoretical or under-theoretical. Civic formation programs are either disproportionally academic, thereby committing the error of not exposing students to the practical mechanics of leadership, service, or statesmanship, or under-theorized where practice is emphasized at the expense of how it is related to theoretical thinking and knowledge.[45] Students are taught either theory without practice or practice without theory.

Of course, there exist some programs that are able to blend theory and practice in their civic formation programs. But even in these situations, these programs are often not considered to be at the core essential of a college's or university's mission. What Aristotle's concept of *phronesis* provides is not only a bridge between theory and practice in the civic formation of students, but it also coordinates the three main activities of American higher education—teaching, research, and public service—into a coherent whole. How this could be accomplished will be briefly discussed below.

THE PARADIGM OF PRUDENCE

As a deliberative intellectual virtue that is both practical and theoretical, *phronesis* is uniquely suited for American higher education. Colleges and universities can cultivate a character in students that requires both theoretical and practical reasoning better than other non-educational institutions. Whereas corporate and government agencies ultimately subordinate theoretical reasoning to practical ends, higher education institutions can orient students' practical reasoning to theoretical ends without losing sight of the world of particulars and contingents, something which liberal education neglects. In other words, the missions of economic utilitarianism and scientific research reduce theoretical reasoning to a practical one while liberal education tends to overlook practical thinking entirely. By navigating between these two extremes, *phronesis* is able to preserve both types of reasoning in order to promote a flourishing of the whole human being.

In a certain sense, *phronesis* is more compatible with the mission of civic formation than economic utilitarianism, scientific research, or liberal education. However, as stated above, the mission of civic formation suffers from the obstacles of curriculum content, over or under theorization, and marginalization from higher education institutions' core mission. With Aristotelian *phronesis*, some of these concerns are allayed. The objectives of such a program would promote both theoretical and practical reason: the former would be learned in the classroom; the latter in practical activity as supervised by faculty. What holds these two types of reasoning together is the ethical formation of the human person which would be at the core of the university's mission. This in turn would require American higher education to take seriously the question what type of human person they would want to cultivate.

Given the diversity of institutions in American higher education, there is no need for a single normative standard imposed on all colleges and universities. For instance, religious institutions may want to incorporate theological beliefs into their ethical understanding of the human person, whereas public institutions may want to focus on responsible and engaged democratic citizens and leaders.[46] There would be flexibility in the curriculum content, but colleges and universities would have to agree to a core set of courses required for all students in order to promote their ethical understanding of what sort of human being they want. Although a discussion of the actual content of a curriculum that would promote *phronesis* is beyond the scope of this particular chapter, I would imagine that it would contain some courses that one may find in a liberal arts curriculum, as these courses tend to deal with questions of ethics. But unlike the liberal arts, this curriculum would also include practical activities in the aim of forming the whole person.

This practical character of the curriculum would be a distinctive feature of the paradigm of *phronesis*: students would have to engage in practical reasoning on a case-by-case basis. One of the criticisms of certain leadership or statesmanship programs is its over-theoretical nature, where students learn concepts that are abstracted from their particular context. The detachment of these concepts, like "two-way communication," from their specific context becomes meaningless to students, as they may apply this concept to the wrong person or at the wrong time. It is only in the specific situation, as Aristotle had observed, where students can exercise their *phronesis*. The conceptualization of leadership or statesmanship without reference to actual practice only gives students confidence without understanding.

If certain programs are over-theoretical, then there are others, such as service-learning, which tend to be under-theoretical and consequently equally negligent of *phronesis*. Although it cannot be *episteme*, *phronesis* is connected with theoretical thinking and therefore is capable of conceptualization only after one has grasped the specific situation in terms of its particularities and contingencies. This connection of *phronesis* with noetic intelligence prevents service-learning activities like internships or study abroad programs from becoming a series of actions that lack any theoretical or ethical direction.

Phronesis not only balances theoretical and practical thinking for its students, but it can also provide coherence to the mission of American higher education. By asking how to cultivate *phronesis* not only in teaching but also in research and public service, colleges and universities can connect these disparate activities under a coherent concept. For example, a state institution's core ethical mission could be to make responsible and engaged democratic citizens and leaders. But how is this accomplished is a question of *phronesis*: what is the proper balance between theoretical and practical courses for students? What sort of research should be conducted; and when and how should certain findings be revealed even if they are contrary to public opinion but for the common good? What ways other than teaching and research can faculty prudentially contribute to supporting a democratic society?[47]

Another advantage of making *phronesis* the prevailing paradigm for higher education institutions is transcending the purported gaps between theory and practice, facts and values, and the sciences and the humanities. As I have shown previously, Aristotle's *phronesis* makes these distinctions irrelevant. *Phronesis* requires theoretical as well as practical reasoning: it obliges students to know facts of specific situations and to be able to make value judgments about them; and it needs science, particularly an understanding of nature, to make ethical judgment possible.[48] Thus, the fragmentation and specialization of academic programs can be returned to a coherent whole under a paradigm of *phronesis*.

This paradigm of *phronesis* therefore calls for a normative understanding of human flourishing specific to a higher education institution that includes both theoretical and practical reasoning and, as a result, directs that institutions' teaching, research, and public service toward this end. American higher education institutions are uniquely suited for such a task because only they are able to cultivate this character that requires both theoretical and practical reasoning aimed at a specific ethical formation. Other institutions in society either lack this combination of theoretical and practical reason or are deficit in an ethical conception of human flourishing. It is only colleges and universities that have the unique resources of students, faculty, and staff that are able to engage in this type of activity.[49]

Granted, *phronesis* may lack a certain branding appeal when compared to other higher education mission statements, but this matter can be easily resolved if there are prudential people in places of authority. Without such a paradigm, colleges and universities often fall prey to a management paradigm with missions that are abstract and have little effect on the lives of students, faculty, and the public.[50] The paradigm of *phronesis* forces administrators, staff, faculty, students, and the public to think what should be the core mission of higher education by asking the question of human flourishing. It forces these groups to ask how American higher education can be relevant. Without asking these questions, and trying to answer them, the future of American higher education will continue to be criticized and called into crisis but without any genuine understanding as to reasons why.

NOTES

I want to thank *The Political Science Reviewer* for granting me and Lexington Books the right to republish this article in this volume.

1. Margaret Spellings, *A Test of Leadership: Charting the Future of U.S. Higher Education* (Washington, DC: U.S. Department of Education, September 2006), accessed February 12, 2012, http://www2.ed.gov/about/bdscomm/list/hiedfuture/reports/pre-pub-report.pdf

2. Richard Arum and Josipa Roksa, *Academically Adrift: Limited Learning on College Campuses* (Chicago: University of Chicago Press, 2011); Richard P. Keeling and Richard H. H. Hersh, *We're Losing Our Minds: Rethinking American Higher Education* (Houndmill, Great Britain: Palgrave Macmillian, 2011).

3. Anthony Kronman, *Education's End: Why Our Colleges and Universities Have Given up on the Meaning of Life* (New Haven: Yale University Press, 2008); Mark William Roche, *Why Choose the Liberal Arts* (Notre Dame: University of Notre Dame, 2010); Martha Nussbaum, *Not for Profit: Why Democracy Needs the Humanities* (Princeton: Princeton University Press, 2012).

4. Allan Bloom, *Closing the American Mind: How Higher Education Has Failed Democracy and Impoverished the Souls of Today's Students* (New York: Simon and Schuster, 1987). Although Bloom defended liberal education, his reasons were different than Kronman's, Roche's, and Nussbaum's. For Bloom, liberal education was reserved for the intellectually-gifted few rather than to serve the many in democratic society.

5. Mark Taylor, *Crisis on Campus: A Bold Plan for Reforming Our Colleges and Universities* (New York: Knopf, 2010).

6. Naomi Schaefer Riley, *The Faculty Lounges, and Other Reasons, Why You Won't Get the College Education You Paid for* (Lanham, MD: Ivan R. Dee, 2011).

7. Andrew Hacker and Claudia Dreifus, *Higher Education? How Colleges are Wasting Our Money and Failing Our Kids—And What We Can Do About* (New York: Times Book, 2010).

8. Lorraine Pangle and Thomas Pangle, *The Learning of Liberty: The Educational Ideas of the American Founders* (Lawrence, KS: University of Kansas Press, 1993), 4–5.

9. Harold Hellenbrand, *The Unfinished Revolution: Education and Politics in the Thought of Thomas Jefferson* (Newark, DE: University of Delaware Press, 1990), 11.

10. Thomas Jefferson, "Jefferson Plans the University of Virginia, 1800," in *American Higher Education: A Documentary History,* ed. Richard Hofstadter et al., (Chicago: University of Chicago Press, 1961), 175.

11. E. L. Johnson, "The 'Other Jeffersons' and the State University Idea," *Journal of Higher Education* 58 (1987): 129, 147; E. H. Roseboom and F. P. Wisenburger, *A History of Ohio* (Columbia: Ohio Historical Society, 1996), 47, 53.

12. John S. Brubacher and Willis Rudy, *Higher Education in Transition* (New York: Harper and Row, 1976), 154.

13. Johnson, "The 'Other Jeffersons,'" 127.

14. The mission of American religious institutions of higher education was slightly different in producing good clergy to serve their faith communities.

15. Bill Reading, *The University in Ruins* (Cambridge, MA: Harvard University Press, 1996), 4.

16. Brubacher and Rudy, *Higher Education in Transition,* 61–64, 288.

17. Laurence Veysey, *The Emergence of the American University* (Chicago: University of Chicago Press, 1965), 62–66.

18. J. C. Scott, "The Chautauqua Movement: Revolution in Popular Higher Education." *Journal of Higher Education* 70 (1999): 389–412.

19. Veysey, *The Emergence of the American University*, 444.

20. Brubacher and Rudy, *Higher Education in Transition*, 177

21. Brubacher and Rudy, *Higher Education in Transition*, 164–165; Veysey, *The Emergence of the American University*, 108.

22. Brubacher and Rudy, *Higher Education in Transition*, 166–168; Christopher Lucas, *American Higher Education* (New York: St. Martin's, 1994), 174–175, 292.

23. Clyde W. Barrow, *Universities and the Capitalist State: Corporate Liberalism and the Reconstruction of American Higher Education, 1894–1928* (Madison, WI: University of Wisconsin Press, 1990), 7, 10; Harold Perkin, "Defining the True Function of the University: A Question of Freedom Versus Control," *Change* 16 (1984): 20–29.

24. Hugh Hawkins, *The Emerging University and Industrial America* (Lexington, MA: D.C. Heath, 1970), xi; Paul Axelrod, *Values in Conflict: The University, the Marketplace, and the Trials of Liberal Education* (Montreal: McGill-Queen's University Press, 2002), 3–7; Henry A. Giroux, "Introduction: Critical Education or Training: Beyond the Commodification of Higher Education," in *Beyond the Corporate University*, ed. Henry A. Giroux et al., (Lanham, MD: Rowman & Littlefield, 2001), 1–11; Eric Gould, *The University in a Corporate Culture* (New Haven: Yale University Press, 2003).

25. Shelia Slaughter, "National Higher Education Policies in a Global Economy," in *Universities and Globalization: Critical perspectives*, ed. Janice Curie et al., (Thousand Oaks, CA: Sage, 1998), 62.

26. Some non-Aristotelian examples of scholars who want to return to judgment for the philosophical and pedagogical purposes are Ronald Beiner and Jennifer Nedelski. *Judgment, Imagination, and Politics: Themes from Kant and Arendt* (Lanham, MD: Rowman & Littlefield, 2001); Philip E. Tetlock, *Expert Political Judgment: How Good Is It? How Can We Know It?* (Princeton: Princeton University Press, 2005); Leslie Paul Thiele, *The Heart of Judgment: Practical Wisdom, Neuroscience, and Narrative* (Cambridge: Cambridge University Press, 2006); Alessandro Ferrara, *The Force of the Example: Exploration in the Paradigm of Judgment* (New York: Columbia University Press, 2008).

27. Benjamin Barber, *Strong Democracy: Participatory Politics for a New Age* (Berkeley: University of California Press, 1984); *The Conquest of Politics: Liberal Philosophy in Democratic Times* (Princeton: Princeton University Press, 1988); Ronald Beiner, *Political Judgment* (Chicago: University of Chicago Press, 1983); Stephen G. Salkever, *Finding the Mean: Theory and Practice in Aristotelian Philosophy* (Princeton: Princeton University Press, 1990); Peter J. Steinberger, *The Concept of Political Judgment* (Chicago: University of Chicago Press, 1993); William Sullivan, *Reconstructing Public Philosophy* (Berkeley: University of California Press, 1986). These scholars reject Martha Nussbaum's contention that Aristotle is too elitist as a guide for democratic politics. Martha Nussbaum, *Therapy of Desire: Theory and Practice in Hellenistic Ethics* (Princeton: Princeton University Press, 1994).

28. Barber, *The Conquest of Politics*, 151, 205; Beiner, *Political Judgment*, 75–79, 85, 106; Michael Walzer, "Democracy and Philosophy," *Political Theory* 9 (August): 393.

29. Mary Ann Glendon, *Rights Talk* (New York: Free Press, 1981); Walzer, "Democracy and Philosophy."

30. Beiner, *Political Judgment*, 16

31. Barber, *The Conquest of Politics*, 209; Sullivan, *Reconstructing Public Philosophy*, 170–173; Steinberger, *The Concept of the Political*, 126–127.

32. Steinberger, *The Concept of the Political*, 117, 279.

33. I follow Arendt and Masters who embrace Aristotle's natural science before recovering *phronesis*. Larry Arendt, "The New Darwinian Naturalism in Political Science," *American Political Science Review* 89 (June): 389–400; Roger D. Masters, *The Nature of Politics* (New Haven: Yale University Press, 1989).

34. Aristotle, *Nicomachean Ethics*, 1134b18–20, 30. All subsequent citations for Aristotle will be in-text. Translations are my own.

35. One possible solution is that Aristotle was suggesting a form of deontological ethics with a universal substance and shifting accidents, making *physei dikaion* absolute in an essen-

tial sense and *kineton pan* absolute only in a formal sense. However, as will be shown, this interpretation is not as persuasive as the one with Aristotle recognizing that *physei dikaion* is substantively paradoxical.

36. The evaluation of moral and ethical situations on a case-by-case basis does not necessarily equate into moral relativism. Aristotle's statement that *physei dikaion* was valid everywhere and that certain actions, such as murder, theft, and adultery were universally evil was a clear rejection of relativism.

37. However, if there were a case that was more ambiguous—whether the United States's atomic bombing of Japan in World War II was justified—then the argument from common sense is finished, as we have reached at the debate about the variability of principle but not the principle itself.

38. Eric Voegelin, *Anamnesis* (Notre Dame: University of Notre Dame Press, 1978), 212.

39. Derek Bok, *Universities in the Marketplace: The Commercialization of Higher Education* (Princeton: Princeton University Press, 2004); Jennifer Washburn, *University, Inc.: The Corporate Corruption of Higher Education* (New York: Basic Books, 2005); Louis Menand, *The Marketplace of Ideas: Reforms and Resistance in the American University* (New York: W.W. Norton and Company, 2010); Gaye Tuchman, *Wannabe U: Inside the Corporate University* (Chicago: University of Chicago Press, 2011).

40. Refer to the third footnote.

41. One of the biggest proponents of assessing the outcomes of transferable skills is the Collegiate Learning Assessment that employs quantitative metrics to evaluate student outcomes. Available at http://www.collegiatelearningassessment.org/.

42. Richard M. Battistoni, "Service Learning and Civic Education," in *Education for Civic Engagement in Democracy*, ed. S. Mann et al., (Bloomington: ERIC, 2000); Susan Komives, *Exploring Leadership: For College Students Who Want to Make a Difference* (San Francisco: Jossey-Bass, 2006); Marcy Shankman, *Emotionally Intelligent Leadership: A Guide to College Students* (San Francisco: Jossey-Bass, 2008); Diana Hess and Patricia G. Avery, "Discussion of Controversial Issues as a Form and Goal of Democratic Education," in *The SAGE Handbook of Education for Citizenship and Democracy*, ed. James Arthur, et al., (Thousand Oaks, CA: SAGE Publications, 2008), 506–518. For more about the relationship between liberal education and civic formation, refer to Richard E. Flathman, "Liberal versus Civic: Republican, Democratic, and Other Vocational Educations: Liberalism and Institutionalized Education," *Political Theory* 24.1 (1996): 4–32; for more about the relationship between research university and civic formation, refer to Barry Checkoway, "Renewing the Civic Mission of the American Research University," *The Journal of Higher Education* 72, no. 2 (2001): 125–147.

43. Bill Hunter, George P. White, and Galen C. Godbey, "What does it mean to be globally competent?," *Journal of Studies in International Education* 10 (Fall 2006): 267–285; Association of American Colleges and Universities, *College Learning for the New Global Century* (Washington, DC: Association of American Colleges and Universities, 2007); James A. Banks, "Diversity and Citizenship Education in Global Times," in *The SAGE Handbook of Education for Citizenship and Democracy*, ed. J. Arthur et al., (Thousand Oaks, CA: SAGE Publications, 2008), 57–70; Paulette P. Dilworth, "Multicultural Citizenship Education," in *The SAGE Handbook of Education for Citizenship and Democracy*, ed. J. Arthur et al., (Thousand Oaks, CA: SAGE Publications, 2008), 424–437; Audrey Osler, "Human Rights Education: The Foundation of Education for Democratic Citizenship in our Global Age," in *The SAGE Handbook of Education for Citizenship and Democracy*, ed. J. Arthur et al., (Thousand Oaks, CA: SAGE Publications, 2008), 455–467; Seyla Benhabib, "Cosmopolitanism and Democracy: Affinities and Tensions," *The Hedgehog Review* 11, no. 3 (Fall 2009): 30–62; Klas Roth, "Peace Education as Cosmopolitan and Deliberative Democratic Pedagogy," in *Global Values Education*, ed. J. Zajda et al., (Heidelberg: Springer, 2009), 49–64.

44. Allan Bloom, *Closing the American Mind: How Higher Education Has Failed Democracy and Impoverished the Souls of Today's Students* (New York: Simon and Schuster, 1987); Roger Kimball, *Tenured Radicals: How Politics Corrupted Our Higher Education* (Chicago: Ivan R. Dee, 1990); *The Long March: How the Cultural Revolution of the 1960s Changed America* (San Francisco: Encounter Books, 2000); Peter Wood, *Diversity: Invention of a Concept* (San Francisco: Encounters Books, 2004); Diane Ravitch, *The Language Police* (New

York: Vintage, 2004); Lee Trepanier and Khalil Habib, *Cosmopolitanism in the Age of Globalization: Citizens Without States* (Lexington, KY: University of Kentucky Press, 2011); Gerson Moreno-Riano, Lee Trepanier, Phillip Hamilton, "Statesmanship and Democracy in a Global and Comparative Context" and "Teaching the American Political Tradition in a Global Context," in *The Liberal Arts in America*, ed. Lee Trepanier (Cedar City, UT: Southern Utah University and Grace A. Tanner Center, 2012), 95–137. *The New Criterion* has consistently pointed out the problems they see in diversity, multiculturalism, and cosmopolitanism in American higher education and society. Available at http://www.newcriterion.com/.

45. An example of this problem can be found in Harry C. Boyle, "Civic Education as Public Leadership Development," where the problem of civic formation is recognized but the solution is more reading and little practice. Similar problems can be found in the works cited in footnotes forty-two and three.

46. I would prohibit colleges and universities that would have mission statements that advocated any activity that violated the "common sense" of society. For example, a college that sought to indoctrinate students into religious violence aimed at the U.S. government should not be permitted, as such mission would be contrary to the Aristotelian understanding of common sense. In fact, such a college would not be fostering *phronesis* but its antithesis and thus would be contrary to proper human flourishing.

47. *Phronesis* also would be able to address some of the criticisms that have focused on college's and universities' organizational and administrative structures (see footnotes five to seven). These problems appear to me secondary in nature to the primary obstacle that higher education institutions lack an ethical understanding of what type of student they want to foster. Once this matter is resolved, then questions of access, tenure, and specialization in scholarship become increasingly irrelevant.

48. Although Aristotle's conception of science and of nature differs from contemporary understanding, there is no reason why contemporary accounts of science still cannot be incorporated into ethical judgments like *phronesis*. In fact, as contemporary science advances in its findings, society finds itself confronting more rather than fewer ethical questions, suggesting an even greater need for *phronesis* today than in Aristotle's time.

49. Specifically, students would be required to learn both theoretical and practical thinking, while faculty's activities would not necessarily be pre-determined in a way that business employees or government officials are. This would allow faculty the freedom to develop ways to best engage students in teaching, their colleagues in research, and the public in service.

50. Graham Peeke, *Mission and Change: Institutional Mission and its Application to the Management of Further and Higher Education* (Buckingham, UK: SRHE and Open University Press, 1994), 8–12, 32.

BIBLIOGRAPHY

Aristotle. *Nicomachean Ethics*. Translated by H. Rackham. Loeb Classical Library 73. Rpt. with corrections. Cambridge, MA: Harvard University Press, 1990.

Arendt, Larry. "The New Darwinian Naturalism in Political Science." *American Political Science Review* 89 (June): 389–400.

Arum, Richard and Josipa Roksa. *Academically Adrift: Limited Learning on College Campuses*. Chicago: University of Chicago Press, 2011.

Association of American Colleges and Universities. *College Learning for the New Global Century*. Washington, DC: Association of American Colleges and Universities, 2007.

Axelrod, Paul. *Values in Conflict: The University, the Marketplace, and the Trials of Liberal Education*. Montreal: McGill-Queen's University Press, 2002.

Banks, James A. "Diversity and Citizenship Education in Global Times." In *The SAGE Handbook of Education for Citizenship and Democracy*, edited by James Arthur, Ian Davies, and Carole Hahn, 57–70. Thousand Oaks, CA: SAGE Publications, 2008.

Barber, Benjamin. *Strong Democracy: Participatory Politics for a New Age*. Berkeley: University of California Press, 1984.

———. *The Conquest of Politics: Liberal Philosophy in Democratic Times.* Princeton: Princeton University Press, 1988.

Barrow, Clyde. W. *Universities and the Capitalist State: Corporate Liberalism and the Reconstruction of American Higher Education, 1894–1928.* Madison, WI: University of Wisconsin Press, 1990.

Battistoni, Richard M. "Service Learning and Civic Education." In *Education for Civic Engagement in Democracy,* edited by Sheilah Mann and John J. Patrick, 29–44. Bloomington: ERIC, 2000.

Beiner, Ronald. *Political Judgment.* Chicago: University of Chicago Press, 1983.

Beiner, Ronald and Jennifer Nedelski. *Judgment, Imagination, and Politics: Themes from Kant and Arendt.* Lanham, MD: Rowman & Littlefield, 2001.

Benhabib, Seyla. "Cosmopolitanism and Democracy: Affinities and Tensions." *The Hedgehog Review* 11, no. 3 (Fall 2009): 30–62.

Bloom, Allan. *Closing the American Mind: How Higher Education Has Failed Democracy and Impoverished the Souls of Today's Students.* New York: Simon and Schuster, 1987.

Bok, Derek. *Universities in the Marketplace: The Commercialization of Higher Education.* Princeton: Princeton University Press, 2004.

Brubacher, John S. and Willis Rudy. *Higher Education in Transition.* New York: Harper and Row, 1976.

Checkoway, Barry. "Renewing the Civic Mission of the American Research University." *The Journal of Higher Education* 72, no. 2 (2001): 125–147.

Dilworth, Paulette P. "Multicultural Citizenship Education." In *The SAGE Handbook of Education for Citizenship and Democracy,* edited by, James Arthur, Ian Davies, and Carole Hahn, 424–37. Thousand Oaks, CA: SAGE Publications, 2008.

Ferrara, Alessandro. *The Force of the Example: Exploration in the Paradigm of Judgment.* New York: Columbia University Press, 2008.

Flathman, Richard E. "Liberal versus Civic: Republican, Democratic, and Other Vocational Educations: Liberalism and Institutionalized Education." *Political Theory* 24, no. 1 (1996): 4–32.

Giroux, Henry A. "Introduction: Critical Education or Training: Beyond the Commodification of Higher Education." In *Beyond the Corporate University,* edited by Henry A. Giroux and Kostas Myrsiades, 1–11. Lanham, MD: Rowman & Littlefield, 2001.

Glendon, Mary Ann. *Rights Talk.* New York: Free Press, 1981.

Gould, Eric. *The University in a Corporate Culture.* New Haven: Yale University Press, 2003.

Hacker, Andrew and Claudia Dreifus. *Higher Education? How Colleges are Wasting Our Money and Failing Our Kids—And What We Can Do About.* New York: Times Book, 2010.

Hawkins, Hugh. *The Emerging University and Industrial America.* Lexington, MA: D. C. Heath, 1970.

Hellenbrand, Harold. *The Unfinished Revolution: Education and Politics in the Thought of Thomas Jefferson.* Newark, DE: University of Delaware Press, 1990.

Hess, Diana and Patricia G. Avery. "Discussion of Controversial Issues as a Form and Goal of Democratic Education." In *The SAGE Handbook of Education for Citizenship and Democracy,* edited by James Arthur, Ian Davies, and Carole Hahn, 506–518. Thousand Oaks, CA: SAGE Publications, 2008.

Hunter, Bill, George P. White, and Galen C. Godbey. "What does it mean to be globally competent?" *Journal of Studies in International Education* 10 (Fall 2006): 267–285.

Jefferson, Thomas. "Jefferson Plans the University of Virginia, 1800." In *American Higher Education: A Documentary History,* edited by Richard Hofstadter and Wilson Smith, 175. Chicago: University of Chicago Press, 1961.

Johnson, E. L. "The 'Other Jeffersons' and the State University Idea." *Journal of Higher Education* 58 (1987): 127–150.

Keeling, Richard P. and Richard H. H. Hersh. *We're Losing Our Minds: Rethinking American Higher Education.* Houndmill, Great Britain: Palgrave Macmillian, 2011.

Kimball, Roger. *Tenured Radicals: How Politics Corrupted Our Higher Education.* Chicago: Ivan R. Dee, 1990.

——. *The Long March: How the Cultural Revolution of the 1960s Changed America.* San Francisco: Encounter Books, 2000.

Komives, Susan. *Exploring Leadership: For College Students Who Want to Make a Difference.* San Francisco: Jossey-Bass, 2006.

Kronman, Anthony. *Education's End: Why Our Colleges and Universities Have Given up on the Meaning of Life.* New Haven: Yale University Press, 2008.

Lucas, Christopher. *American Higher Education.* New York: St. Martin's, 1994.

Masters, Roger D. *The Nature of Politics.* New Haven: Yale University Press, 1989.

Menand, Louis. *The Marketplace of Ideas: Reforms and Resistance in the American University.* New York: W.W. Norton and Company, 2010.

Moreno-Riano, Gerson, Lee Trepanier, and Phillip Hamilton, "Statesmanship and Democracy in a Global and Comparative Context." In *The Liberal Arts in America,* edited by Lee Trepanier, 128148. Cedar City, UT: Southern Utah University and Grace A. Tanner Center, 2012.

——. "Teaching the American Political Tradition in a Global Context." In *The Liberal Arts in America,* edited by Lee Trepanier, 149–166. Cedar City, UT: Southern Utah University and Grace A. Tanner Center, 2012.

Nussbaum, Martha. *Therapy of Desire: Theory and Practice in Hellenistic Ethics.* Princeton: Princeton University Press, 1994.

——. *Not for Profit: Why Democracy Needs the Humanities.* Princeton: Princeton University Press, 2012.

Osler, Audrey. "Human Rights Education: The Foundation of Education for Democratic Citizenship in our Global Age." In *The SAGE Handbook of Education for Citizenship and Democracy,* edited by James Arthur, Ian Davies, and Carole Hahn, 455–467. Thousand Oaks, CA: SAGE Publications, 2008.

Pangle, Lorraine and Thomas Pangle. *The Learning of Liberty: The Educational Ideas of the American Founders.* Lawrence, KS: University of Kansas Press, 1993.

Peeke, Graham. *Mission and Change: Institutional Mission and its Application to the Management of Further and Higher Education.* Buckingham, UK: SRHE and Open University Press, 1994.

Perkin, Harold. "Defining the True Function of the University: A Question of Freedom Versus Control." *Change* 16 (1984): 20–29.

Ravitch, Diane. *The Language Police.* New York: Vintage, 2004.

Reading, Bill. *The University in Ruins.* Cambridge, MA: Harvard University Press, 1996.

Riley, Naomi Schaefer. *The Faculty Lounges, and Other Reasons, Why You Won't Get the College Education You Paid for.* Lanham, MD: Ivan R. Dee, 2011.

Roche, Mark William. *Why Choose the Liberal Arts.* Notre Dame: University of Notre Dame, 2010.

Roseboom, E. H. and F. P. Wisenburger. *A History of Ohio.* Columbia: Ohio Historical Society, 1996.

Roth, Klas "Peace Education as Cosmopolitan and Deliberative Democratic Pedagogy." In *Global Values Education,* edited by Joseph I. Zajda and Holger Daun, 49–64. Heidelberg: Springer, 2009.

Salkever, Stephen G. *Finding the Mean: Theory and Practice in Aristotelian Philosophy.* Princeton: Princeton University Press, 1990.

Scott, J. C. "The Chautauqua Movement: Revolution in Popular Higher Education." *Journal of Higher Education* 70 (1999): 389–412.

Shankman, Marcy. *Emotionally Intelligent Leadership: A Guide to College Students.* San Francisco: Jossey-Bass, 2008.

Slaughter, Shelia. "National Higher Education Policies in a Global Economy." In *Universities and Globalization: Critical perspectives,* edited by Janice Curie and Janice Newson, 45–70. Thousand Oaks, CA: Sage, 1998.

Spelling, Margaret, Secretary of Education. *A Test of Leadership: Charting the Future of U.S. Higher Education.* Washington, DC: U.S. Department of Education, September 2006. Accessed February 12, 2012. http://www2.ed.gov/about/bdscomm/list/hiedfuture/reports/prepub-report.pdf

Steinberger, Peter J. *The Concept of Political Judgment.* Chicago: University of Chicago Press, 1993.

Sullivan, William. *Reconstructing Public Philosophy.* Berkeley: University of California Press, 1986.

Taylor, Mark. *Crisis on Campus: A Bold Plan for Reforming Our Colleges and Universities.* New York: Knopf, 2010.

Tetlock, Philip E. *Expert Political Judgment: How Good Is It? How Can We Know It?* Princeton: Princeton University Press, 2005.

Thiele, Leslie Paul. *The Heart of Judgment: Practical Wisdom, Neuroscience, and Narrative.* Cambridge: Cambridge University Press, 2006.

Trepanier, Lee and Khalil Habib. *Cosmopolitanism in the Age of Globalization: Citizens Without States.* Lexington, KY: University of Kentucky Press, 2011.

Tuchman, Gaye. *Wannabe U: Inside the Corporate University.* Chicago: University of Chicago Press, 2011.

Veysey, Laurence. *The Emergence of the American University.* Chicago: University of Chicago Press, 1965.

Voegelin, Eric. *Anamnesis.* Notre Dame: University of Notre Dame Press, 1978.

Walzer, Michael. "Democracy and Philosophy." *Political Theory* 9 (August): 379–399.

Washburn, Jennifer. *University, Inc.: The Corporate Corruption of Higher Education.* New York: Basic Books, 2005.

Wood, Peter. *Diversity: Invention of a Concept.* San Francisco: Encounters Books, 2004.

Chapter Two

Relevance in Higher Education

A Modest Proposal

Jon M. Fennell

What is this thing, "relevance?" To what degree does it comport with the concept "higher education" and the meaning of "university?" We often hear that higher education in our time finds itself situated in "an era of relevance." How did we arrive at such a juncture? What does it bode for the future? In addressing these questions, let us begin by exploring the conceptual under-pinnings of, and some of the historical background to, the contemporary call for relevance in higher education. After this I will offer a modest proposal.

CONCEPTUAL UNDERPINNINGS AND HISTORICAL BACKGROUND

Anyone who lived through or has studied the infamous "60s" knows that there is nothing new about the call for relevance in higher education. Now, the "60s" as a social phenomenon does not neatly correspond to the interval marked by years beginning with the digits "196." It began around 1963 and ended in the mid-1970s. While we might hesitate to say that the 60s, strictly speaking, began in the universities, it certainly is true that the drama associat-ed with that designation played out there as much as, if not more than it did in any other setting. This was a time of turmoil for higher education, with the passion and disruption, generally speaking, being directly proportional to the prestige of the institution. In the forefront of the unrest were such universities as Berkeley, Columbia, and Cornell. But scarcely any college or university was untouched. And, to the degree that 60s impatience and dissatisfaction was there directed inward, the call for relevance figured prominently. To illustrate what this meant—and to illumine some problems and confusion related to that concept—let us examine the work of three writers from these times.

The first of the three authors is Walden B. Crabtree who, at the time he published his article in January 1971, was an assistant professor of education at the University of Akron. In an essay titled "An Age of Irrelevancy," Crabtree begins, quite appropriately, by examining the meaning of "relevance."[1] He states, "Relevance is a special case of meaning,"[2] by which he means that something is relevant when it is understood as assisting in the solution of what one experiences as a problem. A relevant thing, he adds, meets a need. Because problems and needs vary from person to person, Crabtree concludes that relevance is intrinsically relative: "it is the individual who is the ultimate judge of what is relevant in his life."[3] So, a college or university is *ir*relevant to the degree that it is unclear to those it serves how the institution addresses problems that are important to them. If a college or university is to be relevant, it must, after establishing that it is the responsibility of each individual to solve his own problems, ask the student "How can I help solve [those] problems?"

Crabtree's essay offers an opportunity to raise a number of troubling questions that accompany the call for relevance in higher education. To begin with, what is to count as a problem or need? Is it the proper role of higher education to respond to *all* problems and needs? Were it in fact to pursue such an end, at what point does the university lose its distinctive nature? Moreover, does responding to some problems and needs make it imprudent or impossible to respond to others? Might a response to some problems and needs be incompatible with an effective response to others? For example, does the attempt to reduce the anxiety of young people and build their sense of security conflict with the goal of acquainting them with important works of history, philosophy, or literature? To what extent is commitment to the collegiate success or self-esteem of ill-prepared students compatible with their experiencing the rewards of honest assessment and having met high academic standards (not to mention with the very existence of such standards)?[4] Pointing to a deeper issue, Crabtree evidently believes that the problems and needs that are to drive policy in higher education must be known to the student. But why must this be the case? He offers no argument for this presupposition and, as we shall see, there is good reason to believe that it is precisely deficiencies of which the student is not aware whose remediation constitutes the primary justification for the university. Crabtree does not allow for the ignorance, immaturity, misunderstanding, or inexperience of the university's clientele. This is strikingly peculiar given that the university's original primary purpose was to complete and make whole those that came to it. There is nothing in and of itself inappropriate in higher education responding to the needs of its clientele. But it is important to recognize that these individuals may be in no position to understand what they most need.

The second of our writers is Charles Frankel who in 1968 published *Education and the Barricades*,[5] the last chapter of which is titled "The Relevant University." Frankel, a prominent academic and intellectual, was between 1965 and 1967 a member of the Johnson administration. In the spring of 1968, Frankel's university (Columbia) was wracked by student protests that severely disrupted academic activity and then turned violent. (He returned to campus after this occurred.) Frankel in his book is attempting to make sense of what happened at Columbia and at other major universities across America. In a phrase that surely reflects the view of many people today, Frankel begins his chapter on relevance by stating that "universities are not what they can be."[6] He adds,

> [T]hese institutions . . . have an obligation to make contact with their students, and to recognize the state of mind and feeling in which so many of these students find themselves. The obligation is not an abstract one. It is immediate and practical. Colleges and universities are not going to be able to do their educational jobs if they do not accept it.[7]

Now, the call for relevance associated with the 60s is not the same as what we are hearing today. Frankel's account clearly indicates that it is discontented students that constitute his primary concern. Today, in contrast, the call for relevance is predicated on a much broader conception of the university's clientele. In legislative declarations about the proper role of higher education we detect a preoccupation with unhappy employers, business leaders worried about American competitiveness, distressed farmers, impoverished minorities, obese or dyslexic children, unemployed workers with unneeded skills, high school dropouts, and unmarried mothers at least as much as we do a concern for the perspectives of uninspired or alienated undergraduates. Granted, the activist students of the 60s understood themselves in large measure to be representing the interests of groups and individuals outside the university. In our time, however, it appears that these external parties have eliminated the student middle man and are calling directly for a responsive university. Or, closer to the truth, politicians and university administrators have found it convenient to portray them as making such a call. Whatever the explanation, the call for relevance is broader and, politically, more deeply rooted than it was in the past. As a result, unlike the 60s hysteria, it is not going away.

The strength and persistence of the contemporary call for relevance threatens to trivialize the bits of good sense that we find in Frankel's chapter on the relevant university. Yet, since good sense is always in short supply, we should not leave these bits unreported. The first of Frankel's valuable

observations is that if the university evolves "into the instrument of any
particular political purpose"[8] it will lose its soul. Now Frankel does not make
this point, but what is the contemporary call for relevance if not a "particular
political purpose?" Frankel is also admirably sensitive to the fact that so
many proponents of relevance in higher education are oblivious to the "mag-
ic" of what the university offers. In saying this Frankel is touching on a vital
matter: At the heart of the traditional conception of the university is reverence for liberal education. Liberal education is a preparation that by design is
intended not to have any useful or practical result. At this point we hear
Dewey rolling over in his grave, so let us promptly clarify the meaning here
of "useful and practical." We are all pragmatists to the degree that we concede that to say that something is worthwhile means that it must make a
difference. But what counts as a difference? If we insist that educational
outcomes must be measureable or that they have a specifiable connection to
vocational or other concrete objectives, we have left the heart of the university behind. Referring to that traditional role of the university, Frankel states,

> To learn detachment, to learn to recognize the limits and ambiguities of one's
> ideals, is a purpose of education. To take people out of their own time and
> place, and out of a demeaning and ignorant preoccupation with themselves, is
> another purpose. And to learn the uses of the useless is a third.[9]

Frankel then says something that is even truer today than it was in 1968: We
cannot know what will remain useful in the decades ahead. Therefore, to
train the young in particular practical skills rather than to establish in them a
general liberal competence is to invite obsolescence and disappointment.[10]
This view was recently echoed by William McGurn. He states, "If the young
people now entering our work force are going to change jobs as often as we
think, the key to getting ahead will not be having one particular skill but
having the ability to learn new skills."[11] Tellingly, McGurn goes on to re-
mark that "[i]n this regard the problem is not so much the liberal arts as the
fluff that too often passed for it." Drawing on *Academically Adrift*, a recent
controversial study of higher education by Richard Arum and Josipa Roksa,
McGurn observes that post-graduate ineptness leading to inability to find
employment is worst in "the majors and programs often thought most practical—education, business and communications." At a time, however, of 9
percent unemployment when untold thousands have in the absence of discernible possibilities simply given up looking for work, I imagine these
observations will meet with little sympathy from politicians who are calling
for the university to engage more effectively with the world.

　　Finally, Frankel, in contrast to Crabtree, recognizes that higher education
betrays the young insofar as it acquiesces to their understanding of their
problems and needs.[12] He observes that the "university cannot, without ques-

tion, give students what they think they want or need. Students are not the best judges; if they were, they would not have to be students."[13] To which one can only say "Amen."

Subsequent to the 60s our third author achieved considerable fame and is therefore now well known. In 1966 and then again in 1969, long before *The Closing of the American Mind*, Allan Bloom wrote an essay that analyzed the state of the American university.[14] In the first of these, "The Crisis of Liberal Education," Bloom, as he later points out, is hopeful. He believes that liberal education, by which he means serious consideration via study of "wise old books"[15] of the most important questions, can be made generally available. Like Frankel, Bloom recognizes that students do not know, and should not be expected to know, what they need or how to attain it. The university's responsibility is to arrange for them to read the important texts and to think about the matters they treat. In outlining his program for the university Bloom is endorsing a sort of relevance. He even employs that bewitching term:

> What our students most want and need is training in a few books in the great tradition which give them models for the serious, rather than the sham, universality, books which integrate the various studies and present their *relevance* to life as a whole.[16]

But excitement regarding Bloom's proposal is perhaps tempered by something he says earlier in the essay and is echoed in his 1987 bestseller: "I am referring to the good students in the better colleges and universities."[17] Bloom's version of relevant education may well be appropriate fare for intellectually and spiritually malnourished students, disruptive or otherwise, at the elite institutions. But one wonders about ordering the same dish for the vocationally oriented and other non-liberal segments of the university's clientele, a population that has grown disproportionately since 1966. While Bloom is preoccupied with cultivating the complete and "serious" man, large numbers of students today are instead largely if not exclusively focused on finding a job and paying the bills—an aspiration that is widely endorsed by parents, administrators, and politicians. (Lest I appear naïve, let me acknowledge that there is also a third category of students—those whose purview extends only so far as the next party and buying the latest electronic gadget. But "relevance" rhetoric seldom extends to it.)

By 1969 when he published his second article, "The Democratization of the University," Bloom has developed a very different perspective regarding the future of higher education. In reading this later essay, we at first have reason to believe that Bloom remains on familiar ground, for he early on states that the university "forms men and women of different tastes from those of the people at large."[18] But it is an indication of a new bitterness in

Bloom that in the introduction to this article he ironically refers to the "folly" of our having established institutions designed to be "a center for reflection and education independent of the regime and the pervasive influence of its principles, free of the overwhelming effect of public opinion in its crude and subtle forms, devoted to the dispassionate quest for the important truths."[19] This effort can be a folly only if it had failed. That it had failed and that it was destined to do so is the major lesson Bloom has learned in the short few years since he wrote the first article.

What is responsible for this failure? Bloom's answer is *unbridled egalitarianism*, which is to say the forceful intrusion of the democratic impulse into a place where it does not belong.[20] As we clarify the meaning of Bloom's allegation regarding the 60s, we become increasingly aware of what is occurring in our own time.

Just over ten years ago I was invited to a regional state university in Illinois as a preliminary step in an effort to woo me to accept a faculty position in foundations of education. My host for the visit was the Dean of the College of Education who, in the course of describing the university's mission, referred to students as "customers" that, he said, it was his job to serve. This single statement by itself captures the development that is responsible for Bloom's pessimistic assessment of higher education. He writes, "[W]hat is going on in our universities today is the triumph of a radical egalitarian view of democracy over the last remnants of the liberal university."[21] This egalitarianism, according to Bloom, is not satisfied with equality of opportunity but instead insists on achieving equality of result—and at any cost. On Bloom's analysis, "[t]he liberal university with its concentration on a humane education and high standards had already [before the 60s] been almost engulfed by the multiversity, which is directed to service of the community and responsive to the wishes of its constituency."[22] Now, with the fervid pursuit of the egalitarian objective by administrators and politicians, the transformation is complete: the university has given way and been conquered. Universities "have lost their neutrality as well as control of their destinies" and "the sense of the university's mission has been lost."[23] In all of this, says Bloom, "[t]he key word is *relevance*."[24] He emphasizes that, of course, the university has always been relevant insofar as genuine liberal education through an interiorization of culture provides us with the spectacles through which one can understand and thereby deal effectively with the world.[25] But in the centuries prior to the 60s (and prior to the decades of preparatory decline) that to which the university was understood to be relevant was development "of a human being possessing intellectual and moral virtue" and "the perfection of the natural faculties, independent of the particular demands of time or place."[26] All of this now is gone, displaced by preoccupation with equality of result and the servicing of any and all demands by the demos. In the name of the people the university is transformed.

All rejoice in the victory of democracy. Predictably, Bloom's assessment is very different: "The true result of all of this is that the most vulgar and philistine things which proliferate in society at large . . . dominate the university"[27] and, almost precisely anticipating the sentiments of that dean in Illinois, he states that the university has become "a market in which the sellers must please the buyers and the standard of value is determined by demand."[28] Today it is a singular college or university where such language is not the dominant discourse. Given this predicament, let us now reflect on where we go from here.

A MODEST PROPOSAL

In looking forward I begin from the conviction that the matters examined by Bloom are far worse today than they were when he wrote these words in 1969. In all but a few rare enclaves, vocational and other practical imperatives are ascendant in higher education, as is rule by a bureaucratic mind proudly in bondage to the regime of political correctness.[29] Yet, dismayed as one may be by this seizure of the university, the decay of traditional liberal studies, and the egalitarianism and consumer orientation that are the causes of both, there is no turning back. The die is cast. But if we cannot return to the past, what might we imagine for the future? Let us muse.

My first idea is an old one. While a graduate student at the University of Illinois, for an entire year I began my day in the canteen of the campus YMCA drinking tea and reading the major works of Dewey. Emerging from my daily devotions one crisp Friday morn during the fall of 1974, I looked about and saw with fresh eyes. The Y was across the street from campus and faced a pair of the University's most handsome and distinguished red brick buildings. From its front steps, you could off to the right see Illinois's huge library. To the rear of the Y was the vast expanse of fraternity and sorority houses that are such a prominent feature in Champaign. This happened to be the day before an important home football game. Because Saturday's contest loomed large and—equally important—Friday night bar life was rapidly approaching, excitement was in the air. Everyone was transported. Here was the good life! And then all of a sudden I realized that the activity that most mattered to me and fellow scholars was altogether tangential to the central concerns of the tens of thousands of people with whom we shared the campus, as well as to the priorities of the legislators and taxpayers who made this remarkable world possible. This initial realization was followed by an even more striking thought: If what my fellows and I cared about were to disappear, practically no one among the many thousands would know or care. This was followed by an additional, two-pronged insight: first, my guild was dispensable; and second, I had up to that point been in the grips of a deep (though gratifying) misunderstanding. At the University of Illinois, liberal education and the life of the mind was not the dog but instead the tail. And it was a small and insignificant tail at that.

All of this was followed by a brainstorm. Earlier in the week I had read that a public school building in Champaign had been vacated and stood empty. What, I now wondered, might be possible if the university allocated just a tiny fraction of its budget—say, a half percent—to genuine and unadulterated liberal studies? The operating budget for the U of I for 2011 was $4.8 billion. One half percent of that figure is $24 million. With such a sum as the yearly budget could we not lease an empty building and fund the facilities and faculty required to teach that small minority of students who care about the things dear to Bloom? What made this prospect especially enticing was that there need not be any opposition to this plan. After all, everything else at the university—the football, the parties, the thousands of bachelor's degrees awarded each year, the credentialing, the alumni nostalgia and support, the use of vast public monies to advance political agendas and consumerist objectives of every sort—would remain unaffected. This would include perpetuation of an enterprise in which, according to a prominent recent study, "at least 45 percent" of students after two years of college showed "no statistically significant gains in critical thinking, complex reasoning, and writing skills."[30] So, this is my first nominee for a modest proposal: Acknowledge that the university is beyond redemption; leave it as it is but provide sufficient crumbs for the small tribe that still cares about such things to conduct liberal education in a quiet annex to the restless behemoth.

But there is another, seemingly very different possibility. In 2008 Charles Murray published a startling book that caused widespread irritation. In *Real Education: Four Simple Truths for Bringing America's Schools Back to Reality*,[31] Murray outlines a proposal that is capable of preserving Bloom's liberal education without requiring any sacrifice of the practical and vocational aspirations of so many students and parents and the agendas of the politicians that are sympathetic toward them. Indeed, Murray promises to deliver on those aspirations in a manner superior to that offered by the existing state of affairs.

Murray begins from two premises. First, far too many young people are going to college.[32] Second, the reason they are doing so is a valid one: They want to secure the admission ticket to a good job. (This is what in some rarefied quarters is called the "exchange value" of the college degree, as opposed to its "use value."[33]) Murray offers the radical idea that we can accomplish this vocational objective in a manner that is considerably more efficient and very much less expensive than the current practice of sending increasingly large hordes of young people off to four years of college each fall.[34] An important secondary advantage of his plan is that the colleges and universities would remain in place but would, to a far greater degree than they currently do, be a place devoted to liberal education and the life of the mind. How does this work?

Before addressing this question, it is worth noting that Murray's plan also pays a dividend of honesty, for not only is "relevance" bad for liberal education, it represents to a considerable degree an impulse that cannot succeed.[35] In this vein David Labaree insightfully observes:

> Like educators, politicians also have an interest that is both idealistic and pragmatic in promoting education as the answer to social problems. One of the primary motives for anyone seeking political leadership is the urge to fix what's wrong in the community, and education offers a plausible mechanism for doing this.[36]

On Labaree's account, despite the politicians' perennial interest during the twentieth and twenty-first centuries in employing education to prompt significant social change, nothing of consequence has ever ensued. This, he says, is because educational innovations, based as they are on an underlying assumption by politicians (as well as most educators) that schools will secure such objectives by "tinkering with the skills and beliefs of *individuals*,"[37] cannot lead to significant change. In other words, while social, political, and economic reforms can be secured only at the level of social, political, and economic policy, politicians and their educational reformers want to realize them through change at "the individual level."[38] If Labaree is correct, then, whatever social and economic improvements that are promised as compensation for undermining liberal education in the name of relevance are illusory. Indeed, it is worse than that, according to Labaree: Assigning an ambitious social problem-solving mission to educational institutions,

> has had a negative effect on these problems by draining money and energy away from social reforms that might have had a more direct impact. Educationalizing social problems has consistently pushed education to expand its scope well beyond what it should do and what it can do, and the result is a record of one failure after another.[39]

I would add that in the process we relinquish an *actual* benefit (however limited in scope its impact may be) for what in principle can be no more than a *prospect* of change. The only winners in the subordination of education to relevance are the entrenched interests that consume the allocated resources and the politicians who propel their careers by, in a single stroke, capitalizing upon these venal constituencies while exploiting the naïve optimism of a population that has never paused to wonder whether the problems of social and economic life are in fact susceptible to straightforward educational remedies. In Labaree's phrasing, this constitutes "a kind of confidence game."[40]

Turning now to the practical side of Murray's proposal, we begin by noting that in Murray's view no more than 20 percent ("and probably closer to 10 percent") of the population possesses the academic ability to engage in genuine college work. But what becomes of the democratic commitment to the liberal education of all, if fewer than 20 percent of our citizens attend college? Murray has an answer. Building upon the core curriculum proposals of E. D. Hirsch, Murray calls for the transformation of the K-12 educational system such that all persons receive a liberal education prior to graduating from high school. This in itself is revolutionary and, I might add, long overdue. But the most interesting and controversial element in Murray's vision is that he would disconnect "four-year residential colleges and universities"[41] from vocational preparation. Success in the great majority of jobs—whether it be that of computer programmer, hotel manager, insurance salesman, television producer, advertising executive, business owner, accountant, drug abuse counselor, city manager, and perhaps even pharmacist or early elementary teacher—does not require four years of college education. So why do so many people who are looking for such jobs but are uninterested in liberal education attend college or university? Murray's answer is that our nation has stupidly fallen into a trap (albeit a trap conducive to the wishes and interests of a number of influential constituencies).[42] At the root of this trap is the belief that possessing a college degree is nearly always necessary in order to be a viable candidate for a good job. Now, this is certainly an accurate reading of the existing white-collar, managerial, and "professional" job market. But, Murray asks, why need this be? Let us instead devise an alternative "admission ticket" for employability—one that does not cost so much and that constitutes a genuine barometer of one's qualifications for the position in question. Murray's model for this vision is the CPA exam. If a candidate passes such an exam, an employer is assured that he can do the job. A college degree is superfluous.[43]

Murray is enthusiastic about the advantages of his proposal. To begin with, students and their parents (and, I would add, taxpayers as well) would be spared a monumental and growing expense that is essentially irrelevant to the vocational objective that is the primary concern of the matriculant. Of even greater importance to Murray, however, is that in severing college and university from access to the job market we eliminate a source of divisiveness and injustice. He asks why these jobs—jobs success in which does not in fact require four years of college education—should be off limits to those who cannot afford such an experience or who lack the academic ability or interest to be successful at it. In Murray's words, "we have made something that is still inaccessible to a majority of the population—the BA—into a symbol of first-class citizenship. . . . Today's college system is implicated in the emergence of class-riven America."[44] For these reasons, Murray asserts that his plan is vindicated politically and economically as well as morally. On all relevant counts it is the right thing to do.

To all of this I would add one other advantage: Were Murray's proposal to be adopted, colleges and universities would have an opportunity to return to their traditional and proper role. Most professors are familiar with the significant differences between the atmosphere of a course that students are required to attend and one which they elect to undertake. Under Murray's plan all students of four-year residential colleges and universities, with the exception of the small minority who require undergraduate coursework to qualify for medical or other specialized professional training, would be pursuing their studies in order to experience their intrinsic worth. A student would not be *putting up with* history, literature, philosophy, or chemistry in order to get a job. Rather, he would take such courses because they are enjoyable and liberating. In contrast, if one were instead interested in landing a good job and getting on with career and family, he would after high school undertake the appropriate training and go to work.

The State of Illinois, of course, is not going to allocate $4.8 billion per year for liberal education. Therefore, we might under Murray's proposal expect the campuses of America radically to shrink as they almost exclusively serve only those students interested in liberal studies and the life of the mind. A more likely scenario, however, especially when we consider the innumerable individuals and large number of entrenched interests that benefit from perpetuation of these institutions (as well as that $4.8 billion!), is that they would adapt themselves to provide the vocational preparation and certification envisioned by Murray. Indeed, this response is entirely predictable in light of recent trends in higher education. As the "bubble theorists" point out,[45] we live in a time of both soaring college costs and passionate calls for increased college enrollments. There is a connection between the two. The actual spending per student in higher education is far greater than any reasonable calculation of the real instructional cost per student.[46] It appears, then, that colleges and universities are spending vast amounts of money on something other than the instruction of their students. This fact has prompted Vance H. Fried and Reihan Salam to ask, "So what is happening to all this money?"[47] Their answer is "that the higher-education industry is enriching itself at the expense of taxpayers and students."[48] Fried and Salam, after concurring with the bubble theorists that universities collect far more in revenue than they spend on the instruction of students, state that "[t]he excess is spent in two ways: economic rents and subsidies for other missions. Economic rents are payments made to college insiders that do not increase the college's output. . . . Subsidies for other missions include the revenue from undergraduate tuition that is spent on graduate education and research"[49] (in addition, I might add, to that spent to support various social and political agendas). The bubble theorists emphasize that to cover this growing expense it is necessary to enroll a greater and greater number of the available cohort. But by doing so, higher education undermines its own market rationale: If everyone has a bachelor's degree, the economic value of having graduated necessarily declines and there is less and less reason to bear such huge expense. (This is already becoming clear to a growing number of underemployed graduates and, more importantly, to their younger siblings.) According to the bubble theorists, this cannot indefinitely continue. As is the case with our nation's entitlement programs, the trends are unsustainable.

The very interests and incentives revealed by the bubble theorists would drive higher education to seize upon Murray's alternative vision should it ever somehow be embraced by policymakers. Were this to be the manner in which Murray's proposal is implemented (and if higher education remained in the business of providing prolonged adolescence for those who wish for and can afford it), we may—in the case of the universities at least, if not so clearly that of four-year colleges—in effect have returned to my earlier proposal. The campus, with the great bulk of its expenditures, activities, and payroll, but now explicitly committed to vocational objectives, would remain much as it is. And again, the minority who possess a genuine interest in and commitment to liberal studies would comprise a community apart. The two worlds, by the way, need not be entirely divorced. The small number of students interested in the life of the mind might, for example, find employment in the larger community. One can imagine such individuals washing dishes in the student union or cleaning toilets in university buildings during the night shift. The young scholar might even find employment serving as the subject of a science experiment in a federally funded research department. Conversely, the small community of liberal learning could well be of service simply by holding fast to its mission. Much as visitors willingly pay admission to a zoological garden, members of the larger community and visitors to campus would marvel at and likely be entertained by the exotic practices of this peculiar guild—not unlike visiting Hampton Court Palace near London. Meanwhile, the close proximity of its vast and overwrought neighbor will serve as a constant reminder to members of the guild of what they have been so fortunate to escape and to which they might easily have fallen victim.

Is this not a refreshing prospect? No longer need we dissemble and no longer are we confused regarding what it is we are doing. And this would be true for both factions—the vocational as well as the liberal—each achieving relevance with the blessings of a clear conscience.

NOTES

1. Walden B. Crabtree, "An Age of Irrelevancy," *Educational Theory* 21, no. 1 (January 1971): 33–41.
2. Ibid., 33.

3. Ibid., 35. Crabtree goes on to add, "The only kind of relevance that exists is a contextual one; it is a relative relevancy, applicable to the problem at hand, perceived and accepted by the individual sufferer" (36).

4. One is here reminded of the systematic mismatch, well documented by Thomas Sowell, between 1) the intellectual ability and academic preparation of students admitted through affirmative action programs and 2) the customary demands and academic standards of the universities that so passionately seek their enrollment. Sowell's conclusions are supported by a recent empirical study at Duke University that has sparked the predictably confused and racially charged controversy. Authored by Peter Arcidiacono, Esteban M. Aucejo, and Ken Spenner, this study concludes that "attempts to increase representation at elite universities through the use of affirmative action may come at a cost of perpetuating under-representation of blacks in the natural sciences and engineering" (5). This is the result of "[w]hite and Asian SAT scores [being] over one standard deviation higher than black SAT scores" (6) and, in response to poor grades, the subsequent abandonment by black students of the more difficult disciplines in favor of the humanities and social sciences where, generally speaking, higher grades come more easily. The authors importantly state that "differences in persistence rates [in the natural sciences, engineering, or economics] are fully explained by differences in academic background" (28). In short, more black students would remain enrolled and do well in the difficult disciplines were affirmative action programs abolished. See "What Happens after Enrollment: An Analysis of the Time Path of Racial Differences in GPA and Major Choice," unpublished paper accessed February 20, 2012 at http://flawedeconomist.blogspot.com/2012/02/background.html.

5. Charles Frankel, *Education and the Barricades* (New York: W.W. Norton and Company, 1968).

6. Ibid., 81.

7. Ibid.

8. Ibid., 82.

9. Ibid., 86.

10. We find this view confirmed in a most unexpected place: "You trust in the present order of society without thinking that this order is subject to inevitable revolutions, and it is impossible for you to foresee or prevent the one which may affect your children." This is Rousseau in *Emile* (New York: Basic Books, 1979), 194.

11. William McGurn, "What's Your Kid Getting from College?" *The Wall Street Journal*, November 1, 2011.

12. What this means, of course, is that insofar as a college or university insists on regarding the student as a customer whose view is "always right," it no longer qualifies as an institution of higher education.

13. Ibid., 87.

14. Both essays are included in Allan Bloom, *Giants and Dwarfs: Essays 1960–1990* (New York: Simon and Schuster, 1990).

15. Ibid., 11. The phrase is taken from the preface to Bloom's book.

16. "The Crisis of Liberal Education," 360. Emphasis added.

17. Ibid., 350. Cf. *The Closing of the American Mind: How Higher Education Has Failed Democracy and Impoverished the Souls of Today's Students* (New York, Simon and Schuster, 1987), 22.

18. "The Democratization of the University," 366.

19. Ibid.

20. In contrast to unbridled egalitarianism is the restrained and thoughtful egalitarianism we associate, for example, with Jefferson and "nature's God." In his reflections on education Jefferson speaks of a natural aristocracy. The assertion of equality is thereby tempered in a manner that is alien and offensive to large (and often the noisiest) swaths of the contemporary university. That the university does not in fact uniformly deliver on its theoretical commitment to equality is clear to anyone who wishes to see. This hypocrisy is of little use or comfort to those who are suffering from the ills mentioned by Bloom, however.

21. Ibid., 367.

22. Ibid.

23. Ibid.

24. Ibid., 369.

25. The educated person sees the world in terms of concepts, images, and categories that, by definition, are unavailable to one that is not educated.

26. Ibid.

27. Ibid., 372.

28. Ibid., 373.

29. Bloom's unhappy tale has been told elsewhere in greater detail, not the least in his own 1987 best-seller. See, too, Julie Reuben, *The Making of the Modern University: Intellectual Transformation and the Marginalization of Morality* (Chicago: University of Chicago Press, 1996) and George Marsden, *The Soul of the American University: From Protestant Establishment to Established Nonbelief* (New York: Oxford University Press, 1994). Common to all these accounts is recognition that the university has retreated from a leadership role in the intellectual and moral development of students. Moral instruction continues, of course, but in a deceptive form. Marsden with clarity describes how religion-based pluralism in higher education has been largely eradicated due to the influence of a powerful orthodoxy that wears the cloak of tolerance, diversity, and (ironically) pluralism (432–33). He goes on to note that the restriction on pluralism is often the consequence of allegiance to a tendentious conception of "the common good" (434).

30. Richard Arum and Josipa Roksa, *Academically Adrift: Limited Learning on College Campuses* (Chicago: The University of Chicago Press, 2011), 36. The authors' figures are based on a study of 24 four-year institutions and the class of 2009. They add that there is strong reason to conclude that learning does not improve in the last two years of college. See pages 36–37. Arum and Roksa go on to state that since so little is learned during the four years, the college experience can have little impact on reducing whatever inequalities in skills and understanding that exist between racial and ethnic groups as they enter higher education. Indeed, their research demonstrates that the gap increases!

31. Charles Murray, *Real Education: Four Simple Truths for Bringing America's Schools Back to Reality* (New York: Crown Forum, 2008).

32. How many? Arum and Roksa offer what can only be called stunning figures: "more than 90 percent of high school students [are] *expecting* to attend college… [and] more than 70 percent of recent high school graduates have enrolled in either a two-year or a four-year institution" (33). These figures are from 2005 and 2001, respectively. The authors, citing Martin Trow, note that "higher education has been transformed from a privilege into an assumed right—and, for a growing proportion of young adults, into an expected obligation" (33). In this latter observation, Arum and Roksa explicitly affirm one of Murray's central assertions. Arum and Roksa elsewhere (54–55) provide an explanation of how this has come to pass: In an era of "college for all," high school counselors are loath to suggest to students that they not attend college. For this reason, "In recent decades, 30 percent of students with C grades in high school and 15 percent with grade averages of C minus or lower have been admitted into four-year colleges" (55).

33. See, for example, David F. Labaree, *The Trouble with Ed Schools* (New Haven: Yale University Press, 2004), for whom this distinction goes a long way toward accounting for the crippled character of schools of education, especially their largely unreflective, though altogether understandable, embracing of pedagogical progressivism. Labaree extends the concept of exchange value to account for the character of American education generally. See *How to Succeed in School without Really Learning: The Credentials Race in American Education* (New Haven: Yale University Press, 1997) as well as *The Trouble with Ed Schools*, 186–7.

34. In a review of two recent books on higher education—one regarding the ordeal of college admissions for students and parents, the other focused on the powerful social and economic pressures that prompt so many people to be in college when they do not want to be there and in fact find books and composition repugnant—John Derbyshire employs the term "stampede" for this phenomenon. He adds that this is a stampede "without direction or purpose, and there's a fiscal cliff up ahead there somewhere, perhaps a civilizational one." See "The Importance of a College Education," *Claremont Review of Books* (Winter 2011/12): 77.

35. What follows is inspired by and is an extension of Labaree, *Someone Has to Fail: The Zero-Sum Game of Public Schooling* (Cambridge: Harvard University Press, 2010), chapter 8.

36. Labaree, *Someone Has to Fail*, 230.

37. Ibid., 231 (emphasis added).

38. Cf. 247: "only the political sphere is able . . . to exert a significant impact on these issues." Even if recourse to education to solve the large problems of society is in principle doomed to fail, it nevertheless serves the interests of both politicians and the educational establishment to continue to make such recommendations. See 230 ff.

39. Ibid., 242.

40. Ibid., 233. Derbyshire refers to the "college rackets" ("The Importance of a College Education," 77).

41. Murray, *Real Education*, 68.

42. An observation from the conclusion of Arum and Roksa's study is refreshingly honest, but nevertheless devastating: "We believe that students, parents, faculty, and administrators are not overly concerned with the lack of academic learning currently occurring in colleges and universities, as long as other organization outcomes more important to them are being achieved" (143). And, as the authors clearly demonstrate, those other outcomes are manifestly being achieved. It might come as a surprise to both Murray and David Labaree that the latter in 2004 predicted the former's startling message: "In the current political and fiscal environment...there is an increasing danger that someone will stand up and make a persuasive case that the emperor is wearing no clothes: that there is no necessary connection between university degrees and student knowledge" (*The Trouble with Ed Schools*, 201-2). And Murray continues to blow the trumpet. In an October 2011 address he declared, "The bachelor of arts degree as it has evolved over the last half-century has become the work of the devil. It is now a substantively meaningless piece of paper—genuinely meaningless, if you don't know where the degree was obtained and what courses were taken." He goes on to ask, "So what happens when a paper credential is essential for securing a job interview, but that credential can be obtained by taking the easiest courses and doing the minimum amount of work? The result is hundreds of thousands of college students who go to college not to get an education, but to get a piece of paper." Unsurprisingly, Murray in this context refers to the "degradation of American college education." See Charles Murray, "Do We Need the Department of Education?," *Imprimis* 41, no. 1 (January 2012). Cf. Labaree in *Someone Has to Fail*: "all that this expansion does is keep inflating the credential requirements for jobs as the credential levels of people in the labor queue keep rising" (248).

43. Murray unfortunately fails to address what Derbyshire refers to as "a Mexican standoff" in higher education ("The Importance of a College Education," 77). Derbyshire refers here to a situation in which all the players in higher education (including the student who would rather be working—and without needing the college credential to get the job) are pointing guns at one another and hence no one can afford to withdraw, or even blink, because the first individuals who opt out of the game may be seriously harmed. It is therefore unclear how Murray's plan would be initiated (at least through voluntary action).

44. Ibid., 103.

45. See, for example, Richard K. Vedder and Andrew Gillen, "Cost Versus Enrollment Bubbles," *Academic Questions*, 24, 2 (Fall 2011): 282–90. It is fascinating to note, given his diametrically opposite pedigree, that David Labaree in *The Trouble with Ed Schools* also offers a bubble theory of higher education. He writes, "There is an element of the confidence game in the market-based pattern of academic life, since the whole structure depends on a network of interlocking beliefs that are tenuous at best. . . . The problem is . . . that when confidence in any of these beliefs is shaken, the whole structure can come tumbling down" (202).

46. Ibid., 290.

47. Vance H. Fried and Reihan Salam, "The College Cartel," *National Review*, LXIV, 5 (March 19, 2012): 29–35. This passage is from page 33.

48. Ibid.

49. Ibid.

BIBLIOGRAPHY

Arcidiacono, Peter, Esteban M. Aucejo, and Ken Spenner. "What Happens after Enrollment: An Analysis of the Time Path of Racial Differences in GPA and Major Choice." Unpublished manuscript, accessed February 20, 2012, http://flawedeconomist.blogspot.com/2012/02/background.html.

Arum, Richard and Josipa Roksa. *Academically Adrift: Limited Learning on College Campuses.* Chicago: The University of Chicago Press, 2011.

Bloom, Allan. *The Closing of the American Mind: How Higher Education Has Failed Democracy and Impoverished the Souls of Today's Students.* New York: Simon and Schuster, 1987.

——. *Giants and Dwarfs: Essays 1960–1990.* New York: Simon and Schuster, 1990.

Crabtree, Walden B. "An Age of Irrelevancy." *Educational Theory* 21, no. 1 (January 1971): 33–41.

Derbyshire, John, "The Importance of a College Education." *Claremont Review of Books* (Winter 2011/12).

Frankel, Charles. *Education and the Barricades.* New York: W.W. Norton and Company, 1968.

Fried, Vance H. and Reihan Salam. "The College Cartel." *National Review*, LXIV, no. 5, March 19, 2012, 29–35.

Labaree, David F. *How to Succeed in School without Really Learning: The Credentials Race in American Education.* New Haven: Yale University Press, 1997.

——. *The Trouble with Ed Schools.* New Haven: Yale University Press, 2004.

——. *Someone Has to Fail: The Zero-Sum Game of Public Schooling.* Cambridge, MA: Harvard University Press, 2010.

Marsden, George. *The Soul of the American University: From Protestant Establishment to Established Nonbelief.* New York: Oxford University Press, 1994.

McGurn, William. "What's Your Kid Getting from College?." *The Wall Street Journal*, November 1, 2011, p. A15.

Murray, Charles. *Real Education: Four Simple Truths for Bringing America's Schools Back to Reality.* New York: Crown Forum, 2008.

——. "Do We Need the Department of Education?." *Imprimis* 41, no. 1 (January 2012).

Reuben, Julie. *The Making of the Modern University: Intellectual Transformation and the Marginalization of Morality.* Chicago: University of Chicago Press, 1996.

Rousseau, Jean-Jacques. *Emile.* New York: Basic Books, 1979.

Vedder, Richard K. and Andrew Gillen. "Cost Versus Enrollment Bubbles." *Academic Questions* 24, no. 2 (Fall 2011): 282-90.

Chapter Three

The Expanding Circuit of Life

Higher Education, Wit, and Relevance

Bryan R. Warnick

If you go to Greece today, you can peel back multiple layers of history: the Bronze Age, the Classical Age, the Roman Period, the Byzantine Period, and so forth, each stage giving way to the next. The transition from the Greek to the Roman period is one of the most instructive when it comes to education. Consider the city of Corinth. If you go there today, you can see little evidence of glories of Classical Greece. Most of it was destroyed when the city and its allies stood, unsuccessfully, against the forces of the Roman Republic in 146 BC. If you go to the site museum in Corinth, however, you can find many beautiful examples of Roman mosaics, which were constructed in the wealthy Roman private homes that followed. In contrast to the Romans, the Greeks usually would not have invested so many resources on expensive ornaments for their private homes. They were people of the *polis*, after all, and they made their mark by commissioning public buildings, temples, theaters, and monuments. As the Roman Republic gave way to empire, as local self-government gave way to distant authoritarian rule, there was little to be gained from continued engagement and investment in public life. Roman citizens turned inward, making their mark in the development of their own private homes and families. The beautiful Corinthian mosaics are a symbol of this inward turn. These mosaics also mark a turn toward educational irrelevance.

Education in Classical Greece had been dominated by the rhetorical education offered by the wandering teachers of rhetoric, the Sophists. The rhetorical education was intimately connected to the Greek practice of debate and argument, of local governance within the *polis*. In the public life of the Greeks, nothing was more valuable than the ability to persuade others through the skillful use of language. After they were conquered, Greek forms of rhetorical and literary education, like other forms of Greek culture more generally, persisted and penetrated the Roman Empire. Where Greek armies had failed, Greek culture was victorious, and schools of rhetoric flourished as never before. This was a mere ghost of an education, however, because it was disconnected from the public culture that gave rhetorical education its meaning and vibrancy. It was a public skill, made obsolete in a private world. When one is governed by distant decrees instead of local debate, there is little use for the skills of persuasion. Rhetoric became a tool for private advantage rather than a way of expressing one's humanity through political engagement. The literary sort of education championed in the rhetorical schools became ripe for criticism by satirists and other social commentators. Juvenal's seventh *Satire* asks the irrelevant teachers of his day: "What harvest will you gather, what fruit, from the tilling of your field?"

The shifting grounds of culture that led to educational irrelevance can be seen again in the Renaissance. I need not rehearse all the new intellectual currents sweeping through Europe during this time. Needless to say, the new interest in classical literary texts, in the development of vernacular literature, and in experimental science and systematic empirical investigation revolutionized the European intellectual landscape. With a few exceptions, however, the medieval universities seemed completely uninterested in these intellectual trends. The traditional systematic doctrines, the forms of textual interpretation, and the methods of logical investigation all left significant room for the voice of religious authority in higher education and were therefore favored by the medieval church that had nurtured and supported the early universities. The new trends did not sit well with these older academic traditions: "Most of the Italian *studia* had continued to develop more or less independently along the lines of their original medieval traditions," writes Christopher Lucas, "and they remained thereafter largely unaffected by the ferment of classical learning."[1] This intellectual mismatch, together with the religious wars that would arise in Europe after the Reformation, led to a decline in European higher education. As Lucas summarizes, "It seems fair to claim that the long span between the latter half of the fifteenth century and the end of the eighteenth century represented a genuine nadir for European universities everywhere."[2] Critics were, once again, unsparing in their criticisms of the irrelevance of universities.

A QUESTION OF WIT

This history raises the question: Where do we stand today? Is there a similar mismatch between our universities and the intellectual, cultural, and political context in which we find ourselves? Are we, like these previous examples, laboring under delusions of relevance in a world that has long passed us by?

To explore this question, I wish to turn to a 2001 film, *Wit*.[3] The screenplay was based on a 1998 play by Margaret Edson, which won the 1998 Pulitzer Prize. The film, staring Emma Thompson, centers on a character named Vivian Bearing, a professor of English literature and specialist in the difficult *Holy Sonnets* of John Donne. At the beginning of the film, she is diagnosed with metastatic, Stage IV ovarian cancer. She promptly begins a highly aggressive experimental therapy, which she deems a "significant contribution to knowledge," under the direction of physician/researcher Harvey Kelekian. We see the long and painful process of Bearing's death as she suffers through eight full cycles of chemotherapy treatments. We see her vomiting, losing her hair, shaking with the chills, groaning, and enduring endless amounts of inhumane poking and prodding. The film deals with the nature of contemporary higher education at its most fundamental level: the relationships we have to our students, the relationships that exist between our research and teaching, the relationships between our scholarship and the surrounding culture. Most centrally, the film deals with how higher education can be relevant to what human beings most cherish—and how it can go wrong.

Vivian Bearing, the central character, describes herself as an "uncompromising" researcher, scholar, and teacher. She has little patience for students who are unmotivated or uncomprehending. She is cold and demanding, and we wince as the film flashes back to give us glimpses of her fairly brutal classroom demeanor. As a former student claims: "If there's one thing we learned in 16th Century Poetry . . . you can forget all about that sentimental stuff. Enzyme kinetics was more poetic than Bearing's class. Besides, you can't just go around . . . thinking about that meaning-of-life stuff all the time. You'd go nuts." Analysis of John Donne's religious poetry became, in Dr. Bearing's classroom, "a puzzle to be solved," "an intellectual game," a contest of "wit" in which the "puzzle takes over."

Over the course of her experimental treatment, Dr. Bearing realizes that she herself has now become nothing more than a puzzle for other researchers to solve. After being treated like an object during an awkward "grand round" where she is examined by a team of medical residents, she tells the audience: "In grand rounds they read me like a book. Once I did the teaching . . . now I am taught." She claims to be "anatomized" by her doctors, becoming identified with her ovaries, uterus, and, most of all, her cancer. Bearing's former student, Jason, now a medical research fellow, has taken to applying Bearing's research-as-puzzle-solving model to his own work with cancer patients. Her poetry class, he says, was "great training for lab research. Looking at increasing levels of complexity. . . . Research is just trying to quantify . . . the complications of the puzzle." Dr. Bearing realizes that in her case the puzzle had taken over, and she, the patient, is nowhere to be seen. The connection between Bearing, in her previous life as the uncompromising teacher of poetry, and Jason, the puzzle-obsessed researcher of cancer, is an explicit theme of the film. The film often flashes back to show us Bearing's unpleasant classroom behavior, and compares her cold behavior to that of Jason. The hero of the film, it turns out, is not Vivian Bearing. Nor is it any of the cancer researchers. The hero turns out to be one of the nurses, whose small acts of human kindness fly in the face of the scholars, professors, and researchers of various stripes that the film depicts, all interested in putting their puzzles before humanity.

The film, though, is more interesting than my initial description indicates. At first it may seem to be an anti-intellectual rant. A key moment of the film, however, occurs in a flashback as we see Dr. Bearing as a young graduate student of the "great E. M. Ashford." Ashford hands back a class paper that Bearing had written, saying, "Your essay on Holy Sonnet VI is a melodrama with a veneer of scholarship unworthy of you to say nothing of Donne. Do it again. Begin with the text, Miss Bearing, not with a feeling." Here we see, or think we see, the film showing us another lamentable example of a professor putting scholarship in front of humanity. It is all about the text, Ashford says, and human emotions are secondary. Our worries continue as Dr. Ashford drones on and on about how young Vivian should have chosen the "Gardner edition," which she claims is more authentically punctuated because it goes back to the "Westmoreland manuscript of 1610." The Gardener edition, Vivian is told, does not include a semicolon in the last line, but a comma. The film seems about to condemn this scholarly nitpicking, the obsessive focus on academic minutia, which is so derided by both ancient and modern critics of higher education. We are presented with the esoteric and seemingly pointless arguing about editions, manuscripts, variant readings, punctuation, and so forth. Such useless trivia seems so unimportant to human life and to the questions we most care about. We believe we have in this moment an example of how higher education becomes irrelevant to humanity.

This is all a feint. The film quickly turns our worry on its head, as Ashford goes on to explain why this all matters. Things of profound human significance hang on favoring the comma instead of the semicolon.

> Nothing but a breath, a comma, separates life from life everlasting. Very simple, really. With the original punctuation restored, death is no longer something to act out on a stage with exclamation marks. It is a comma. A pause. In this way, the uncompromising way, one learns something from the poem, wouldn't you say? Life, death, soul, God, past, present. Not insuperable barriers. Not semicolons. Just a comma.

It is precisely through uncompromising scholarship, Ashford says, which helps us to "learn something" of significance from the poem. You start with the text, Ashford seems to say, but you do not end there. You end with, as philosopher John Dewey would say, the "problems of men." It was in this moment, Bearing reflects, when she was introduced to proper relationship between research, teaching, and human life. "*Simple human truth.* Uncompromising scholarly standards. They're connected," she realizes, although at this time she finds that she is unable to realize what connection there is. Only when she is dying of cancer, desperate for human contact with her aloof researchers, does she realize what her mentor was trying to tell her.

As an audience, we are brought back to this connection at the end of the film. Ashford comes to visit her former student in the intensive care facility, just as Bearing is about to die. Ashford reads to Bearing a selection from a children's book she had recently purchased for a grandchild, *The Runaway Bunny*, by Margaret Wise Brown. Even here, Ashford does not renounce careful scholarship, as she carefully reads to Bearing the detailed information regarding the edition of the children's book she is holding. As she reads the book, Ashford realizes that there is a connection between the text (a mother bunny's loyalty to her child) and the questions of life and death that are facing her dying student. The text, carefully and uncompromisingly considered, becomes an allegory of the soul and its relationship to God. It becomes relevant in the most profound way possible.

There are three points that I think the film helps me make about education. First, the film suggests that contemporary higher education can become irrelevant, I would argue, just as rhetorical education became irrelevant in the Roman Empire and as the medieval university became irrelevant to the intellectual life of the Renaissance. With the Romans, rhetoric became a puzzle, a puzzle that trumped all other human concerns. In the Renaissance, Aristotelian logical analysis, aimed at ever more esoteric theological questions, also became a puzzle-solving exercise that took on a life of its own, with intrinsic standards trumping exterior connections. The film *Wit* suggests this same danger can often be found lurking in the corners of our contemporary libraries and laboratories.

Second, I think the point of the film is not to champion one subject matter as being more relevant to human life than another. Cancer research can become irrelevant to human concerns, in some contexts, and in the minds and hearts of some researchers. At the same time, a children's book can speak to the questions of the most profound gravity and meaning. It is not so much, then, the content area that is, by itself, relevant or irrelevant. It is how scholars handle content, and how that content is framed and articulated to the larger public. A study of the NGC 7129 stellar cluster can be an enormous exercise of irrelevance, producing "knowledge for its own sake," or it could be, in some small way, an attempt to locate the place of human beings in the larger universe. The scholar-educator should be able to articulate the larger connections, while at the same time relentlessly pursuing the necessary puzzle solving.

Finally, the type of relevance that *Wit* describes is not always found within narrow utilitarian questions. Unfortunately, a narrow utilitarian vision of relevance seems to be behind the recent demands for relevance in higher education. While some research questions, such as those involved in cancer research, have obvious connections to pressing practical problems, *Wit* seems to have in mind a scholarship that addresses questions of human meaning. These are the big, enduring questions, rather than simply the pressing practical problems of the moment. These are the questions that philosopher Nel Noddings has in mind: "Who am I? What kind of person will I be? Who will love me? How do others see me?"[4] These larger questions give meaning and purpose to the more utilitarian questions involved in something like cancer research. They tell us why we want to cure cancer, and what limits to this pursuit there may be. These enduring questions are always relevant and they should be at the heart of university life. The critics of the university are correct that the university needs to be relevant; they err, however, by looking only at immediate needs and problems rather than on the enduring questions of meaning that haunt human life.

RELEVANCE THROUGH WISDOM

The sort of relevance that is called for has to do with how knowledge is connected. It is in forging connections between ideas that we are able to produce the knowledge that becomes significant to human life. How do the puzzles we pursue relate to each other? How does cancer relate to the metaphysical poetry of John Donne or to children's literature?

As an example of how connections forge meaning, consider the film *Nostalgia de la Luz* (*Nostalgia for the Light*), by Chilean filmmaker Patricio Guzman.[5] It deals with the seemingly different activities occurring in Chile's Atacama desert. On the one hand, you have astronomers taking advantage of the dry conditions to observe the ancient light coming from distant galaxies; on the other hand, you have mothers of the political prisoners who were killed during the reign of dictator Augusto Pinochet looking for the thousands of bodies that were dumped in the same desert some thirty-five years ago. The film attempts to make the connection between these activities, namely, that they are both exploring the past in a way that situates our identities in the present: "Los que tienen Memoria son capaces de vivir en el frágil tiempo presente, los que no la tienen, no viven en ninguna parte."[6] The film connects astronomy, history, anthropology, art, and political science in a way that speaks to issues of central concern to human life.

It is through forging these sorts of connections that meaning is made. The university is seen as most relevant when it is a place, not only to produce bits of knowledge, but also to make connections among them. John Henry Newman championed this as the particular strength of the university. He describes the university as essentially a place of gathering, where people with very different talents and interests come together:

> This I conceive to be the advantage of a seat of universal learning, considered as a place of education. An assemblage of learned men, zealous for their own sciences, and rivals of each other, are brought, by familiar intercourse and for the sake of intellectual peace, to adjust together the claims and relations of their respective subjects of investigation. They learn to respect, to consult, to aid each other. Thus is created a pure and clear atmosphere of thought, which the student also breathes, though in his own case he only pursues a few sciences out of the multitude. [7]

Alfred North Whitehead also argued the idea that universities find their relevance as places to forge connections. "During the school period the student has been mentally bending over his desk; at the University he should stand up and look around," he stipulates. [8] Elsewhere, he argues, "There is only one subject matter for education, and that is Life in all its manifestations." Contemporary universities, for Whitehead, would lose their relevance by supplying lists of disconnected subjects. "Can such a list be said to represent Life, as it is known in the midst of the living of it? The best that can be said of it is, that it is a rapid table of contents which a deity might run over in his mind while he was thinking of creating a world, and had not yet determined how to put it together." [9]

I also think this idea is, in the end, what Ralph Waldo Emerson was getting at in his 1837 address, *The American Scholar*. Emerson begins his essay with the myth of the divided man. According to this myth, there was originally one person, encompassing the full range of human wisdom, functions, and activities. In our social state, though, this original person has become separated through divisions of labor, and we therefore experience a lack of wholeness in our existence. Using this myth as a starting point, Emerson argues that the idea behind education is to find again those connections to our lost powers and abilities, to have a range of experiences representative of the whole of the human race. We put together the work of our minds and our hands, the work of our heads and our hearts, the work of our passions and our intellects. We can engage in thought and scholarship, then, but our full humanity should remain central. In Emerson's terms, we should be "Man Thinking," forging connections, instead of being "mere thinkers."

HOW WE CAN BECOME CONNECTORS

If the university finds its relevance through the gathering of scholars, making real human meaning through connections, how do we develop and nurture this relevance? Emerson's essay, I believe, also offers some helpful suggestions in this regard. We develop our powers, as scholars and human beings, by extending the range of our experiences. If we are to make connections, we must have something to connect.

For Emerson, the need to connect has several implications. First, if we want universities to be relevant in this way, we should promote a wide-ranging, first-hand experience with Nature. Emerson writes, "Ever the winds blow; ever the grass grows. Every day, men and women, conversing, beholding and beholden. The scholar is he of all men whom this spectacle most engages."[10] The journey into Nature, for Emerson, is really a journey of self-discovery. Emerson was thinking here of the Kantian "turn to the subject," where the human subject experiences and objectifies Nature through systems of categories imposed by an active mind. We experience Nature only through mental categories that we ourselves have constructed. Emerson extrapolates from this, as do the Romantics, that we learn about ourselves as we study Nature. One way to connect research to humanity, then, in a way that breaks scholarship free from aimless puzzle solving, is to contemplate what we learn about *ourselves* through our investigations of Nature. We should more often ask: Why did we ask this question? Why did we approach our study in the way that we did? Why did we find this to be important? And what does this all say about us?

The second way to connect the scholar to a wide range of experiences is through books. Emerson, of course, has a great respect for books, but most striking in his discussion is the warning he provides. If scholars are to connect their studies with humanity, they cannot be overly focused on the writings of others.

> Books are written by thinkers, not by Man Thinking. . . . Meek young men grow up in libraries, believing it their duty to accept the views, which Cicero, which Locke, which Bacon, have given, forgetful that Cicero, Locke, and Bacon were only young men in libraries, when they wrote these books. Hence, instead of Man Thinking, we have the bookworm. Hence, the book-learned class, who value books, as such; not as related to Nature and the human constitution, but as making a sort of Third Estate with the world and the soul. Hence, the restorers of readings, the emendators, the bibliomaniacs of all degrees.[11]

Third, we have Emerson's famous call to action. While Emerson reminds us to experience Nature, it is through action that we develop a relationship with

Nature. In Nature we can find self-knowledge, but action is the key that propels us into the relationships that make self-knowledge possible.

> The world,—this shadow of the soul, or other me—lies wide around. Its attractions are the keys which unlock my thoughts and make me acquainted with myself. I run eagerly into this resounding tumult. I grasp the hands of those next me, and take my place in the ring to suffer and to work, taught by an instinct, that so shall the dumb abyss be vocal with speech. I pierce its order; I dissipate its fear; I dispose of it within the circuit of my expanding life. So much only of life as I know by experience, so much of the wilderness have I vanquished and planted, or so far have I extended my being, my dominion. I do not see how any man can afford, for the sake of his nerves and his nap, to spare any action in which he can partake. It is pearls and rubies to his discourse. Drudgery, calamity, exasperation, want, are instructors in eloquence and wisdom. The true scholar grudges every opportunity of action past by, as a loss of power. [12]

To be relevant, then, universities must allow for a broad range of human experiences. They must provide "the circuit," Emerson says, of a constantly "expanding life." They use books, but also provide students with experiences in Nature through action. Universities should hire faculty who are not only book learned, but who bring with them a range of human experiences. It is not the length of the CV, Emerson would say, it is the breadth that matters.

At this point, the film *Wit* again might have something to add to Emerson's list. It is not simply experience with Nature, Books, and Action that is required, but something more specific. Ashford's advice to the young Bearing, when she was a young graduate student who had written a bad paper, was not to go back to the library. It takes scholarship to understand poetry, to be sure, but Ashford implies that it also takes experience living in the world, experience with the agonies and ecstasies, the joys and sorrows. To learn from poetry, to make it relevant, one needs, most of all, to love. "Vivian, you're a bright young woman. Use your intelligence. Don't go back to the library, go out. Enjoy yourself with friends." This advice, unfortunately, is advice that the studious young Bearing simply cannot accept. It is the full engagement with human relationships, however, that gives scholars a sense of what is most important. Knowing the human world, in an intimate way, is what allows us to make our work relevant to the most pressing human questions. Having people to care about, to talk with and to laugh with, exposes the questions that are most important to consider, and the type of answers that will be most significant. "Simple human truth. Uncompromising scholarly standards." They *are* connected. In these connections we find wisdom, and in wisdom, we find relevance.

NOTES

1. Christopher J. Lucas, *American Higher Education: A History* (New York: St. Martin's Press, 1994), 76.
2. Ibid., 94.
3. Emma Thompson and Mike Nichols, *Wit*. DVD. Directed by Mike Nichols. United States: Avenue Pictures Productions, 2001.
4. Nel Nodding, *The Challenge to Care in Schools: An Alternative Approach to Education* (New York: Teachers College Press, 1992), 20.
5. Patricio Guzman, *Nostalgia for the Light*. DVD. Directed by Patricio Guzman. Chile: Atacama Productions, 2011.
6. "Those who remember are able to live in the fragile moment of the present, those who do not, do not live anywhere."
7. John Henry Newman and Frank M. Turner, *The Idea of a University* (New Haven: Yale University Press, 1996), 77.
8. Alfred North Whitehead, *The Aims of Education and Other Essays* (New York: The New American Library, 1949), 37–38.
9. Ibid., 18.
10. Ralph Waldo Emerson, *Selected Essays* (Harmondsworth, Middlesex: Penguin Books, 1982), 85.
11. Ibid., 88.
12. Ibid., 92.

BIBLIOGRAPHY

Emerson, Ralph Waldo. *Selected Essays*. Harmondsworth, Middlesex: Penguin Books, 1982.
Guzman, Patricia. *Nostalgia for the Light*. DVD. Directed by Patricio Guzman. Chile: Atacama Productions, 2011.
Lucas, Christopher J. *American Higher Education: A History*. New York: St. Martin's Press, 1994.
Newman, John Henry and Frank M. Turner. *The Idea of a University*. New Haven: Yale University Press, 1996.
Nodding, Nel. *The Challenge to Care in Schools: An Alternative Approach to Education*. New York: Teachers College Press, 1992.
Thompson, Emma and Mike Nichols. *Wit*. DVD. Directed by Mike Nichols. United States: Avenue Pictures Productions, 2001.
Whitehead, Alfred North. *The Aims of Education and Other Essays*. New York: The New American Library, 1949.

II

Historical Perspectives of Relevance

Chapter Four

Virtue, Happiness, and Balance

*What Jefferson Can Still Teach Us
about Higher Education*

Michael Schwarz

In 2011 the National Governors' Association's Center for Best Practices, which describes itself as "the nation's only dedicated consulting firm for governors and their key policy staff," released a report entitled "Degrees for What Jobs? Raising Expectations for Universities and Colleges in a Global Economy." Whatever it might have done for expectations, the report's title alone raises hackles on Humanities professors grown weary of utilitarian prescriptions for higher education. Predictably, the report insists that universities and colleges should "drive economic growth" by linking "students' academic success" to the "needs of the marketplace." It does not deny, but neither does it acknowledge, any other purpose in higher education. Thus, according to the National Governors' Association's policy consultants, universities and colleges demonstrate their relevance to society by preparing students to enter the job market.[1]

One hundred and ninety-three years earlier, an elderly Thomas Jefferson laid out a very different plan for higher education. On August 4, 1818, Jefferson drafted the famous "Rockfish Gap Report," a detailed administrative and curricular plan that paved the way for the chartering of his University of Virginia. As much as any single document can encapsulate decades of serious thought, the Rockfish Gap Report probably best represents Jefferson's mature understanding of higher education and its purposes. This incipient university, Jefferson declares, will cultivate in students "habits of reflection and correct action, rendering them examples of virtue to others, and of happiness within themselves."[2] Nowhere does Jefferson suggest that Virginia's governors should use the institution as a driver of economic growth. According to the Rockfish Gap Report, Jefferson believed that his university would demonstrate its relevance to society in part by forming thoughtful young men of character.

What are we to make of these two very different reports on higher education, separated by nearly two centuries? It is tempting, perhaps, to showcase the 2011 NGA Report as proof of intellectual and societal declension, but this little report should not bear that much symbolism. Likewise, it would be unfair to denounce the conventional, market-oriented ideas that originated with consultants in the NGA Center's Economic, Human Services, and Workforce Division and then contrast those ideas with the celebrated work of a Pantheon-level Founding Father. Jefferson, moreover, lived in a pre-industrial age before compulsory education and improved standards of living swelled the ranks of middle- and lower-middle-class college students. So his purposes, some might argue, cannot be ours.

On the other hand, Jefferson seems to have a perpetual claim on our attention. "If Jefferson was wrong, America is wrong. If America is right, Jefferson was right," biographer James Parton famously declared in 1874.[3] Notwithstanding a slew of critical studies published at least since the 1960s, and notwithstanding the 1998 revelation of DNA evidence that appears to confirm Jefferson's paternity of at least one child by a slave mistress, Parton's nineteenth-century judgment holds. As the great historian Gordon Wood has observed, Jefferson's "ideas about liberty and democracy left such a deep imprint on the future of his country that, despite persistent attempts to discredit his reputation, as long as there is a United States he will remain the supreme spokesman for the nation's noblest ideals and highest aspirations."[4] Most important of all, Jefferson fought to ensure that those ideals became institutionalized. In the half century between the Declaration of Independence and his 1826 death, Jefferson did more than any of his famous contemporaries to promote educational reform, particularly in Virginia. "No one can doubt my zeal for the general instruction of the people," Jefferson wrote in 1821. After all, "Who first started that idea? I may surely say, myself."[5] Jefferson's Rockfish Gap Report, therefore, commands the attention of historians and educators alike. Its goals stand in marked contrast to those articulated in the 2011 NGA Report, which, however careful we must be not to invest with too much significance, does seem representative of a market-oriented way of thinking about relevance in higher education. If we are to understand the Rockfish Gap Report, however, we must examine it in the context of Jefferson's broad thinking about education, which evolved over more than four decades.

In sum, Jefferson's ideas about how institutions of higher learning can perform functions relevant to both individuals and societies appear more persuasive than those contained in the NGA Report, in part because of Jefferson's noble ideals and high aspirations, but also because Jefferson's prescription for higher education does not ignore the practical reasons why human beings seek to educate themselves. Jefferson's approach deserves our consideration not simply because he answered the relevance question with classic Jeffersonian erudition and lucidity but because he understood, as advocates of market-oriented reforms apparently do not, that people choose education for a variety of reasons, that institutions can promote the broadly defined interests of both the individual and the society, and that the best system of higher education will always be a balanced one.

By the time Jefferson penned the Rockfish Gap Report he already had spent more than four decades thinking about public education. In the late 1770s, as a member of the Virginia legislature, he drafted "A Bill for the More General Diffusion of Knowledge," which, along with concurrent bills abolishing primogeniture, entail, and the Anglican Church establishment, Jefferson later described as part of a "system by which every fibre would be eradicated of antient or future aristocracy; and a foundation laid for a government truly republican."[6] In this sense, Jefferson's education bill pursued the same objectives as the Revolution itself.

Jefferson and his contemporaries were born into a monarchical society, albeit one whose monarchism was slowly eroding. As Gordon Wood explained more than twenty years ago, monarchical society was rooted in the divinely ordained truth that some human beings were born better than others. Hierarchy was natural. People divided neatly into patricians and plebeians. Political authority depended on birth and title. To advance in this society required not merit but patronage. John Locke, Voltaire, even Benjamin Franklin—all had patrons. What mattered was not your quality but whether anyone in a higher station of life would take notice of you, and even then, without a hereditary title you could never become anything more than a commoner.[7] In a more immediate sense, too, Jefferson's world had monarchical trappings. Virginia, oldest of all British North American colonies, had its origins in what historian David Hackett Fischer has called one of the "four folkways" to America, the mid-seventeenth-century emigration of "distressed cavaliers" who fled the Puritan revolution in England, bringing with them to Virginia an intense royalism and a determination to impose South England's bifurcated society upon the unsuspecting tidewater.[8] Of course, Virginia also had its representative assembly, the House of Burgesses, and the New World's frontier proved remarkably resistant to the impositions of the Old, which meant that all the seventeenth-century cavalier expatriates could not transform Virginia into a second England. Jefferson's own lineage, in fact, is a microcosm of this very odd society, partly egalitarian and partly aristocratic. His father, Peter Jefferson, came from a relatively obscure family. His mother, Jane Randolph, hailed from one of the FFVs, the first families of Virginia, whose patriarchs had dominated the colony since the late seventeenth century. "They trace their pedigree far back in England and Scotland," Jefferson later wrote of his mother's family," to which let everyone ascribe the faith and merit he chooses."[9]

Having come of age in this strange Virginia society, where aristocratic and republican sensibilities coexisted, Jefferson well understood that privilege, backed by power, posed a constant threat to liberty. In 1774, his political anxieties awakened by the imperial crisis that followed the Boston Tea Party, Jefferson wrote and circulated a pamphlet entitled *A Summary View of the Rights of British America*, warning against what we might call a revival of Old-World-style feudalism. Early in the text, Jefferson identifies "an error in the nature of our land holdings." American colonists, like their Saxon ancestors, ought to have held their property "in absolute dominion, disencumbered with any superior, answering nearly to the nature of those possessions which the feudalists term allodial." Alas, English settlers in North America had been duped into believing that "all lands belong originally to the king." Jefferson also notes that in the seventeenth century the settlers' lands had been "parted out and distributed among the favorites" of the Stuart kings and "by an assumed right of the crown alone, were erected into distinct and independent governments."[10] The history of some royal and all proprietary colonies did indeed follow this pattern.[11]

Why, in the midst of a trans-Atlantic dispute over rights and taxation, did Jefferson bother raising the issue of seventeenth-century proprietary grants and his ancestors' presumably allodial landholdings? By 1774, ample evidence suggested that aristocrats in England and would-be aristocrats America, enthralled by the prospect of mass tenancy and exorbitant quitrents, hoped to advance their century-old feudal claims through the agency of the Crown. This "feudal revival" left few colonies untouched. Thomas Penn had reasserted his family's claims as early as the 1730s. Lord Baltimore did likewise in Maryland. The enormous Fairfax claim in Virginia owed its legitimacy to this revival. So, too, did the great estates that bore the names of famous New Yorkers, such as Cortlandt Manor and Rensselaerswyck. In South Carolina, on the eve of the Revolution, wealthy planters in significant numbers called for lifetime nobility in the upper house of the legislature.[12] The consequence of all this should be obvious: if the structure of American society in the late eighteenth century appeared conducive to a revival of feudalism backed by Crown authority, then we might conclude that the bustling, acquisitive, interest-driven, middle-class democracy that greeted Alexis de Tocqueville in the second quarter of the nineteenth century emerged not as a consequence of natural social development but through revolutionary convulsions.

It was in this broad context of monarchism and feudalism that Jefferson made his initial exertions on behalf of public education. His "Bill for the More General Diffusion of Knowledge," part of that "system" by which he would wipe out aristocracy, envisioned a three-tiered pyramidal structure of publicly funded schools whereby Virginia would guarantee all of its children the most basic education in reading, writing, and arithmetic, supplemented by an introduction to Greek, Roman, English, and American history, all of which Jefferson hoped would help ensure the republicanization of Virginia's next generation. Good laws and a republican constitution would do much to secure the Revolution, but these alone would not suffice, for all forms of government at one time or another, regardless of their benign origins, had descended into tyranny. The "most effectual means of preventing this," Jefferson declared, "would be, to illuminate, as far as practicable, the minds of the people at large, and more especially to give them knowledge of those facts, which history exhibiteth, that, possessed thereby of the experience of other ages and countries, they may be enabled to know ambition under all its shapes, and prompt to exert their natural powers to defeat its purpose." A republic, too, needed its leaders, which is why "those persons, whom nature hath endowed with genius and virtue, should be rendered by liberal education worthy to receive, and able to guard the sacred deposit of the rights and liberties of their fellow citizens." True to the egalitarian creed he had drafted in 1776, Jefferson believed that Virginia would draw its future statesmen from all ranks of society, so he insisted that these guardians of republican liberty "should be called to that charge without regard to wealth, birth or other accidental condition or circumstance" and that they "should be sought for and educated at the common expense of all."[13]

Having outlined this breathtakingly democratic vision for education in Virginia, Jefferson proceeded to describe in detail how the statewide system would work. Qualified electors in each county would choose three Aldermen who then would meet and divide their county into "hundreds." Electors who resided within these hundreds then would select a convenient location for a school, where all children would receive three years' education at the public expense. The Aldermen then would appoint an overseer, responsible for approximately ten of these schools, to "superintend" both teachers and curriculum. Next, the overseers from multiple counties would gather to choose the location of a grammar school, where students would learn Latin, Greek, English grammar, geography, and advanced mathematics. But the overseers' most important function would be to identify in the hundred schools boys of "promising genius and disposition" and invite these children, "whose parents are too poor to give them farther education," to proceed to the nearest grammar school for at least one additional year free of charge. There the process would become even more selective. Some boys would be sent home after one year; all except one would be sent home after two years or else continued at their parents' private expense. The one boy "of the best genius and disposition" would continue "four years longer on the public foundation" and thereafter would be "deemed a senior." Finally, a handful of the most promising seniors would enjoy three years free tuition at the College of William and Mary, the apex of the Jeffersonian educational pyramid.

Alas, Jefferson's bill failed. The men who ruled Virginia in the 1770s saw no reason why wealthy taxpayers should bear the burden of sending poor children to school, even for a few years. Not for the last time did Virginia's elites reveal the limits of their own revolutionary egalitarianism. In 1796 the Virginia legislature revived Jefferson's plan in a modified form only to see the local "oligarchs," as Jefferson called them, refuse to act on the bill. [14]

Although the failure of Jefferson's plan probably contributed to Virginia's eventual decline in the nineteenth century, one might speculate that had the bill succeeded in the 1770s its results would have fallen short of Jefferson's expectations. [15] Much depended upon the College of William and Mary, Jefferson's alma mater and the only institution of higher education in the entire state. In fact, for half a century William and Mary had existed as one of only three colleges in all of British North America. Since 1745, seven additional colleges had opened their doors, and three more were in the works by the time Jefferson drafted his bill, so the third quarter of the eighteenth century certainly qualifies as an era of unprecedented activity in college founding. [16] Whether it also might have qualified as an era of innovation in higher education is a bit more dubious. [17] Though it was capable of producing an Enlightenment lawyer such as Jefferson, William and Mary remained an Anglican institution. Professors and students alike conformed to the 39 Articles of the Elizabethan Religious Settlement. The school's main purpose was to produce Anglican ministers. Both the college and the legislature thus resisted Jefferson's attempts to bring chairs and curricula in line with the Revolution's republican currents. Furthermore, freedom of conscience in Virginia was still a few years away, so Jefferson's educational reform efforts encountered resistance not only from dedicated Anglicans but also from religious dissenters who feared that by placing William and Mary College at the head of his system Jefferson risked further empowering the Episcopal establishment. [18] Even while serving as a member of the College's Board of Visitors Jefferson managed only modest reforms. [19] Like his efforts to bring public education to Virginia's children, Jefferson's hopes of republicanizing William and Mary remained elusive. In fact, he would never attempt it again.

What are we to make of Jefferson's initial exertions on behalf of public education? That these exertions failed is no measure of their merit. Jefferson's proposed system of graduated and symbiotic institutions—hundreds, grammar schools, and a secularly reformed College of William and Mary—had no precedent anywhere in Colonial America. [20] His purposes aligned with the larger goals of the American Revolution, at least as he understood them. Hence he did not yet view educational reform in economic terms. His motives were entirely political and civic: destroy aristocracy, instruct Virginians in their rights, and uncover the state's natural leaders who otherwise would labor in obscurity. The hundreds alone constituted an ambitious experiment in local self-government. It remained to be seen whether a system of public schools, sweeping and innovative, and crowned by a worthy institution of higher learning, could be made to serve Virginia's needs in the way Jefferson intended.

Decades passed before Jefferson again could focus his attention on education. As president of the United States between 1801 and 1809 he took several bold steps in this direction. First, despite having once opposed the idea, Jefferson helped establish the United States Military Academy at West Point.[21] Then, in his Sixth Annual Message to Congress, a speech that revealed powerful strains of nationalism, he proposed using surplus federal revenues toward the construction of roads, canals, and, most notably, a national university—all, of course, with the classic Jeffersonian proviso that Congress would require a constitutional amendment in order to act on these recommendations.[22] President Washington once had toyed with the idea of a national university, and within twenty years a group of southern politicians would skewer President John Quincy Adams for proposing a similar institution, albeit without the insistence upon a constitutional amendment.[23] Each time the idea went nowhere.

Shortly after retiring from the presidency, Jefferson abandoned his national efforts and renewed his focus upon educational reform at the state level. Like his political thinking, which seemed to oscillate between nationalism and state sovereignty, Jefferson's ideas on education proved flexible enough to respond to Virginia's changing circumstances. Gone were the revolutionary days when Jefferson would think to propose public education as part of a systematic assault on aristocracy. The republican revolution of 1776, thanks in no small part to Jefferson's ascension to the presidency, was finally secure. And yet Virginia since the Revolution had not fared well in relation to her sister states. Many of her sons had struck out for the greener pastures of Kentucky and points west. Once-prosperous tobacco planters found no escape from the tightening noose of debt, preferring to sell their slaves southward rather than emulate their northern brethren who had adopted plans of gradual emancipation. "Virginia," in the words of Jefferson biographer Merrill Peterson, had "slid into deeper ignorance than she had known at her birth."[24] By the second decade of the nineteenth century, Jefferson would come to define the relevance of his educational system not by republicanization but by statewide regeneration.

In some respects the road to Rockfish Gap and the chartering of the University of Virginia began in 1814. Peter Carr, Jefferson's nephew, was spearheading efforts to establish a private academy in Albemarle County, Jefferson's home. Hoping to secure funds and lend legitimacy to the endeavor, Carr enlisted his famous uncle in the project. The immediate result was a detailed letter from Jefferson to Carr in which the retired Sage of Monticello

laid out plans for an entire system of education similar to the one he had
sketched during the Revolution, albeit with new wrinkles. Apart from his
fellow Virginians' stubborn reluctance to fund universal primary education—a reluctance made more intractable by the state's recent decline—
Jefferson knew that the principal obstacle to his system remained the absence
of a suitable university. "I have long entertained the hope that this, our native
State, would take up the subject of education," Jefferson told Carr, "and
make an establishment, either with or without . . . William and Mary." By
this time Jefferson seems to have given up on his alma mater. He also seems
to have concentrated his thinking about this new private academy, for he
advised his nephew that they and the Albemarle Academy's trustees "must
ascertain with precision the object of our institution." Could he already have
envisioned a broader role for the Albemarle Academy? Indeed, within less
than two years Jefferson and his allies in the Virginia legislature would
transform Albemarle Academy into Central College, which suggests that
Jefferson already had begun to shift his attention from elementary to higher
education.[25]

Meanwhile, Jefferson continued to instruct his nephew in both structure
and curricula. At the base of the Jeffersonian pyramid stood the elementary
or "hundred" schools. Jefferson had described these in detail during the
Revolution, and his letter to Carr adds little of consequence to the subject,
which further suggests that the elementary schools no longer occupied first
place in his thoughts.[26] At the pyramid's second level Jefferson chose to
replace the old grammar schools with what he calls "general schools,"
though the change involved more than semantics, for the general schools
constituted the "second grade of education" and "professional schools" occupied the "third grade of education." Clearly, Jefferson intended a modification of the old three-tiered system, for he imagined that elementary students,
"destined to the pursuits of science," would "proceed to the college," which
would "consist, 1st of general schools; and 2nd, of professional schools" (the
"college" he envisioned here differed in scope from the university he later
established, though, as we shall see, the curriculum was quite similar). With
regard to the college's precise structure, however, Jefferson's ideas advanced
no further.

With regard to curriculum and prospective students, however, Jefferson's
letter to Carr laid the groundwork for a truly novel and balanced institution.
The grammar schools would consist on one hand of students "destined for
learned professions" who eventually will require professional training, and
"the wealthy" on the other hand, who "may aspire to share in conducting the
affairs of the nation." To suit these students' respective needs, Jefferson
suggested dividing the general school's curriculum into three departments:
Language, Mathematics, and Philosophy, under which he classified a number
of humanistic and scientific subfields, such as History, Zoology, and Ethics.

For the professional schools Jefferson also proposed three departments: one encompassing Fine Arts and Civil Architecture, another that includes Rural Economy, Military Architecture and Projectiles, Medicine, and what he calls "Technical Philosophy," and a third devoted to Theology, Ecclesiastical History, and Law. In addition to leisured gentlemen who wished to hone their musical or artistic skills, the professional school promised to attract would-be lawyers, physicians, ecclesiastics, military men, and agriculturalists. Furthermore, the department that housed Technical Philosophy would appeal to Virginians engaged in dozens of different trades: mariner, carpenter, clockmaker, machinist, optician, metallurgist, druggist, brewer, distiller, painter, soapmaker, and any others who might hope "to learn as much" of science "as shall be necessary to pursue their art understandingly." He even suggested an evening trade school "so as not to interrupt the labors of the day" and "maintained wholly at the public expense."[27] It would be difficult to imagine a demographic of white men in Virginia for whom Jefferson's prospective college offered nothing. It would be even more difficult perhaps, at least in the early nineteenth century, to imagine a better-conceived blend of classical and humanistic learning with practical education.

Jefferson's letter to Carr and subsequent work on behalf of Central College laid the foundation for the 1818 Rockfish Gap Report and the establishment of the University of Virginia. In the nearly four years since his nephew Peter Carr had enlisted his aid on behalf of Albemarle Academy, Jefferson had worked through back-channels and with allies in the Virginia legislature to secure approval and public funding for his university. Having transformed Albemarle Academy into Central College, Jefferson proceeded with designs for what he called an "academical village," a series of smaller buildings running parallel to one another along a gently sloping and terraced piece of land only a few miles from Monticello.[28] Here, of course, were the architectural origins of UVA. He also managed to defeat rival plans for an educational system, including one proposed by the Virginia Federalist Charles Fenton Mercer.[29] In the spring of 1818, Jefferson was named as one of more than a dozen commissioners charged with determining a site for the University of Virginia—Lexington, Staunton, and Central College were the finalists—and drawing up plans for both governance and, most important of all, curriculum. The group of commissioners, which included national figures such as Jefferson and James Madison as well as prominent Virginia statesmen such as Spencer Roane, John Taylor, and William Cabell, met from August 1–4 at Rockfish Gap tavern in the Blue Ridge Mountains. There they settled on a location for the university, Jefferson's Central College site, as well as a statement of philosophy, penned by Jefferson, outlining what they viewed as the objectives of higher education and how the University of Virginia would achieve those objectives.

As he had done on two prior occasions, Jefferson began the substantive portion of his Rockfish Gap Report by alluding to the primary schools. Unlike his Revolutionary-era "Bill for the More General Diffusion of Knowledge," and in keeping with the 1814 letter to Carr, Jefferson did not dwell upon these schools other than to note that if the legislature ever saw fit to create them they would provide a useful foundation in reading, writing, arithmetic, geography, and history, as well as basic instruction in individual rights and responsibilities—many of the same benefits he had identified forty years earlier. Jefferson probably felt conflicted about the primary schools. He had been frustrated on this subject in his younger days, so he reconciled himself to defeat and then came to hope that time and circumstances would do for statewide public education what he also hoped they would do for slavery; as it turned out, neither hope was realized until after the Civil War. More important, Virginia likely would fund either primary schools or his university but not both. At seventy-five years old, Jefferson believed he could accomplish more through the university than through a statewide network of schools, so he finally abandoned the three-tiered system of symbiotic institutions and concentrated all his efforts on the University of Virginia.

UVA could not achieve all that Jefferson hoped from a broad-based system, but he certainly believed it could satisfy what he called "the objects of that higher grade of education." Here the institution would prove its relevance both to individuals and to society. Higher education, Jefferson wrote, should "develop the reasoning faculties of our youth, enlarge their minds, cultivate their morals, and instill into them the precepts of virtue and order." It should "form them to habits of reflection and correct action, rendering them examples of virtue to others and of happiness within themselves." A modern liberal arts professor could not say it better. Higher education, too, had its civic purposes. It must "form the statesmen, legislators and judges" and "expound the principles and structure of government," all for the sake of "banishing all arbitrary and unnecessary restraint on individual action" and leaving human beings "free to do whatever does not violate the equal rights of another." Finally, as a complement to his libertarian prescription for government, and recalling perhaps the novel and practical features of the plan outlined in his 1814 letter to Carr, Jefferson charged his embryonic university with the responsibility to "harmonize and promote the interests of agriculture, manufactures and commerce, and by well-informed views of political economy to give a free scope to the public industry." This was not quite the expansive vision for general and professional schools he had developed four years earlier, but for an early-nineteenth-century university it was as liberal and practical an approach to higher education as any yet seen.

In his earlier documents promoting educational reform Jefferson had moved swiftly from the philosophical to the curricular, but at Rockfish Gap—perhaps anticipating ecclesiastical resistance to his secular university—he chose instead to pursue the philosophical question until, in his mind, he had answered every possible objection. Many Americans in the twenty-first century have a difficult time understanding why, for example, the Founders did not eradicate slavery and elevate the condition of women, in part, I think, because we no longer live in a world in which it is necessary to *declare* that all men are created equal. To recover a centuries-old mindset, therefore, and return to a time when such declarations were necessary requires an extraordinary leap of imagination. Likewise, we no longer live in a world in which it is necessary to declare that public education is a good thing, so it is not always easy to appreciate Jefferson's arguments on its behalf. "Some good men," Jefferson began, "consider the learned sciences as useless acquirements," while others think that schooling "should be left to private and individual effort." But "an establishment embracing all the sciences which may be useful and even necessary in the various vocations of life," complete with all the buildings and supporting materials, is something "far beyond the reach of individual means, and must either derive existence from public patronage, or not exist at all." Happily, a majority of the Virginia legislature had come to accept that "the advantages of well-directed education, moral, political and economical, are truly above all estimate." Others, however, were so sure. Some believed, for instance, that human beings were fixed by nature and therefore insusceptible of improvement. For these naysayers Jefferson reserved his strongest and lengthiest rebuttal. "What, but education," he asked, "has advanced us beyond the condition of our indigenous neighbors? And what chains them to their present state of barbarism and wretchedness, but a bigotted veneration for the supposed superlative wisdom of their fathers, and the preposterous idea that they are to look backward for better things, and not forward, longing, as it should seem, to return to the days of eating acorns and roots, rather than indulge in the degeneracies of civilization?"[30] Rhetorically, it might have been useful for Jefferson to compare opponents of publicly-funded higher education to those eastern Indians, such as Tecumseh, who resisted assimilation and the advance of civilization.[31] As was the case forty years earlier, however, his real target was not the Indians but rather the ecclesiastical mind. The "doctrine," he said, which holds that "the condition of man cannot be ameliorated, that what has been must ever be, and that . . . we must tread with awful reverence in the footsteps of our fathers" is itself the "genuine fruit of the alliance between Church and State," whose beneficiaries, "finding themselves but too well in their present condition, oppose all advances which might unmask their usurpations . . . and fear every change, as endangering the comforts they now hold."[32] Despite three decades of life under his celebrated Virginia Statute for Religious Freedom (1786), Jefferson still regarded the traditional bond between church and state as an impediment to moral, political, and economic progress. That he should have to make such arguments on behalf of education in the first place reminds us of the obstacles he encountered with every effort at reform.

Having dispensed with the likely objections to his university, Jefferson proceeded to lay out the proposed curriculum. Incorporating and expanding upon the academic departments he envisioned in his 1814 letter to Carr, Jefferson divided the university's curriculum into ten "branches of learning," each "within the powers of a single professor." In the future Jefferson would have to temper his expectations of both the number and the quality of the professors UVA would attract. For now, however, he sketched an ambitious curriculum that strikes the modern reader as heavy on the arts and sciences. Two professors would teach Languages, one each for Ancient and Modern. As one might expect from Jefferson the scientist, UVA's curriculum also included one professorship each for Mathematics, Physico-Mathematics, Physics, Botany/Zoology, and Anatomy (even in 1818 the Humanities had to fight for scraps from the Natural Sciences' table). The three remaining professors would teach Government, Law, and Rhetoric, respectively. The Rockfish Gap Report's precise grouping of sub-disciplines differs in arrangement from that which appears in the 1814 Carr letter, but the identity of those sub-disciplines, that is, what those ten professors actually would teach, is remarkably similar. For instance, Military Architecture, which Jefferson envisioned as part of the professional schools' curriculum, appears in the Rockfish Gap Report under Mathematics. Likewise, UVA's Department of Anatomy encompasses Medicine, and Rhetoric covers the Fine Arts. Gone is the school of Technical Philosophy with its innovative evening program, but the sciences Jefferson hoped would enable craftsmen of all types "to pursue their art understandingly" remained in place. Though one doubts that Jefferson could have imagined UVA's curriculum as a perfect blend of the general and professional schools he envisioned in 1814, the curriculum spelled out in the Rockfish Gap Report contains enough of the classical, the humanist, and the practical to allow us to conclude that Jefferson's overall plan for higher education was indeed a balanced one. [33]

While there was nothing in the political climate of the nineteenth century's second decade comparable to the revolutionary-era assault on aristocracy, some scholars nonetheless have suggested that Jefferson fashioned the University of Virginia with overtly political goals in mind. There is a bit of truth in the assertion, at least in the years following the Rockfish Gap Report. Many Virginians had grown wary of sending their children northward to be educated at schools whose environment was becoming more hostile to southerners. [34] Likewise, Jefferson soon began gauging the winds of a gathering political and socio-economic storm. The Panic of 1819 accelerated the decline of Virginians's financial fortunes. That same year, Chief Justice John Marshall's opinion in the *McCulloch v. Maryland* case appeared as the boldest strike yet on behalf of nationalism and consolidated government, prompting Jefferson to denounce Marshall for having turned the Constitution into "a thing of wax in the hands of the judiciary."[35] The Missouri Crisis of 1820, "like a fire bell in the night," awakened Jefferson to the real dangers of sectional strife. "A geographic line," he wrote, "coinciding with a marked principle, moral and political, once conceived and held up to the angry passions of men, will never be obliterated."[36] In a sign, perhaps, that he continued to think of politics in eighteenth-century terms, Jefferson later attributed the Missouri agitation to discredited Federalists who, "despairing of ever rising again under the old division of whig and tory, devised a new one, of slave-holding & non slave-holding states, which, while it had a semblance of being Moral, was at the same time Geographical, and calculated to give them ascendancy by debauching their old opponents to a coalition with them."[37] Northern politicians professing anti-slavery principles, in other words, merely sought to unite with Pennsylvania and New York, weaken the Virginia-dominated Jeffersonian Republican Party, and thereby revive New England's long-dormant electoral hopes. Six months before he died, in fact, Jefferson explicitly identified the political characters coalescing around the John Quincy Adams administration as the remnants of the long-ago vanquished Federalist Party, who now embraced Marshall-style consolidation as "a next best blessing to monarchy" and "perhaps the surest stepping-stone to it."[38] There is no question, then, that after 1818 Jefferson began to perceive of the University of Virginia in political terms, not as bastion of states-rights thinking, as some have suggested, but as a bulwark against what he perceived as a Federalist revival. "In the selection of our Law Professor," he wrote to Madison in February 1826, "we must be rigorously attentive to his political principles." At the time of the Revolution, Jefferson recalled, "our lawyers were then all whigs." But the legal profession since those days had begun to "slide into toryism, and nearly all the young brood of lawyers now are of that hue."[39] In Jeffersonian parlance, Toryism and monarchism served as shorthand for Federalism. As he began to despair of the nation's future, he projected more and more of that desperation onto the university.

All of this occurred, however, in the years following the Rockfish Gap Report, where four decades of Jeffersonian thinking on education crystallized into plans for the University of Virginia. Having failed to reform his alma mater William and Mary, and having given up trying to persuade his contemporaries of the need for a structured, symbiotic, three-tiered system of public education that began at the primary-school level, Jefferson did the best he could. His university, while far from complete by 1818, was unlike anything yet seen in America: a secular institution (it had no chair of divinity), laid out in the brilliantly original style of an "academical village," that promised to educate Virginia's youths in a classical and humanistic tradition while also opening avenues for professional training. The University of Virginia would form statesmen and judges—preferably Republican ones—but it also would train physicians, botanists, and anyone whose work in the sciences someday might add to Virginians' well-being and material comforts. It was not a perfect institution, but it was a perfectly balanced architectural and spiritual representation of its founder.

The 2011 NGA Report, on the other hand, falls short of the Jeffersonian standard for higher education. This is meant as an indictment not of the report itself and certainly not of its authors but of the mindset of the people the report serves: policymakers, in this case state governors, who hope to use public higher education in order to spur job growth in their states. They think this approach is desirable, of course, because at some point we all seem to have agreed that economic growth is the responsibility of elected officials, many of whom know very little about the myriad forces that drive complex economies. They think it is acceptable to drive economic growth through education policy because, having made economic growth their top priority, they are likely to view all other public institutions as tools waiting to be applied to whatever broad purposes the policymakers' whims might dictate. They think it is possible to do these things because, having subordinated the Humanities to the "practical" disciplines, they lack the perspective and humility that comes, for example, from serious study of History. Perhaps all of this is unfair to the intelligent and well-meaning public servants who try their best to confront serious social and economic challenges. But these are precisely the sort of people who ought to know enough to reject the NGA Report's advice on higher education.

The NGA Report declares that "a growing number of governors and state policymakers have come to recognize that higher education . . . cannot help drive economic growth in their states unless students' academic success is linked to the needs of the marketplace." This is all well and good if the report means to advise policymakers on how to encourage business schools and other pre-professional schools to tailor their training to the market. But the report does not stop there. "Given the longstanding independence of institutions of higher education—and their emphasis on broad liberal arts education," the NGA consultants lament, "getting such institutions to embrace a more active role in a state's economic development is often challenging." One way policymakers can get institutions to embrace such things, of course, is to "incentivize" by using "performance-based funding" to produce "outcomes aligned with state strategic goals," including the development of "industry oriented curricula" and "new efforts to meet the workforce needs of specific key sectors."[40] One hardly need guess how many of these incentive-based funds would find their way into the English Department.

In the end, the NGA Report offers an inferior approach not because it imagines that relevant higher education should produce tangible economic benefits—Jefferson, too, believed as much—but because it imagines *no other kind of relevance.* The economic challenges of the twenty-first century, while novel in their particulars, are by no means unprecedented in their urgency. Jefferson's contemporaries also wished a competence and perhaps even a promising profession. The University of Virginia could help them achieve it. But Jefferson's institution also aspired to mold reflective men of character and virtue who knew their own rights and could be trusted with those of others. Modern policymakers would do well to emulate the Sage of Monticello.

NOTES

1. Erin Sparks and Mary Jo Waits, *Economic, Human Services, and Workforce Division, NGA Center for Best Practices*, "Degrees for What Jobs? Raising Expectations for Universities and Colleges in a Global Economy" (March 2011), accessed January 14, 2012, http://www.nga.org/files/live/sites/NGA/files/pdf/1103DEGREESJOBS.PDF. (Hereafter cited as "NGA Report").

2. Thomas Jefferson, "Report of the Commissioners for the University of Virginia," August 4, 1818, in *Thomas Jefferson: Writings*, ed. Merrill Peterson (New York: Library Company of America, 1984), 457–73. (Hereafter cited as "Rockfish Gap Report").

3. James Parton, *Life of Thomas Jefferson, Third President of the United States* (Boston: James R. Osgood and Company, 1874), iii.

4. Gordon Wood, *Empire of Liberty: A History of the Early Republic, 1789-1815* (Oxford and New York: Oxford University Press, 2009), 277.

5. Jefferson, "Jefferson to General James Breckenridge, February 15, 1821," in *Writings*, 1452–54.

6. Jefferson, "Autobiography, 1743–1790," in *Writings*, 44.

7. Gordon Wood, *Radicalism of the American Revolution* (New York: Alfred A. Knopf, 1992).

8. David Hackett Fischer, *Albion's Seed: Four British Folkways in America* (Oxford and New York: Oxford University Press, 1989).

9. Jefferson, "Autobiography, 1743–1790," in *Writings*, 3.

10. Jefferson, "A Summary View of the Rights of British America," in *Writings*, 105–22.

11. For a superb analysis of Jefferson's *Summary View* as well as the place of history in his education and political philosophy, see Trevor Colbourn, *The Lamp of Experience: Whig History and the Intellectual Origins of the American Revolution* (Chapel Hill: University of North Carolina Press, 1965), 193–225.

12. Rowland Berthoff and John M. Murrin, "Feudalism, Communalism and the Yeoman Freeholder: The American Revolution Considered as a Social Accident," in *Essays on the American Revolution*, ed. James Hutson et al. (Chapel Hill: University of North Carolina Press, 1973), 256–88. See also Alan D. Watson, "The Quitrent System in Royal South Carolina," *The William and Mary Quarterly*, Third Series, 33, no. 2 (April 1976): 183–211.

13. Jefferson, "A Bill for the More General Diffusion of Knowledge," in *Writings*, 365–73.

14. Merrill D. Peterson, *Thomas Jefferson and the New Nation* (London, Oxford, and New York: Oxford University Press, 1970), 965.

15. Virginia's slide into ignorance and secession is the subject of Susan Dunn, *Dominion of Memories: Jefferson, Madison and the Decline of Virginia* (New York: Basic Books, 2007).

16. Beverly McAnear, "College Founding in the American Colonies, 1745–1775," in *Essays in American Colonial History*, ed. Paul Goodman (Freeport, New York: Books for Libraries Press, 1967), 586–601.

17. Though the institutions had the same basic conservative mission of training ministers and inculcating values, the curriculum did receive something of a jolt with the appearance of

Newton, Locke, and the Scottish philosophers. See Henry May, *The Enlightenment in America* (Oxford, London, and New York: Oxford University Press, 1976), 32–34.

18. A now-classic study of the intersection between political and religious life in the eighteenth-century Old Dominion is Rhys Isaac, *The Transformation of Virginia, 1740–1790* (Chapel Hill: The University of North Carolina Press for the Institute of Early American History and Culture, 1982).

19. Jefferson, "Autobiography," in *Writings*, 43; Cameron Addis, *Jefferson's Vision for Education, 1760–1845* (New York: Peter Lang, 2003), 20–22.

20. Peterson, *Jefferson and the New Nation*, 151.

21. See the collection of essays in Robert M.S. McDonald, *Thomas Jefferson's Military Academy: Founding West Point* (Charlottesville: University of Virginia Press, 2004).

22. Jefferson, "Sixth Annual Message," in *Writings*, 524–31.

23. The best account of the Adams administration and its ordeal appears in George Dangerfield, *The Era of Good Feelings* (New York: Harcourt, Brace and Company, 1952).

24. Peterson, *Jefferson and the New Nation*, 965.

25. Jefferson, "Jefferson to Peter Carr, September 7, 1814," in *Writings*, 1346–52.

26. Roy Honeywell, *The Educational Work of Thomas Jefferson* (Cambridge, Mass.: Harvard University Press, 1931) makes this case. For this and other sources, see the very useful bibliographic essay in Addis, *Jefferson's Vision for Education*, 153–62.

27. Jefferson, "Jefferson to Peter Carr, September 7, 1814," in *Writings*, 1346–52.

28. This "academical village" is The Lawn at present-day UVA, with the Rotunda at one end and Cabell Hall at the other. Jefferson apparently designed this village from scratch, with no known model in existence. See Peterson, *Jefferson and the New Nation*, 968–69.

29. The political history of UVA's founding has been amply and ably described elsewhere. See especially Addis, *Jefferson's Vision for Education*, chapter 2.

30. Jefferson, "Rockfish Gap Report," 457–62.

31. Jefferson always maintained in any case that whites and Indians were probably equal in the faculties of mind. See, for instance, "Notes on the State of Virginia," Query XIV, in *Writings*, 266.

32. Jefferson's hostility toward the clergy is well documented. See Jefferson, "Jefferson to Mrs. Samuel Smith, August 6, 1816," in *Writings*, 1403–05: "But I have ever thought religion a concern purely between our God and our consciences, for which we were accountable to him, and not to the priests. I never told my own religion, nor scrutinized that of another. I never attempted to make a convert, nor wished to change another's creed. I have ever judged of the religion of others by their lives, and by this test, my dear Madam, I have been satisfied yours must be an excellent one, to have produced a life of such exemplary virtue and correctness. For it is in our lives, and not from our words, that our religion must be read. By the same test the world must judge me. But this does not satisfy the priesthood. They must have a positive, a declared assent to all their interested absurdities. My opinion is that there would never have been an infidel, if there had never been a priest. The artificial structures they have built on the purest of all moral systems, for the purpose of deriving from it pence and power, revolts those who think for themselves, and who read in that system only what is really there."

33. Jefferson, "Rockfish Gap Report," 462–64.

34. Dunn, *Dominion of Memories*, 61–68.

35. Jefferson, "Jefferson to Judge Spencer Roane, September 6, 1819," in *Writings*, 1425–28.

36. Jefferson, "Jefferson to John Holmes, April 22, 1820," in *Writings*, 1433–35.

37. Jefferson, "Jefferson to Albert Gallatin, December 26, 1820," in *Writings*, 1447–50.

38. Jefferson, "Jefferson to William Branch Giles, December 26, 1825," in *Writings*, 1509–12.

39. Jefferson, "Jefferson to James Madison, February 17, 1826," in *Writings*, 1512–15.

40. Sparks and Waits, "NGA Report," 1–3.

BIBLIOGRAPHY

Addis, Cameron. *Jefferson's Vision for Education, 1760–1845.* New York: Peter Lang, 2003.
Berthoff, Ronald and John M. Murrin. "Feudalism, Communalism and the Yeoman Freeholder: The American Revolution Considered as a Social Accident." In *Essays on the American Revolution,* edited by James Hutson and Stephen Kurtz, 256–88. Chapel Hill: University of North Carolina Press, 1973.
Colbourn, Trevor. *The Lamp of Experience: Whig History and the Intellectual Origins of the American Revolution.* Chapel Hill: University of North Carolina Press, 1965.
Dangerfield, George. *The Era of Good Feelings.* New York: Harcourt, Brace and Company, 1952.
Dunn, Susan. *Dominion of Memories: Jefferson, Madison and the Decline of Virginia.* New York: Basic Books, 2007.
Fischer, David Hackett. *Albion's Seed: Four British Folkways in America.* Oxford and New York: Oxford University Press, 1989.
Honeywell, Roy. *The Educational Work of Thomas Jefferson.* Cambridge, Mass.: Harvard University Press, 1931.
Isaac, Rhys. *The Transformation of Virginia, 1740–1790.* Chapel Hill: The University of North Carolina Press for the Institute of Early American History and Culture, 1982.
Jefferson, Thomas. "A Bill for the More General Diffusion of Knowledge." In *Thomas Jefferson: Writings,* edited by Merrill Peterson, 356–73. New York: Library Company of America, 1984.
———. "A Summary View of the Rights of British America." In *Thomas Jefferson: Writings,* edited by Merrill Peterson, 105–22. New York: Library Company of America, 1984.
———. "Autobiography, 1743–1790." In *Thomas Jefferson: Writings,* edited by Merrill Peterson, 3–101. New York: Library Company of America, 1984.
———. "Jefferson to Albert Gallatin," December 26, 1820. In *Thomas Jefferson: Writings,* edited by Merrill Peterson, 1477–50. New York: Library Company of America, 1984.
———. "Jefferson to General James Breckenridge," February 15, 1821. In *Thomas Jefferson: Writings,* edited by Merrill Peterson, 1452-54. New York: Library Company of America, 1984.
———. "Jefferson to James Madison," February 17, 1826. In *Thomas Jefferson: Writings,* edited by Merrill Peterson, 1212–15. New York: Library Company of America, 1984.
———. "Jefferson to John Holmes," April 22, 1820. In *Thomas Jefferson: Writings,* edited by Merrill Peterson, 1433–35. New York: Library Company of America, 1984.
———. "Jefferson to Judge Spencer Roane," September 6, 1819. In *Thomas Jefferson: Writings,* edited by Merrill Peterson, 1425–28. New York: Library Company of America, 1984.
———. "Jefferson to Mrs. Samuel Smith," August 6, 1816. In *Thomas Jefferson: Writings,* edited by Merrill Peterson, 1403–05. New York: Library Company of America, 1984.
———. "Jefferson to Peter Carr," September 7, 1814. In *Thomas Jefferson: Writings,* edited by Merrill Peterson, 1346–52. New York: Library Company of America, 1984.
———. "Jefferson to William Branch Giles," December 26, 1825. In *Thomas Jefferson: Writings,* edited by Merrill Peterson, 1509–12. New York: Library Company of America, 1984.
———. "Notes on the State of Virginia," Query XIV. In *Thomas Jefferson: Writings,* edited by Merrill Peterson, 256–75. New York: Library Company of America, 1984.
———. "Report of the Commissioners for the University of Virginia," August 4, 1818. In *Thomas Jefferson: Writings,* edited by Merrill Peterson, 455–73. New York: Library Company of America, 1984.
———. "Sixth Annual Message." In *Thomas Jefferson: Writings,* edited by Merrill Peterson, 524–31. New York: Library Company of America, 1984.
May, Henry. *The Enlightenment in America.* Oxford, London and New York: Oxford University Press, 1976.
McAnear, Beverly. "College Founding in the American Colonies, 1745–1775." In *Essays in American Colonial History,* 586–601, edited by Paul Goodman. Freeport, NY: Books for Libraries Press, 1967.

McDonald, Robert M. S. *Thomas Jefferson's Military Academy: Founding West Point.* Charlottesville: University of Virginia Press, 2004.

Parton, James. *Life of Thomas Jefferson, Third President of the United States.* Boston: James R. Osgood and Company, 1874.

Peterson, Merrill D. *Thomas Jefferson and the New Nation.* London, Oxford and New York: Oxford University Press, 1970.

Sparks, Erin and Mary Jo Waits. *Economic, Human Services, and Workforce Division, NGA Center for Best Practices,* "Degrees for What Jobs? Raising Expectations for Universities and Colleges in a Global Economy" (March 2011). Accessed January 14, 2012, http://www.nga.org/files/live/sites/NGA/files/pdf/1103DEGREESJOBS.PDF.

Watson, Alan D. "The Quitrent System in Royal South Carolina." The William and Mary Quarterly, Third Series, 33, no. 2 (April 1976): 183–211.

Wood, Gordon. *Radicalism of the American Revolution.* New York: Alfred A. Knopf, 1992.

——. *Empire of Liberty: A History of the Early Republic, 1789–1815.* Oxford and New York: Oxford University Press, 2009.

Chapter Five

Toward a Neo-Perennialist Philosophy of Liberal Education

Wayne Willis

Perennialism was a twentieth century movement in education, and especially higher education, that saw education as essentially the engagement of students in learning and thinking critically about those historic ideas that are a part of the historic canon of western literature through a study of the liberal arts. It never placed much stock in the idea that education should be relevant, in the sense of immediately practical, to our everyday problems. As such perennialism itself, one might argue, has become irrelevant to contemporary discourse of higher education, which seems preoccupied with immediate political, economic, and social problems. It is the contention of the current author, however, that perennialism as a philosophy of higher education can be relevant to higher education in the twenty-first century and that the education it offers can be relevant to contemporary students. Both, it is argued, will require a revision of some of perennialism's key themes.

HISTORICAL BACKGROUND

When William Rainey Harper became the founding president of the University of Chicago in 1891, he aspired to create a great university that would nurture the highest intellectual, moral, and spiritual capacities of the best and brightest young people both to help them achieve their potentials as human beings and to prepare them for leadership in their respective communities. One of the biggest barriers to this, he believed, was the growing demand for post-secondary education among students who were not capable of doing traditional university studies. He believed that of those who came to college at the time, only about 10 percent were actually "fitted" for legitimate university work.[1] His solution was the creation of a school within the university for these other students, one that he called the "junior college," an institution that would provide advanced high school studies. After two years in this junior college, most students would go on to the world of work, and a small number of the highest achievers would be allowed to continue into the second two years of real university studies. Without such a separation in studies, the whole university would, he believed, become watered down, and our best and brightest would not experience the rigor and excellence that they needed.

A generation later, the second boy wonder of the University's college presidency was aboard, Robert Maynard Hutchins. His concerns were different. He believed that a very large portion of the population was capable of doing legitimate university studies. The problem was that we were providing them with an inferior curriculum. Under the influence of both student interests and commercial pressures, the curriculum was shifting away from the traditional classical content to more utilitarian subjects—a trend, which he believed was highly destructive for our society. To put it in terms of relevance, what is relevant for the short term to an individual's career plans may not be relevant to the needs of the larger society, or, for that matter, relevant to the long term self-actualization of the individual. Hutchins argued that rather than change the curriculum for the new audience of higher education, we should maintain the traditional academic curriculum but provide new teaching methods and additional study time for these new students to master it. The challenge would be to change not the *what*, but the *how* of higher education. What we must not do, he argued, is abandon it for career-oriented studies and whatever commercial interests will fund.[2]

By the 1940s, Harvard's president James Conant was echoing the sentiments of Harper, not Hutchins. In his day, 11 percent of high school graduates were enrolling in college, and he argued that was far too many. If we let in students who are not the most elite achievers in high schools, we will water down the standards of the universities, and the whole culture will suffer.[3]

By the 1960s, it became clear that both classicists like Hutchins and the elitists like Conant would lose out, and American higher education would embrace almost all students and teach them almost anything they wanted to study. Not only that, but universities would be so responsive to funding from government and corporate sources, that they would do almost anything to get the money. Clark Kerr argued in 1963 in *The Uses of the University* that the very term "university" was no longer appropriate in American higher education because its prefix implied a unity of purpose that was alien to the institution. He said they could more appropriately be called "multiversities." He did not necessarily see this as a bad thing.[4]

In their recent book, Richard Keeling and Richard Hersh see this lack of clarity about purpose as highly problematic, as the title of their book on rethinking American higher education bluntly asserts, *We Are Losing Our Minds*.[5] They argue that universities have become so sidetracked by various social forces that they no longer see student learning as central to their mission. A curious affirmation of this is the fact that my own institution adopted a mission statement in the 1990s that made no reference to anyone learning anything. Our mission was simply to offer programs—a mission which we fulfilled admirably. Thankfully, we have since adopted a new mission statement, which does in fact place a priority on student learning.

In 2002 the National Academy for Academic Leadership published *A Field Guide to Academic Leadership*, a book which all academic department chairs at my institution were instructed to buy and read.[6] It seems to reflect the realities that Kerr described in the fact that nowhere in it is there any discourse about the purposes of a university. It repeatedly states that universities must change in response to the needs of the changing world in order to survive, but it articulates no central purpose, no historic mission, no specific thing that universities have to offer that world, nor does it invite the reader to consider whether the forces pressing against us are legitimate ones or whether our world will be a better place if we yield to them or resist them. Indeed, one might get the impression that a university has no higher goal than simply to exist.

I confess that this strikes me as an appalling state of affairs. The historic mission of the university, to nurture the highest intellectual and moral qualities in our young people, is hardly obsolete. Indeed, one might argue that those qualities are more urgently needed now than ever before, and one might hope that university leaders would stand tall in defending that mission and opposing those who would turn us into anything less. In fact, it sometimes seems that those policy makers whose task is to lead us don't even believe in our mission.

It is especially ironic that in this age of high stakes assessment and accountability that we do not have a clear sense of our purpose. After all, how can you tell if an institution is doing its job well if no one knows what is its job? The purpose of this chapter is to look at one well-defined vision of higher education and consider how it might inform current discourse. Here I am referring to the shared vision Robert Maynard Hutchins, Mortimer Adler, Mark Van Doren, and others often labeled by education textbooks as "perennialism." When the influx of large numbers of non-academically minded students began to pour into the universities, contributing to universities becoming more and more confused about their purpose, the perennialists offered a clear vision for higher education, one that merits reconsideration.

Perennialism is a movement in educational thought that emphasizes the nurture of the shared goal of intellectual development for all young people, through the study of a common core curriculum built around the classics of Western civilization, and rooted in Aristotelian philosophy. It sees the central purpose of education (as opposed to training) as the nurture of the highest element of human nature, our rationality, for the sake being the very best human beings we can be. Education is an activity of essentially intrinsic value—not utilitarian. Indeed, from an Aristotelian perspective, as soon as one's motives move from intrinsic to extrinsic, learning ceases to be education and becomes mere training. Given the muddled use of the language today, the "education" referred to by Aristotle and the perennialists is more clearly referred to as "liberal education." One happy byproduct of that liberal education is that we become better citizens for the democratic society.

COMMENTARY ON PERENNIALISM

George Kneller's little book, *Introduction to the Philosophy of Education*, described perennialism more specifically in terms of six main beliefs, and here I propose to comment on those six and to offer my own critique of how well they have stood the test of time for the three-quarters of a century since Hutchins so eloquently offered this model. [7]

> *1. Despite differing environments, human nature remains the same everywhere; hence, education should be the same for everyone.*

A focus on the nurture of the human being as a human being strikes me as one of the most compelling parts of the perennialist philosophy of education. Any educational purpose that focuses on utility ultimately either cast the human as an object to be used by others for their purposes, or begs the question of what is the use of a human being. A logical and ethically defensible philosophy of education must begin with an analysis of human nature.

Perennialists like Hutchins and Adler begin, and end, with an Aristotelian definition of the human as rational creature, whose highest good is found in the nurture of the mind. There are at least two major problems with this: 1) there is plenty in human behavior to raise questions about our actual capacity to live rationally, both from the standpoint of modern existential and postmodern thought, as well as the traditional religious idea of original sin; 2) people with the most highly developed rational skills do not in fact seem "happier," in the Aristotelian sense (or "self-actualized," to use Maslow's term) than other less rationally developed people. Just visit the English department of any university and tell me if the faculty there seems to be more self-actualized human beings than the rest for their rigorous training in the humanities.

The problem here may lie, at least partly, with too narrow a definition of rationality—a definition that focuses on bookish subjects. Aristotle himself had a broader definition of the rationality of an educated person, as reflected in his curriculum, than the modern perennialists. For example, Aristotle considered practical skills like home economics to have an intrinsic element that made them legitimate liberal arts subjects.[8] Also, consider the idea of "human flourishing" in today's virtue ethics literature.[9] Or to put it in more widely understood language, consider Howard Gardner's broad definition of intelligence.[10] To say that human beings are essentially rational creatures, and then limit your educational goals to linguistic and logical-mathematical skills is to ignore an enormous part of the intellectual functions of the human mind. Where do Mihaly Csikszentmihalyi's creative geniuses fit in the narrow perennialist view of human nature?[11] Surely his idea of flow merits consideration in the analysis of human flourishing.

What about the cabinetmaker whose enormous skills and excellence in execution bring him joy—is this not a part of what it means to be self-actualized? What about the classical or folk musician who has refined his musical skills to the top percentile of human achievement, and who brings great joy to himself and his community, but has never read Plato? Is this skill not a highly intelligent one and is his self-actualization not comparable to the classicist who knows the intricacies of Plato's *Meno*, but cannot clap in rhythm? Surely a more holistic theory of human nature is called for.

Many have attacked the perennialist idea that education should be the same for everyone, but that sameness is much less problematic when the flourishing of human nature is expanded to include more than the bookish rationality of humanities scholars inherent in the perennialist vision. If one accepts that education ought to help a human being reach his/her potential as a human being, a broader examination of the concept of human flourishing would be an excellent place to start designing a new post-perennialist theory of liberal education.

It might be worth noting that Dewey's concept of "industrial arts," was much more akin to Aristotle's liberal arts than the narrowly utilitarian vocational classes that emerged in the twentieth century. As Dewey conceived it, industrial arts was in a broad analysis of the role of industry in culture, and given Dewey's own criticisms of industrialization, presumably not just a naïve endorsement of all things industrial. Perhaps there is a place for industrial arts, so conceived, in a genuine liberal arts program. In a pragmatically driven culture with little emphasis on the intrinsic, the historical, and the purely intellectual, the addition of industrial arts to the core of liberal arts studies might generate a new interest in the liberal arts from those with more practical and less bookish interests. In fact, the absence of such practical content is part of what makes traditional liberal education seem irrelevant to many contemporary students (and their parents.)

> 2. *Since rationality is man's highest attribute, he must use it to direct his instinctual nature in accordance with deliberately chosen ends.*

This is the perennialist response to the romanticism of Rousseau and the progressives who had a profound confidence in the ability of young people to follow a nurturing path by following their own impulses. Perennialists see their opponents going to an extreme of child-centered education and tend to go the polar opposite, suggesting, for example, that students not have electives in the curriculum until they get their bachelors degree (as Hutchins argued in *The Higher Learning in America*) or that the only elective in high school should be *which* foreign language to take (as Adler et al. argued in the 1980s in *The Paideia Proposal*[12]). As argued above, this seems to take far too narrow a definition of human nature and what constitutes human flourishing.

While one might well agree with Adler that children are in no position to decide without guidance what they should study, their impulses are not entirely counter-productive. Small children are following their own natural impulses when they learn to talk, to walk, and to evoke their parent's affection. They do not need externally created lessons and standards to develop these profoundly important and remarkably sophisticated human skills. If they are genetically programmed to learn these basic skills needed to survive and flourish, perhaps we should not ignore their natural impulses toward learning at later stages of life. Indeed, perhaps our schools would be much more productive learning environments, if, as Dewey pointed out, they built on those positive natural impulses instead of resisting them.

It does seem that even Aristotle placed a higher value on the natural impulses of children to learn than do his modern perennialist disciples. He has great confidence in the instinctive impulse to know, that is, the intrinsic value of learning, to motivate students. In this area, modern perennialist may be more Calvinistic than Aristotelian. The Calvinist connection is not just speculative—Adler said that children are the least perfect of all human beings.[13] One might also wonder if this is an area where Aristotle's Golden Mean would be useful. Does it really have to be Adler's "no electives," or extreme romanticists "no requirements?" As noted above, if students do not seem to have a natural impulse to learn our curriculum, perhaps it is partly because we have defined learning too narrowly around books and abstract ideas. A broader definition of liberal education that embraces the whole gamut of natural human developmental interests would surely be experienced by students as more relevant.

3. It is education's task to import knowledge of eternal truth.

One can well appreciate the perennialists' opposition to a kind of popular relativism that rejects all rational standards for truth and treats all values as mere personal preferences. And surely Adler and Hutchins would feel their conviction about this even more strongly if they could see today's news media with its casual disregard for fact in favor of political partisanship. Nevertheless, the perennialists went too far in building their whole philosophy of education on the idea of absolute truths.

If the pragmatism of Dewey and a whole host of other early twentieth century thinkers (C. S. Pierce, William Heard Kilpatrick, and Theodore Brameld, for example) was not enough to discredit the idea of absolute truth that can be known with certainty, surely Einstein's cosmology and Heisenberg's quantum science has. It is ironic that conservative thinkers since the Enlightenment have tried to find an absolute foundation on which to build morality to give it the same validity and reliability as science, only to find that the most rigorous science itself lacks objectivity. That may sound like bad news, but it is not. The great moral problem is that people assume that if there is no objective certainty, then everything is arbitrary. Not so, and even science can show us otherwise. While science may not be able to achieve absolute certainty, that does not mean that scientists consider all knowledge equally valuable or have abandoned the quest for better models for understanding reality. The debates in science are as vigorous today as they were 150 years ago, and the passion of today's scientist is no less now than that of Galileo or Newton. This is in no way to suggest that education or philosophy of education should adopt the methods or assumptions of science, but rather, by analogy, to show that the absence of absolutes need not lead to the kind of pop relativism which assumes that if absolutes are not attainment, all ideas are equally defensible.

Richard Bernstein's arguments in *Beyond Objectivism and Relativism* strike me as highly relevant here.[14] The modernist quest for certainty has fostered a false moral dichotomy, and to get bogged down in that quest and dichotomy is, I would argue, morally destructive. A recognition that absolutes are not attainable, indeed may not exist, need not throw our world into moral chaos, and for perennialists to insist that it will in some ways is to foster a self-fulfilling prophecy. Instead of feuding over the existence of absolutes, those of us in the humanities should acknowledge the wisdom of the ages, that generally love is better than hate, kindness is better than spite, peace is better than war, health is better than illness, flourishing is better than suffering, and use their resources to try to make the world a better place. To put any of these principles on hold until we can prove them with certainly is to abandon the world to chaos.

It is worth noting that in the introduction to the 1995 edition of Hutchins's *The Higher Learning in America*, Harry S. Ashmore notes that Hutchins attributed *to Dewey* the characterization of metaphysical truths as "fixed" and "eternal." Distancing himself from this characterization, Hutchins offered his own view of that "research, in the sense of the development, elaboration and refinement of principles, together with the collection and use of empirical materials to aid in these processes, is one of the highest activities of a university and one in which all of its professors should be engaged."[15] If the narrow absolutism often associated with perennialism makes it (and higher education) seem less and less relevant to contemporary discourse, Hutchins's disclaimer and embracing of empirical methods should offer at least a partial remedy.

   4. Education is not an imitation of life but a preparation for it.

   Perennialists here reacted to the progressives' insistence that education is life itself and the progressive quest to make schooling more present-centered and more authentic (more relevant?). It would seem to me that the perennialists' insights were rooted in a proper understanding of the egocentrism of the young that inhibits their ability make wise long-term judgments. A student living absorbed in the present will not appreciate the fact that much achievement in life depends upon delayed gratification, self-discipline, and even self-sacrifice. If they only do those things that seem important to them in the present, their potential for self-actualization in the future may be seriously inhibited. While Hutchins and Adler were originally reacting to the progressivism of the 1920s and 30s, even today there is a tendency to define "relevance" as applicable in the short term, and to neglect the importance, even "relevance" of preparation for the long-term realities of life.

   On the other hand, a ten-year-old who is told that he should study something he finds meaningless that he should do so because in ten years he will be glad he did, is not likely to engage with it in any meaningful way and hence will be unlikely to learn it any way. The challenge for the perennialist becomes a methodological one—how to engage young people in tasks that are of long-term relevance, but not of immediate relevance to them. The answer, I suspect, lies in calling upon that intrinsic intellectual inquisitiveness of human nature that is a part of the Aristotelian philosophy. I think we often underestimate the interest students have in big philosophical and moral questions. Even little kids ask about why people die and why people suffer. They are curious about why other families have different religions or morals, why some kids are good athletes and others are not, and why some people are so mean. The problem may be that we stifle these questions, and impose on them low-level academic questions about states and capitals that do not in fact speak to their innate drive to learn. In his defense, by all accounts, Mortimer Adler was very good at activating students' natural curiosity, even when teaching elementary school children.

   5. The student should be taught certain basic subjects that will acquaint him with the world's permanencies.

The point here seemed to be less about the "permanencies" than a reaction to progressive era combined disciplines like social studies, rather than history, geography, for example because these combined disciplines were perceived to be "watered down"—less rigorous, less intensive versions of their traditional predecessors. While a concern about the watering down of the curriculum was probably legitimate then and is presumably more so now, that problem is not necessarily the same as or due to the integration of subject matter. Surely the interdisciplinary study of subjects much broader than the social studies is not only legitimate, but inherent in the perennialist agenda itself. Surely even Adler would acknowledge that any careful study of his hero, Aristotle, is an interdisciplinary matter, given the great one's writings about philosophy, politics, psychology, and science. Indeed, any study of *The Great Books of the Western World* will be an inherently interdisciplinary task. The problem is not with interdisciplinary studies themselves, but with the possibility of a superficial study of those disciplines. And on that issue, I believe the perennialists' concerns remain dead on target.

As for the use of the term "permanencies" here, I would note that the failure to establish absolutes does not preclude an appreciation of those insights that passed the test of time. Indeed an idea becomes perennial precisely because it has shown its relevance to multiple generations. The term "perennial" seems to capture this idea without imposing the burden of unproven absolutes, and Kneller was well advised to use it here.

> *6. Students should study the great works of literature, philosophy, history, and science in which men through the ages have revealed their greatest aspirations and achievements.*

The problem of canon inherent in this proposal is even bigger today than it was in the 1930s and 40s.[16] Hutchins and Adler actually took on a very practical task relative to the canon—Hutchins used his clout at *Encyclopedia Britannica* to get them to publish as a single set what he and his kindred spirits considered the canon of Western civilization, known as *The Great Books of the Western World*, and Adler produced a detailed index of the set, called *A Syntopicon: An Index to The Great Ideas*. While any such canon is subject to the claim of individual bias on the part of its selectors, the biggest problem then and now may be the focus that Hutchins and Adler placed on *Western* literature, which itself is highly biased toward one part of civilization, the West, as well as upper class male writers. To limit the canon in such a way seems spectacularly parochial today, and it is hard to look back and see how it even made sense to Hutchins and Adler in the first half of the century. While a certain blindness to issues of gender is understandable for the time they first popularized these ideas, but relative to the Western bias, they were familiar with Lao Tsu, Confucius, and the Buddha, and it seems strange to have framed education in such a way as to value their ideas less than those of Erasmus or Rousseau. And I might add, both of them lived long enough that they could have corrected their earlier biases, but I have not come across any such correction in my readings of their later works.

I might add that their Western civilization seems even more ironic when one considers how it contradicts both points one and three in Kneller's summary. Both of these points have to do with the universality of both human nature and truth. To say that education is about the universal in human nature and the universal in truth, and then propose an education that is culture-specific seems hypocritical to this reader.

Of course, more recent critics of the perennialist will point out that even in the West, their canon is narrow in its almost exclusive inclusion of Caucasian male writers. Admittedly the sexist nature of education and culture in the past substantially limited the production of great works of literature to males with relatively fair skin, but surely even one committed to a great books canon could find ways to explore elements of a cultural heritage that were manifested in other ways than in "great books."

Indeed, the bookishness of the perennialist philosophy of education is one of its greatest problems. As noted above, the intellectual life is about more than just literature or literature and numbers, and some of our greatest achievements were by people who were not writers, and in some cases were not fond of books. Socrates, himself, was no fan of book learning, and Jesus, though he cites the Torah, never, to our knowledge, wrote a book or even a letter, and he seemed more interested in the existential realities of life than in the propositional analysis of great ideas. Is there room for a Socrates or a Jesus in a perennialist school?

Finally, even if one buys into the idea of a canon of literature, there is the problem of reaching a consensus of what should be in it. Hutchins and Adler solve this to some degree by saying that classics have to have passed the test of time, therefore, only old books need to be considered. This is hardly satisfactory to today's relevance driven policy makers, who seem to define relevance in the most immediate and practical terms and for whom something written five years ago is passé and classic status means nothing. Nor is it satisfactory to book lovers who think that great literature is still being produced and is recognizable at most in a matter of a decade or two rather than a century or two.

Of course, once we include recent literature and non-Western literature to the canon, the sheer number of books far exceeds what any one student can be expected to read and understand in his/her basic education—even when the college years are included. In that case, how are educators to decide which great books to include in the curriculum and which not to?

Is the problem insurmountable? Is the answer to simply abandon the idea of great books and happily invite every teacher to teach whatever he or she happens to like? Surely not. Surely not all of our judgments about good literature are purely arbitrary. I have seen Wynton Marsalis argue on television that in the history of music, America's most noted contribution is jazz, and that American school children should be familiar with their country's great contribution. And I would add that while there may be great and wonderful arguments about which jazz performers are the very best, it is not capricious to say that the Louis Armstrong, Billie Holliday, and Miles Davis are among the greats. I would note that Marsalis is not saying that jazz is better than every other kind of music, but that because of its unique role in the history of music American children ought to be taught about it.

What we must do, it seems to me, is to avoid the assumption that we must refrain from making judgments at all if we cannot objectively prove that this is the absolute good. Surely there is a good Aristotelian golden mean somewhere on the issue of great literature in the school curriculum.

I suspect that at least part of the answer lies in humbly acknowledging that what we are teaching is not THE great books, but SOME of the great books and then be open to some negotiations on what is included and what is not. It does seem to me that if we want to start by asking people who love the content to identify what they consider the best. It makes no sense to ask someone who does not love jazz to identify the great jazz recordings, to ask someone who does not love science to identify the great scientific achievements, to ask someone who does not love novels to identify the great novels, etc. This, by the way, is what I think often happens when policy makers set the curriculum.

One additional problem with the great books idea, focused on classics of previous centuries, is that it ignores the fact that some of the greatest social and moral problems of our generation are genuinely new ones, not on the radar of Moses or Cicero. For example, nuclear weapons add to the problem of war a new dimension that our predecessors did not anticipate. More recently, mass media and advertising has turned the "village" it takes to raise a child over to a highly skilled group of manipulators whose goal is not to enhance the children's development but to exploit them for their money. I do not think Quintilian could have imagined such a village. Thanks to digital technologies, our privacy is under assault in ways that few could have imagined prior to 1850. The point is that educational discourse that includes only the classics will neglect some of the most compelling and urgent problems facing anyone today trying to live life as fully as Aristotle intended.

In light of these significant criticisms, one might well wonder why this author is even bringing up this largely discarded approach to higher education. The answer is that I believe, despite its problems, perennialism provides a far superior conception of the purposes of higher education than anything I see in current discourse where our mission seems little more elevated than increasing enrollments of universities and employability of graduates. While young people immersed in a materialist and entertainment-driven culture may not see the relevance of broad intellectual development, it does remain as relevant as ever to their self-actualization and to the democratic society's effective functioning. Actually, the characterization of America's problems in Chris Hedges's *Empire of Illusion: The End of Literacy and the Triumph of Spectacle* and Neil Postman's older book, *Amusing Ourselves to Death,* would suggest it is more relevant than ever. Both suggest that a shrinking of literary abilities and the capacity for critical thought put our culture at risk. A step back further to reread Aldous Huxley's *Brave New World* may evoke a sense that it was terrifyingly prophetic, and the perennialist vision may be the antidote to the poison of contemporary anti-intellectualism.[17]

In our increasingly fragmented society, a common body of knowledge is more relevant to the common good than ever. (E.D. Hirsch, Jr. has some valid points here.[18]) In an age of anti-intellectualism, we need more than ever to nurture the minds of young people, especially our best and brightest. In a world of consumerism, we need young people who can see beyond crass materialism. In a world of spectacularly manipulative advertising and political campaigns, we need young people who are disposed to critically examine the messages with which they are bombarded. In a world of narrow specialization, we need young people who have a view of the larger context of everything, so they can make the judgments about complex issues that are essential to intelligent voting. In a world of entertainment, we need young people who value work and are willing to put forth the effort to match the achievements of previous generations.

This ability to see complexities of a problem in their larger context, make sound judgments in light of them, and then act upon those sound judgments is what was traditionally known as wisdom, and wisdom is never irrelevant. I do not believe that currently fragmented higher educational ideals and practices, driven by economic rather than moral concerns and developing at best technical expertise and superficial knowledge, are fostering such wisdom, and a new perennialism, shed of its unnecessary baggage, can.

NOTES

1. Thomas Wakefield Goodspeed, *A History of the University of Chicago: 1891–1916* (Chicago: The University of Chicago Press, 1916), 144.

2. Robert Maynard Hutchins, *The Higher Learning in America* (New Brunswick: Transaction Publishers, 2008)

3. Steven E. Tozer, Guy Senese, and Paul Violas, *School and Society: Historical and Contemporary Perspectives* (New York: McGraw Hill, Inc., 1994), 227.

4. Clark Kerr, *The Uses of a University,* fifth ed. (Cambridge, MA: Harvard University Press, 2001), 5.

5. Richard P. Keeling and Richard H. Hersh, *We're Losing Our Minds: Rethinking American Higher Education* (New York: Palgrave Macmillan, 2012).

6. Robert M. Diamond, ed., *Field Guide to Academic Leadership* (San Francisco: Josey-Bass, 2002).

7. George Kneller, *Introduction to the Philosophy of Education* (New York: J. Wiley, 1964), 42–46.

8. Wayne Willis, "Liberating the Liberal Arts: An Interpretation of Aristotle," *JGE: The Journal of General Education* 39, no. 4 (1988): 193–205.

9. Roger Crisp and Michael A. Slote, *Virtue Ethics* (Oxford: Oxford University Press, 1997).

10. Howard Gardner, *Frames of Mind: The Theory of Multiple Intelligences* (New York: Basic Books, 1983).

11. Mihaly Csikszentmihalyi, *Flow: The Psychology of Optimal Experience* (New York: Harper and Row, 1990).

12. Mortimer Adler, et al. *The Paideia Proposal, An Educational Manifesto* (New York: Macmillan, 1982).

13. Mortimer Adler, "Education," *Time*, March 17, 1952. vol. LIX no. 11, 76.

14. Richard J. Bernstein, *Beyond Objectivism and Relativism: Science, Hermeneutics, and Praxis* (Philadelphia: University of Pennsylvania Press, 1983).

15. Robert Maynard Hutchins, *The Higher Learning in America* (New Brunswick: Transaction Publishers, 2008), xxiv.

16. See for example, John Guillory. *Cultural Capital: The Problem of Literary Canon Formation* (Chicago: University of Chicago Press, 1995) and numerous essays in Lee Morrissey's *Debating the Canon: A Reader from Addison to Naffisi* (New York: Palgrave Macmillan, 2005).

17. Aldous Huxley, *Brave New World* (New York: Perennial Classics, 1998).

18. In *Cultural Literacy*, Hirsch deals with the a problem parallel to the problem of canon, the problem of core content, without falling into the trap of objectivism and absolutism by characterizing decisions about shared academic content as contemporary judgments subject to revision as the culture changes. See E. D. Hirsch Jr., Joseph F. Kett, and James S. Trefil, *Cultural Literacy: What Every American Needs to Know* (New York: Vintage Books, 1988).

BIBLIOGRAPHY

Adler, Mortimer. "Education." *Time*. March 17, 1952. vol. LIX no. 11. 76–79.

———. *The Paideia Proposal: An Educational Manifesto*. New York: Macmillan, 1982.

Bernstein, Richard J. *Beyond Objectivism and Relativism: Science, Hermeneutics, and Praxis*. Philadelphia: University of Pennsylvania Press, 1983.

Crisp, Roger and Michael A. Slote. *Virtue Ethics*. Oxford: Oxford University Press, 1997.

Csikszentmihalyi, Mihaly. *Flow: The Psychology of Optimal Experience*. New York: Harper and Row, 1990.

Diamond, Robert M. ed. *Field Guide to Academic Leadership*. San Francisco, California: Jossey-Bass, 2002.

Gardner, Howard. *Frames of Mind: The Theory of Multiple Intelligences*. New York: Basic Books, 1983.

Goodspeed, Thomas Wakefield. *A History of the University of Chicago: 1891–1916*. Chicago: The University of Chicago Press, 1916.

Guillory, John. *Cultural Capital: The Problem of Literary Canon Formation*. Chicago: University of Chicago Press, 1995.

Hirsch Jr., E. D., Joseph F. Kett, and James S. Trefil. *Cultural Literacy: What Every American Needs to Know*. New York: Vintage Books, 1988.

Hutchins, Robert Maynard. *The Higher Learning in America*. New Brunswick: Transaction Publishers, 2008.

Huxley, Aldous. *Brave New World*. New York: Perennial Classics, 1998.

Keeling, Richard P. and Richard H. Hersh. *We're Losing Our Minds: Rethinking American Higher Education*. New York: Palgrave Macmillan, 2012.

Kerr, Clark. *The Uses of a University, fifth edition.* Cambridge, MA: Harvard University Press, 2001.

Kneller, George. *Introduction to the Philosophy of Education.* New York: J. Wiley, 1964.

Morrissey, Lee. *Debating the Canon: A Reader from Addison to Naffisi.* New York: Palgrave Macmillan, 2005.

Tozer, Steven E., Guy Senese, and Paul Violas. *School and Society: Historical and Contemporary Perspectives.* New York: McGraw Hill, Inc., 1994.

Willis, Wayne. "Liberating the Liberal Arts: An Interpretation of Aristotle." *JGE: The Journal of General Education* 39, no. 4 (1988): 193–205.

Chapter Six

Academic Freedom and the Role of the Humanities

James Scott Johnston

Debates regarding the relevance of higher education to the public are sometimes pitched at the level of institutions, and when distinctions are made regarding these institutions, they concern "type." For example, it is common to hear of debates regarding the public investment in university education, or junior college education. Also common are debates regarding the worth of a college education—particularly salient given the high unemployment rate of recent college graduates, the high cost of undergraduate tuition, and the steadily declining economic worth of an undergraduate degree. Equally prevalent are debates regarding the sorts of undergraduate degrees awarded, and whether awarding these presently makes sense, given current circumstances. For example, granting undergraduate degrees in the liberal arts and sciences has increasingly come under fire as a result of the present difficulty of these graduates in obtaining gainful employment. If we are to judge by the rhetoric surrounding 9/11, the humanities are indeed in dire shape. At least one book has been devoted to the systematic devolution of academic freedoms in light of the "Patriot Act" and other, post-9/11 legal interventions.[1]

These are all very important debates; however, they are not my concern. My concern is with the challenges to the disciplines in light of the public scrutiny on higher education. Specifically, I am concerned with the humanities, and the response of the humanities to the ongoing assaults from public interests. One way—the chief way—that the humanities has historically defended itself from public intervention is through claims to professional autonomy. And these claims are in turn defended on the basis of academic freedom. I want to examine the role of academic freedom more closely in this regard. It will be my thesis that academic freedom still provides the best measure against public condemnation of the humanities, but that the humanities must do a better job of convincing the public what it does best—the articulation and dissemination of the historical self-understanding of the disciplines to society. Only if academic freedom is maintained can the humanities perform this service for the public. But only if this role is undertaken by the humanities is public support for the humanities likely to be forthcoming. Delineating how academic freedom serves the project of historical self-understanding is a major concern of this chapter.

PART ONE: ACADEMIC FREEDOM AND THE PUBLIC INTEREST

In 1902, John Dewey wrote "Academic Freedom," an essay diagnosing the basic anxiety of academics in regard to their relationship with the public. This essay was to become prophetic, both for the development of North American higher education's self-understanding and the development of the American Association of University Professors. In the essay, Dewey judged that,

> The general public may be willing enough to admit in the abstract the existence of a science of political economy, sociology, or psychology, but when these dare to emerge from a remote and technical sphere, and pass authoritative judgment upon affairs of daily life,—when they come in contact, that is, with the interests of daily life,—they meet with little but skepticism or hostility or, what is worse, sensational exploitation. [2]

Dewey's strategy to deal with public skepticism was for the disciplines to become more scientific—in effect, to remedy the "backwardness of some of our sciences" through constant and patient attention to modes of context-based, empirical inquiry as opposed to speculative and/or dogmatic claims. [3] Dewey, of course, was concerned about the "new" social sciences of psychology, sociology, and economics: the humanities, at least in the context of "Academic Freedom," were not in his purview. However, Dewey would be the first to admit that no claim for the relevance of higher education can be made without explicit attention to the humanities, because it is through the humanities that our historical self-understandings are brought to light and to bear on the other disciplines. And only if this bringing to light is undertaken can a cohesive case be made to the public that higher education is relevant.

What was the basis of Dewey's argument on behalf of the sciences and social sciences in respect of academic freedom? And what, for that matter, did the committee empanelled to draft the 1915 "Declaration of Principles on Academic Freedom and Academic Tenure" rest on as a sufficient (if not necessary) grounding for the general principles of Academic freedom? The answer in both cases is the public. I shall discuss each of these further, and comment on the relationship between the two arguments at the end of this section. Dewey was the first president of the AAUP (1915) and on behalf of the organization wrote several essays, addresses, and newspaper articles discussing matters of public importance. The most important of these is his inaugural address to the Association, given January 1, 1915, and published later that month in *Science*.[4] Dewey tied the importance of the goals of the organization to the formation and maintenance of an intelligent public. I quote at length.

> I am a great believer in the power of public opinion. In this country nothing stands against it. But to act, it must exist. To act wisely, it musts be intelligently formed. To be intelligently formed, it must be the result of deliberate inquiry and discussion. It can not be developed in corners here and there; it can not be the voice of a few, however wise. It must be formed democratically; that is, cooperatively. All interests, however humble, must be heard; inquiry and conference must glean all the experiences available; decision must be based upon mutual consultation.[5]

Dewey thought the problems endemic to the American professoriate did not reside in the relationship between trustees and faculty, rather in the use of "methods of control developed decades ago, before anything like the existing type of university was thought of."[6] Needless to say, his recommendation to improve the relationships between trustees and faculty consisted in reconstructing these methods. For neither the trustees nor the faculty could be held responsible for the systematic failures. In fact, to Dewey it was a wonder how well these worked together, given the failures. "A system inherently absurd in the present situation has been made workable because of the reasonableness and goodwill of the governors on one side and, even more, of the governed on the other."[7]

What the system required, then, was reconstruction. In discussing this reconstruction, Dewey avers to the claims made in his 1902, "Academic Freedom." "The best way to put educational principles where they belong— in the atmosphere of scientific discussion—is to disentangle them from the local circumstances with which they so easily get bound up in a given institution."[8] For Dewey, this was to generalize the discussion along scientific lines; disseminating the "fruits" of the scientific research into educational policy. While not wishing to downplay the hard work the committee on academic freedom and tenure had done, Dewey is keen (more keen if we are to judge by his statements) that faculty effort should be directed to the scientific establishment and dissemination of higher educational policy. Dewey rhetorically asks,

> Let us cultivate a like social sense of the wide educational interests we have in common; of our dependence upon one another as institutions and as teach-

ers. . . . Shall we not require of ourselves a similar scientific spirit as we try to
settle educational questions? A more intense consciousness of our common
vocation, our common object and common destiny; and a more resolute desire
to apply the methods of science, methods of inquiry and publicity, to our work
in teaching—these are the things which call for the existence of organized
effort.[9]

Dewey's urge to have faculty work on behalf of sustaining a common
interest is not incidental: it is built into his social philosophy. It is the same
spirit that infuses such works as *The Public and its Problems*. Interestingly,
Dewey thought that the academic dismissals of faculty by boards of trustees
the committee investigated in 1915 were isolated events; he was to be proven
wrong by the many and continued challenges on academic freedom after his
tenure as president.[10]

The public loomed large in the subsequent 1915 "Declaration of the Principles on Academic Freedom and Academic Tenure."[11] A committee of fif-
teen members was empanelled to create the "Declaration" at the very first
official meeting. The document was produced for the second meeting (December 31, 1915) by Edwin Seligman of Columbia University and Arthur
Lovejoy of Johns Hopkins, and was signed by the remaining thirteen members.[12] The document famously concentrates on *Lehrfreiheit*—the freedom
of the teacher to conduct research, to teach, and to make extramural utterances.[13] The first section of the "Declaration" is given over to an examination and declaration of the general principles, and it is this section I wish to
concentrate upon.

The first discussion topic in regard to general principles is the basis of
academic authority. The "Declaration" distinguishes between proprietary institutions, such as religious colleges, and public institutions. In the case of the
former, boards of trustees are well within their mandates to expect faculty to
operate within the guidelines set by the institutions in matters of scholarship
and teaching. However, as the "Declaration" notes, these institutions are
becoming rarer.[14] Far more common are public institutions, whose mandates
lie elsewhere. The "Declaration" asks (rhetorically): "Can colleges and universities that are not strictly bound by their founders to a propagandist duty
ever be included in the class of institutions that we have just described as
being in a moral sense proprietary? The answer is clear. If the former class of
institutions constitutes a private or proprietary trust, the latter constitutes a
public trust."[15] In the case of these latter institutions, "The trustees are trustees for the public . . . ,"[16] and there is an absolute dichotomy between these
and proprietary institutions. "They [public colleges] cannot be permitted to
assume the proprietary attitude and privilege if they are appealing to the
general public for support. Trustees of such universities or colleges have no
moral right to bind the reason or the conscience of any professor."[17]

The second discussion topic in regard to academic principles is the nature of the academic calling. Here the committee put forth a decidedly *Bildung*-esque set of claims regarding the importance of ". . . men of the highest ability, of sound learning, and of strong and independent character," for the ". . . dignity of the scholar's profession. . . ."[18] The function of the scholar's profession is said to be ". . . to deal at first hand, after prolonged and specialized technical training, with the sources of knowledge; and to impart the results of their own and of their fellow-specialists' investigations and reflection, both to students and to the general public, without fear or favor."[19] In regard to the role of the general public, the "Declaration" states,

> The lay public is under no compulsion to accept or to act upon the opinions of the scientific experts whom, through the universities, it employs. But it is highly needful, in the interest of society at large, that what purport to be conclusions of men trained for, and dedicated to, the quest for truth, shall in fact be the conclusions of such men, and not echoes of the opinions of the lay public, or of the individuals who endow or manage universities.[20]

Now this prior statement may seem to suggest that the faculty has an obligation only to itself, and the lay public is not to interfere in the carrying-out of the faculty's "quest for truth." But in fact, the obligation on the part of the public to not interfere with the faculty's "quest for truth" is met by a reciprocal obligation of the faculty to inquire, develop, and use the knowledge gleaned from study and investigation for the benefit of the public. In fact, the obligation of the faculty is to the profession *and* the public. In speaking on the nature of the relationship between the university trustees and the faculty, the "Declaration" maintains,

> The latter [faculty] are the appointees, but not in any proper sense the employees, of the former [trustees]. For, once appointed, the scholar has professional functions to perform in which the appointing authorities have neither competency nor moral right to intervene. The responsibility of the university teacher is primarily to the public itself, and to the judgment of his own profession; and while, with respect to certain external conditions of his vocation, he accepts a responsibility to the authorities of the institution in which he serves, in the essentials of his professional activity his duty is to the wider public to which the institution itself is morally amenable.[21]

The third discussion topic in regard to academic principles is the function of the academic institution. The three purposes are:

a. to promote inquiry and advance the sum of human knowledge;
b. to provide general instruction to the students; and
c. to develop experts for various branches of the public service.[22]

The promotion of inquiry and the advancement of the sum of human knowledge are considered in terms of scientific, social-scientific, and spiritual disciplines. The spiritual disciplines are tied closely to freedom.[23] The instruction of students is tied to respect, and respect is in turn tied to ". . . their confidence in his [the teacher's] intellectual integrity."[24] The "Declaration" continues; "It is clear, however, that this confidence will be impaired if there is suspicion on the part of the student that the teacher is not expressing himself fully or frankly, or that college and university teachers in general are a repressed and intimidated class who dare not speak with that candor and courage which youth always demands in those whom it is to esteem."[25] The "Declaration" then discusses the role of experts for the public service. The training of such experts has, accordingly, in recent years, become an important part of the work of the universities; and in almost every one of our higher institutions of learning the professors of the economic, social, and political sciences have been drafted to an increasing extent into more or less unofficial participation in the public service. Beyond this, "To be of use to the legislator or the administrator, he [the faculty member] must enjoy their [the publics'] complete confidence in the disinterestedness of his conclusions."[26] Finally, in terms of the university as a whole, the *Declaration* makes clear that "The responsibility of the university as a whole is to the community at large, and any restriction upon the freedom of the instructor is bound to react injuriously upon the efficiency and the *morale* of the institution, and therefore ultimately upon the interests of the community."[27]

The above should be enough to dispel the claim that, from the AAUP's inception, the faculty has a vested interest *only* in their disciplinary societies or practices, or that there is no professional or moral connection between the public at large and the scholarship of the faculty.[28] In fact, as we see, the converse is the case—the public is the overriding concern of the faculty in conducting their scholarship and teaching. This is also made clear in subsequent 1940 "Statement of Principles on Academic Freedom and Tenure," and the 1970 "Interpretive Comments"—both which uphold the initial 1915 "Declaration."[29] Though the faculty are to be protected (through academic freedom) from public intrusion into the role, scope, and matter of their inquiry, scholarship, and teaching, it is for the purpose of the public that inquiry, scholarship, and teaching are conducted.

PART TWO: THE PRESENT CRISIS: THE HUMANITIES FACE IRRELEVANCE

The rhetorical, rallying cry of the demise of the humanities is at least as old as the "Declaration." In 1918, Thorstein Veblen made reference to the humanities in his critique of corporate interests on the scholarship of the faculty, suggesting that they were imperiled by the attention given to ". . . pecuniary interests."[30] Of course, the most famous of addresses was Robert Hutchins's, published in 1936 as part of *The Higher Learning in America*. For Hutchins, the humanities functioned to instill in the university a sense of ". . . unity . . . ;" though the modern university behaved as an ". . . encyclopedia . . . ," through training the student to appreciate and practice the intellectual virtues, the humanities could elevate the student's attention to higher things, the chief of these being metaphysics.[31] But in order to do this, the university must place checks on overweening scientism—a scientism he claimed Dewey supported.[32]

Scientism is no longer the bugbear of the humanities. The rise of the sociology of knowledge, with its attendant pessimism regarding the certainty of the epistemic claims of the sciences, seems to have cooled the utopian rhetoric with which Hutchins had to deal. If we are to judge the recent literature on the subject, far more prevalent since at least the 1970s has been the role of the culture wars on the humanities, and, since the 1990s, the so-called rise of neo-liberalism. A quick survey of the literature demonstrates politically polarized accounts of the demise of the humanities are in abundance. I will not address these, other than to note two important distinguishing characteristics. The first is the role played by novel methodologies and theorizations in the crisis. The second is the turn to academic freedom as a bulwark against encroachment by the politically inspired antagonists of higher education. I will finish with my considered opinion on the role of academic freedom in regard to the current crisis in the humanities.

Intramural Conflicts

We can follow the pattern of the 1915 "Declaration" and divide disputes over the crisis in the humanities according to intramural and extramural.[33] Extramural disputes concern impingements upon academic freedom from outside the institution—as in the case of calls for a professor to be fired from her position for making supposedly incendiary statements (think of Ward Churchill's "little Eichmanns" claim). Intramural disputes concern impingements upon academic freedom from inside the institution or discipline (think tenure disputes that arise as a result of disciplinary disagreements). The role played by novel methodologies and theorizations concerns both types of disputes, but especially the latter. Not surprisingly, those on the side of the novel methodologies and theorizations are suspicious of disciplinary interventions to deny or otherwise downplay their scholarly achievements. The 1915 "Declaration" and the earlier pronouncements of faculty on behalf of academic freedom do not offer much support to them. Joan Scott for example, chastises Dewey for neglecting to envision that disciplinary societies and professional organization might take a dim view to certain scholarships and in effect, secure ". . . consensus by exclusion."[34] Judith Butler seconds this concern. In unambiguous fashion, Butler claims, "If an account of knowledge and knowledge production is meant to secure [that] academic freedom, it should agree with the ways knowledge is pursued now. Accordingly, if the 1915 "Declaration" assumes that all knowledge follows the model of a conception of a scientific progress that few, if any, scientists still embrace, then a clear need emerges to establish the value of knowledge inquiry in the arts, humanities, and social sciences, in ways that describe well those practices and their values."[35]

Scott and Butler are keen to disassociate the methodologies and theorizations of post-modernism, post-structuralism, feminist studies and cultural studies from the scientism they see evident in the earlier, 1915 "Declaration," as well as the recent attacks on these from within the disciplines. These attacks are well known to us, and concern a broad range of literatures from various disciplines within the humanities, drawn from distinctive political positions, and constituted of multifarious arguments. They encompass, for example, Allan Bloom's *The Closing of the American Mind* and Martha Nussbaum's *Cultivating Humanity*. Both want to "save" the humanities; and both believe that these novel methodologies and theorizations are damaging to its reputation. Several concerns are evidenced; however, the two chief concerns (shared by both authors mentioned) are the nihilism at the core of the post-modern project (evident in the essentialization of difference and the fracture of any ideal that is stable, certain, or unified) and the impregnable jargon that makes the claims inimical to scrutiny.[36] Both Bloom and Nussbaum fear for the humanities in regard to the (American) public.[37] The corresponding fear on the part of those practicing novel methodologies and theorizations is that those in disciplines in the humanities inimical to these methodologies and theorizations will close ranks and shut them out. Thus, authors such as Scott and Butler champion the view of humanities as an open-ended pursuit in which the disciplinary attitudes and views of others should not be allowed to intrude on individual scholarship.

Scott attacks the critics of post-modernism by running them together with proponents of disciplinarity in the humanities. Doing so allows her to make the claim, "Despite their opposition to one another, these two examples...both represent attempts to build community—in one case a disciplinary community, in the other a political community—on a foundation of immutable truth."[38] Scott thinks that if this is the case, if immutable truth is what grounds both disciplinary and political activity in the humanities, a critique of this truth ought to serve as sufficient means to break up these hegemonies: "If we think of communities and disciplines not as common essences, not as bodies of people who are the same . . . but as provisional entities called into being to organize relations of difference, then standards and rules become heuristic practices around which argument is expected and change anticipated."[39] The standards and rules are then amenable to transformation, as they are both historically conditioned and historically responsive to whatever scholarship is going on within the disciplines at the time. (The role of the public in all of this is curiously overlooked or unstated.)

Extramural Conflicts

Increasingly, extramural conflicts have been seen by the courts as evidence of infringement of individual rights.[40] Justice Frankfurter's concurrence of Chief Justice Warren's opinion in *Sweezy vs. New Hampshire* (1957) seems to be the *locus classicus* of this turn. "For society's good . . . inquiries into these problems [those studied by the social sciences], speculations about them, stimulation in others of reflection upon them, must be left as unfettered as possible. . . . This means the exclusion of governmental intervention in the intellectual life of the university."[41] Frankfurter and Warren both tied this unfettering to the first amendment rights of an individual, in similar ways to press freedoms.[42] Subsequent court opinions have favored this reading (for example, *Tinker vs. Des Moines*, 1969; *California vs. Bakke*, 1978). Nevertheless, the articulation of individual rights in respect of academic freedom does not protect the professor from the scrutiny of her disciplinary society, nor is she permitted to practice her profession free from university restraints. It is rather the case that "If the First Amendment protects the interests of individual persons to speak as they wish, academic freedom protects the interests of society in having a professoriat that can accomplish its mission."[43]

One the salient concerns of the 1970 interpretation of the Declaration was to distinguish between the invocation of the First Amendment, which applies to the state, and the role and scope of the First Amendment in proprietary institutions such as private colleges.[44] In the invocation of the First Amendment, the interpretation cited the 1964 "Committee A Statement on Extramural Utterances," which read, "The controlling principle is that a faculty member's expression of opinion as a citizen cannot constitute grounds for dismissal unless it clearly demonstrates the faculty member's unfitness for his or her position. Extramural utterances rarely bear upon the faculty member's fitness for the position. Moreover, a final decision should take into account the faculty member's entire record as a teacher and scholar."[45] The opinion of the 1970 interpretation of the "Declaration" was that few proprietary colleges existed that did not adhere to the principles of academic freedom, and that it was no longer necessary to endorse such a departure of the principle.

Extramural conflicts permeated the earliest challenges to academic freedom, and continue to do so today, if we are to judge by such sensational cases as Ward Churchill's (in which the AAUP *did not* support his case, because a faculty committee voted for dismissal).[46] But constitutional challenges to breaches of academic freedom by themselves do little to ease the reluctance of non-academic, private, or public interests to support the humanities; they merely constitute a rear-guard action. Indeed, if anything, they draw attention to the most egregious uses of these freedoms (as with the Ward Churchill matter). In light of the downsizing of humanities departments and the closing of university programs, academic freedom comes too late on the scene. The indifference—even hostility—toward the humanities cannot be dealt with solely through First Amendment rights. It has to be overcome through persuasion. We have to persuade both private and public interests that the humanities are beneficial. And, if we are to preserve the humanities (and not transform them into something less than recognizable) we have to do so without reconstituting the humanities as an instrumental means to some non-humanistic end.

Several attempts at such persuasion have been offered. Martha Nussbaum's work (*Cultivating Humanity*, and more recently, *Not for Profit*) operate in this vein. One means of attacking the indifference to the humanities has been to demonstrate that the liberal arts are not elitist. Nussbaum attempts to demonstrate this by connecting the tradition of the liberal arts to the founding fathers and early American educators. She also reminds us of the unique importance of the two-year liberal arts model for American university education and its necessity for the stability of democratic institutions.[47] Many others have concurred. Yet, it is doubtful that appeals to history, tradition, or even the stability of democratic institutions will persuade in an era were humanities undergraduates are increasingly finding employment opportunities negligible, and graduate programs in the humanities (not to say gainful employment post-PhD) drying up. Other means of persuasion have to be tried, and this means novel claims and arguments on behalf of the humanities. I will attempt a different, though complementary argument to those, above. I will argue that the humanities have the function of articulating the historical and present self-understandings of the disciplines to society. It is in this regard that the humanities' usefulness to society resides.

PART THREE: THE HUMANITIES AS THE PURVEYOR OF HISTORICAL SELF-UNDERSTANDING: ARTICULATING THE HERMENEUTIC TASK

It should be patently obvious that one of the roles of the humanities is to carry out the hermeneutical task of understanding the various conceptual and practical concerns in society on their own terms, and linking these to the conceptual and practical concerns of the various disciplines. I say "should be" because I am not at all certain that this actually occurs. To judge by the disputes in the 1980s and 1990s between the various branches of the humanities (English, comparative literature, history, philosophy), discord rather than concord seems the norm. Essentializing difference—a preferred strategy of post-modernist, post-colonialist, and cultural studies, thwarts the role of such an understanding.[48] Thankfully, we are entering a "post-post-modernist" phase of scholarship, and the retrieval of hitherto unacceptable discourses is now underway. The discourse I want to retrieve in defense of the humanities is the *Geisteswissenschaftlich* tradition—the tradition of the "human sciences" made plausible by German Idealism and post-Idealism. I will not rehearse the history of Idealism (or its objections) other than to note certain pivotal claims for the project of retrieval. I will begin with Hegel's contribution to our conceptual understanding, move to Wilhelm Dilthey's explication of the human sciences, and finish with Gadamer's understanding of "historically effected consciousness."

The first claim is that our conceptual apparatus (that which we use to understand) is historical. This is Hegel's claim. This is of course in contradistinction to (metaphysical) realism, which wanted to say that essential features of the world resided *in* the world (the view Hegel called "sense-certainty").[49] But it was also claimed, in contradistinction to Fichte and Kant, that our conceptual apparatus was not transcendental; it depended not on some vaunted "thing-in-itself," but was rather wholly and completely immanent. The concepts develop as a result of tensions internal to the concepts themselves, and not as a result of external forces.[50] Historical forces, of course, condition concepts; but the concepts themselves remain at a descriptive level distinctive from those.[51] Thus, Hegel can consider conceptual development alone in a *Science of Logic*, and the actual, practical working out of concepts in various treatises such as the *Philosophy of Nature* and the *Philosophy of Mind* (both in the *Encyclopedia*).

The second claim is that our concepts are irreducibly normative, and our conceptual apparatus informs concerns such as experience, nature, and history at an entirely different descriptive level than that provided in the *Science of Logic*. That is to say, while we can concentrate on the conceptual apparatus itself in a text such as the *Science of Logic*, the actual operation of the concepts lies elsewhere, in experience, nature, and history. So for example, to say nature is rational is to say we cannot help but understanding nature from a conceptual (rational) standpoint.[52] The same is true for history. While we are obviously not operating at the level of concepts *simpliciter*, we are nevertheless considering concepts as we take in historical events and form historical understandings from them.

The third claim is that our awareness of the processes of historical understandings is historical self-understanding—self-consciousness. That is to say, self-consciousness is, in respect of experiential and historical concerns, historical. While we can fairly understand the logical development of concepts as separate and apart from our self-awareness, when we come to our role in the development of the concepts (what Hegel calls Reflection), we invoke self-consciousness.[53] It is only through reflection that we can trace the development of concepts historically, and it is this development that gives us the wherewithal to make judgments about this or that concept in relation to experiential and historical affairs. This is what Hegel famously calls the Notion; the concept reflecting into itself for itself, or, absolute subjectivity.[54] These three claims—that our conceptual apparatus is historical, that concepts are irreducibly normative and play out in experience, nature, and history, and that subjectivity—the reflection on the part of the self into the concept—are vital ingredients in the retrieval of the self-understandings of the disciplines.

These three claims have been at the nexus of a variety of hermeneutical enterprises stretching from Wilhelm Dilthey to Hans-Georg Gadamer. Dilthey's task was to distinguish at a phenomenological level, the human sciences from the natural sciences.[55] For Dilthey, the "causes" in scientific research are explained hypothetico-deductively, whereas human "causes" are experienced.[56] Lived experience is the realm of "being conscious," and included feelings, perceptions, representations, as well as the attitudes toward these.[57] Dilthey calls this realm, the "psychic nexus."[58] The psychic nexus is a shared nexus; though each of us has different ingredients that make our psychic nexus comprehensive, there is a great overlap because each of us participates in a shared culture and history. This allows for the possibility of *Verstehen*—understanding. Understanding is the capacity to realize oneself in another's context because one is already in, or can place oneself within, that context. The recognition of lived experience through the human sciences Dilthey calls "historical consciousness."[59] Historical consciousness is not consciousness in an objective, scientific mode; it is consciousness acquired through interpretation.

It was this notion of historical consciousness that Gadamer thought so valuable for his own articulation of "historically effected consciousness."[60] Gadamer adopts (with certain reservations) Dilthey's famous take on the hermeneutic circle, adapting it to the concerns of texts rather than Being. "Fundamentally, understanding is always a movement in this kind [hermeneutic] of circle, which is why the repeated return from the whole to the parts, and vice versa, is essential. Moreover, this circle is constantly expanding, since the concept of the whole is relative, and being integrated in ever larger contexts always affects the understanding of the individual part."[61] Texts generate infinitely many meanings. As one grapples with the text, one adds to the circle of understanding. Not only is one interpreting the text, but the received responses to the text. A larger and larger cluster of meanings builds up from ongoing interpretations of the text. While the text has its origin with an author writing from a particular perspective, and within a particular social and historical context, with the expansion of the interpretive circle *the text becomes the means for generating a tradition for others.*

> A written tradition is not a fragment of a past world, but has already raised itself beyond this into the sphere of the meaning that it expresses. The ideality of the world is what raises everything linguistic beyond the finitude and transience that characterize other remnants of past existence. It is not this document, as a piece of the past, that is the bearer of tradition but the continuity of memory. Through it tradition becomes part of our own world and thus what it communicates can be stated immediately. Where we have a written tradition, we are not just told a particular thing; a past humanity itself becomes present to us in its general relation to the world.[62]

The products of the disciplinary discourses (science, social science, humanities) are primarily textual. (And if they are not, they are often enough oral and can be converted to text.) This is true even in our so-called digital age. Social practices inhering in the disciplines are more difficult to get at, but can be gotten through qualitative methods, including interviews and observation, and these can be converted into text. There is thus a connection between the Heideggerian-styled "hermeneutics of being," and the Gadamerian-inspired "hermeneutics of text." The point is we can understand the disciplines' self-understandings through textual means. And that which we cannot understand through textual means, we have recourse to through qualitative methods. It is the interpretation of the text (or data in the case of social practices) that constitutes the link between the past (memory) and the present. What the humanities can do is furnish this link. They can do it through comparative and critical textual analysis; policy analysis; document analysis; and they can complement the analysis of discourse (speech) and behavior (social practice) in the critical social sciences. In this way, they generate historical consciousness that the public can then use to form opinions on matter of expedience (such as, say, legislation or social practices). This much is uncontroversial to all except the most cynical of humanities scholars.

What is controversial is the role of the humanities *to* the public. That is to say, what, if any, obligations do the various disciplines constituting the humanities, as well as humanities departments and individuals therein, place themselves under in consideration of their roles to the public? To judge by recent developments in the humanities, the answer is few, if any. I believe this has to change if we are to persuade the public that the humanities have relevance. The obligation I am most concerned with is the corresponding duty that follows from the First Amendment right to academic freedom. The corresponding obligation to operate in the public interest (however broadly defined), I argue, necessitates finding ways to be relevant to the public that are neither subserviently instrumental, nor arrogantly stand-offish. However, if this is to be, the corresponding obligation to utilize one's academic freedom in pursuit of the public interest must be met. In terms of the role of the humanities, I suggest there is a broad obligation to craft our scholarship in

the public interest. Joan Scott and Judith Butler champion the view of humanities as an open-ended pursuit in which the disciplinary attitudes and
views of others (including other humanities scholars) should not be allowed
to intrude on individual scholarship.[63] I find this too stand-offish. While it is
quite correct to say that the hermeneutic enterprise consists in a variety of
models and approaches—the "hermeneutics of suspicion" being one of those
practiced recently by many in the humanities—the scholarship produced is
necessarily a product of the public interest.[64] This means we have a responsibility (to be defined) in what counts as acceptable scholarship *for* the public
interest. If the public doesn't see the humanities as offering itself in the
public interest, it *will* police the resultant scholarship in a very heavy-handed
manner. One may argue that this is precisely what is happening. While I am
not suggesting we police the borders of our scholarship in quest of malcon-
tents who do not demonstrate a public utility, if we are to avoid this state of
affairs we must nevertheless regulate this scholarship ourselves.

Now it might be thought we can continue on, Rorty-like, with our endless
conversation, adding here and there to the hermeneutic circle that humanities
scholarship has constructed. The problem with this is from the point of view
of the public, the circle is impenetrable; hyper-specialization and the abstruse
technical jargon of many of the discourses help render the circle imperme-
able to the public.[65] While scholars in the humanities may well understand
what is taking place in various disciplinary disputes, what is at stake, and
how this contributes to an ongoing conversation, the public is likely bewil-
dered. Our obligation to the public interest runs deeper than simply publishing our scholarship and resting satisfied that we are contributing to a larger
conversation; we must let the public in on this conversation as well. But there
is a problem: there are scholars that often argue against hermeneutical approaches and against the possibility of a consistent conversation. These
scholars often argue there are epistemic breaks that in effect deny that a
tradition exists or that a conversation is occurring. This is the corollary to the
essentialization of difference in certain scholarship. Yet, we cannot continue
to essentialize difference in our scholarship if we are meet our public obligations: at some point, we must connect up our conversations (including those
that essentialize difference) to make them available (and comprehensible) to
the public.

The hermeneutic enterprise I have in mind thus is unifying rather than
differentiating; it is inclusive rather than exclusive. It does not essentialize
difference. Rather, it stresses the unity of interpretative findings—the essentialization of difference being one of them. It operates, then, as a model of
"unity in difference," making the movements or particulars of discourse (the
differences) readily visible, yet connecting these to a larger discourse in
which they are seen to be a part. If the public interest is what academic
freedom obligates us to do, then we have a professional ethical and pedagogi-

cal responsibility to present our findings in such a way that they are comprehensible to the public. And this means finding and articulating the links between the various discourses, however fractured and differential they first appear.

The difficulty as I see it will not be in convincing the public that the historical enterprise is valuable and that the humanities are best poised to carry it out. The difficulty will rather be convincing recalcitrant or otherwise suspicious humanities scholars (and in some cases, large swaths of a discipline) that this is the project in which our scholarship should be involved. Those that already practice the "hermeneutics of suspicion" are unlikely to accommodate those (such as myself) that would like to see a wholesale turn to the project of historical self-understanding of the disciplines. But short of fiat (which would violate long-cherished tenets of academic freedom and undo the very safeguards of academic privilege), I see no other way than the persuasive route to accomplish this.

FINAL THOUGHTS

I return to Dewey, and to the prescient claim he made as president at the first meeting of the AAUP in 1915: "A more intense consciousness of our common vocation, our common object and common destiny; and a more resolute desire to apply the methods of science, methods of inquiry and publicity, to our work in teaching—these are the things which call for the existence of organized effort."[66] For Dewey, this was a socio-political rather than an epistemological claim.[67] What the humanities seems to lack in the turn to essentializing difference is precisely this "common vocation," and "common object," to say nothing of a "common destiny." While not going as far as Dewey's rhetoric regarding the methods of science would suggest, I think it behooves us in the humanities to get better at the "publicity" necessary for the ongoing support of our scholarship. Our vocation implies the academic freedom needed to operate relatively unimpeded in the pursuit of our teaching and scholarship.

Academic freedom gives us the right, under the First Amendment, to pursue our scholarship and teaching unimpeded by most intramural and extramural considerations. But we must not forget that Academic Freedom implies an obligation to the public interest. Beyond any instrumental purpose such scholarship and teaching may have, there exists an obligation that we craft our scholarship and teaching such that it can be articulated in the public domain. If we are granted the right to academic freedom, we are also charged with the responsibility to the public interest, in whose name we operate: the vocation is inclusive of this obligation. A way (one way) I believe we can best serve our public obligation is to consider the humanities as that enterprise that articulates the self-understandings of the disciplines—historical and current—and articulates these understandings to and for the public. This is a unifying accomplishment, as opposed to one that emphasizes the essential difference between or within, disciplinary self-understandings.

NOTES

1. Barbara Doumani, ed., *Academic Freedom after September 11*, (New York: Zone Books, 2006).

2. John Dewey, "Academic Freedom," in *The Middle Works of John Dewey*, vol. 2, ed. Jo Ann Boydston (Carbondale, IL: Southern Illinois University Press, 1972), 122.

3. Dewey, "Academic Freedom," 123.

4. John Dewey, "Annual Address to the American Association of University Professors," in *The Middle Works of John Dewey*, vol. 8, ed. Jo Ann Boydston (Carbondale, IL: Southern Illinois University Press, 1979), 100.

5. Ibid. 100.

6. Ibid.

7. Ibid., 100–101.

8. Ibid., 101.

9. Ibid., 103.

10. Dewey, "Annual Address of the President to the American Association of University Professors," in *The Middle Works of John Dewey*, vol. 8, ed. Jo Ann Boydston. (Carbondale, IL: Southern Illinois University Press, 1979), 106; Louis Menand, "The Limits of Academic Freedom," in *The Future of Academic Freedom*, ed. Louis Menand (Chicago: the University of Chicago Press, 1996), 7.

11. Matthew Finkin and Robert Post, *For the Common Good: Principles of American Academic Freedom* (New Haven: Yale University Press, 2009), 42.

12. AAUP, "1915 Declaration of Principles on Academic Freedom and Academic Tenure," *Policy Documents and Reports* (Baltimore, MD: Johns Hopkins Press, 2006), 291.

13. Ibid., 292.

14. Ibid., 293.

15. Ibid.

16. Ibid.

17. Ibid.

18. Ibid., 294.

19. Ibid.

20. Ibid.

21. Ibid., 295.

22. Ibid.

23. Ibid. This section of the "Declaration" reads, "Finally, in the spirit life, and in the interpretation of the general meaning and ends of human existence and its relation to the universe, we are still far from a comprehension of the final truths and from a universal agreement among all sincere and earnest men."

24. Ibid., 296.

25. Ibid.

26. Ibid.

27. Ibid.

28. As Barbara Doumani suggests, in reference to perceived understandings by the American courts in regard to First Amendment Rights. See Barbara Doumani, "Between Coercion and Privatization: Academic Freedom in the Twenty-First Century," in *Academic Freedom after September 11*, ed. Barbara Doumani, (New York: Zone Books, 2006), 12.

29. AAUP, "1940 Statement of Principles on Academic Freedom and Tenure," in *Policy Documents and Reports* (Baltimore, MD: Johns Hopkins Press, 2006) 3; AAUP, "1970 Inter-

pretive Comments," in *Policy Documents and Reports* (Baltimore, MD: Johns Hopkins Press, 2006), 5.

30. Thorstein Veblen, *The Higher Learning in America* (New York: Hill and Wang, 1918), 200.

31. Robert Hutchins, *The Higher Learning in America* (New Haven: Yale University Press, 1936), 93, 99.

32. Robert Hutchins, "Education for Freedom," *Christian Century* (November 15, 1944), 1315.

33. AAUP, "Declaration," 292.

34. Joan Scott, "Academic Freedom as an Ethical Practice," in *The Future of Academic Freedom*, ed. Louis Menand (Chicago: University of Chicago Press, 1996), 169.

35. Judith Butler, "Academic Norms, Contemporary Challenges: A Reply to Robert Post," in *The Future of Academic Freedom*, ed. Louis Menand (Chicago: University of Chicago Press, 1996), 111.

36. Allan Bloom, *The Closing of the American Mind* (New York: Simon and Shuster, 1988); Martha Nussbaum, *Cultivating Humanity: A Classical Defense of Reform in Liberal Education* (Cambridge, MA: Harvard University Press, 1997), 65.

37. Bloom, *Closing of the American Mind*, 27; Nussbaum, *Cultivating Humanity*, 13.

38. Scott, "Academic Freedom as an Ethical Practice," 172.

39. Scott, "Academic Freedom as an Ethical Practice," 174.

40. Philippa Strum, "Why Academic Freedom: the Theoretical and Constitutional Context," in *Academic Freedom after September 11*, ed. Barbara Doumani (New York: Zone Books, 2006), 153–54.

41. Justice Felix Frankfurter, in Strum, "Why Academic Freedom," 148.

42. Strum, "Why Academic Freedom," 154.

43. Finkin and Post, *For the Common Good*, 39.

44. AAUP, "Interpretive Comments," 6.

45. AAUP, "Interpretive Comments," 6.

46. Cary Nelson, *No University is an Island: Saving Academic Freedom* (New York: New York University Press, 2010), 244.

47. Martha Nussbaum, "The Liberal Arts are not Elitist," *Chronicle of Higher Education*, February 28, 2010, accessed February 12, 2012, http://chronicle.com/article/The-Liberal-Arts-Are-Not/64355/; See also Andrew Delbanco, "College at Risk," *The Chronicle Review*, February 26, 2012, accessed February 26, 2012, http://chronicle.com/article/College-at-Risk/130893/.

48. William Schroeder, *Continental Philosophy: A Critical Approach* (London: Blackwell, 2005), 157.

49. G. W. F. Hegel, *Phenomenology of Spirit*, trans. by A. V. Miller (Oxford: Oxford University Press, 1977), 57.

50. G. W. F. Hegel, *Science of Logic*, trans. by A. V. Miller (Highlands, NJ: Humanities Press, 1969), 8.

51. Hegel, *Science of Logic*, 11.

52. G. W. F. Hegel, *Encyclopedia of the Philosophical Sciences in Outline: the Philosophy of Nature*, trans. by Steve Taubeneck (New York: Continuum, 1990), 111.

53. Hegel, *Science of Logic*, 18.

54. Hegel, *Science of Logic*, 21.

55. Wilhelm Dilthey, "The Formation of the Historical World in the Human Sciences," in *Wilhelm Dilthey: Selected Works*, vol. III, ed. by R. Makkreel, et al. (Princeton: Princeton University Press, 2000), 141.

56. Ibid., 141–42.

57. Ibid., 46.

58. Ibid.

59. Gadamer's "historically effected consciousness" is similar, and indeed, is indebted, to this.

60. Hans-Georg Gadamer, *Truth and Method*, second edition, trans. by J. Weinsheimer, et al. (New York: Crossroad, 2004), 335.

61. Gadamer, *Truth and Method*, 190. Note how this compares with Hegel; for Hegel, the whole is never merely the sum of its parts, but its parts are not dissolved in the whole.

62. Gadamer, *Truth and Method*, 390.

63. Scott, "Academic Freedom as an Ethical Practice," 169; Butler, "Academic Norms, Contemporary Challenges," 111.

64. Paul Ricoeur, *Freud and Philosophy: An Essay on Interpretation* (New Haven: Yale University Press, 1970), 32. The *locus classicus* of the hermeneutics of suspicion for Ricoeur were Marx, Nietzsche, and Freud.

65. While it is not my intention to develop a specific argument against hyper-specialization in the humanities, it must be said that such specialized discourses must also be linked to the broader historical conversation the humanities is responsible to the public for generating. This may or may not limit the nature of the specific disciplinary conversations; but it does mandate that the scholarship and teaching produced is amenable to the public.

66. Dewey, "Annual Address to the American Association of University Professors," 103.

67. Thus, Richard Rorty is quite right in his attribution of "socio-political" to Dewey's intent. See Richard Rorty, "Does Academic Freedom Have Philosophical Presuppositions?" in *The Future of Academic Freedom*, ed. Louis Menand (Chicago: Chicago University Press, 1996), 35.

BIBLIOGRAPHY

American Association of University Professors. "1915 Declaration of Principles on Academic Freedom and Academic Tenure." *Policy Documents and Reports*, 291–305. Baltimore, MD: Johns Hopkins Press, 2006.

——. "1940 Statement of Principles on Academic Freedom and Tenure." In *Policy Documents and Reports*, 3–6. Baltimore, MD: Johns Hopkins Press, 2006.

——. "1970 Interpretive Comments." In *Policy Documents and Reports*, 7–9. B altimore, MD: Johns Hopkins Press, 2006.

Bloom, Allan. *The Closing of the American Mind*. New York: Simon and Shuster, 1988.

Butler, Judith. "Academic Norms, Contemporary Challenges: A Reply to Robert Post on Academic Freedom." In *Academic Freedom after September 11*, edited by Barbara Doumani, 107–142. New York: Zone Books, 2006.

Delbanco, Andrew. "College at Risk." *The Chronicle Review*, February 26, 2012. Accessed February 26, 2012. http://chronicle.com/article/College-at-Risk/130893/.

Dewey, John. "Academic Freedom." In *The Middle Works of John Dewey*, vol. 2, edited by Jo Ann Boydston, 53–66. Carbondale, IL: Southern Illinois University Press, 1972.

——. "Introductory Address to the Annual Address to the American Association of University Professors." In *The Middle Works of John Dewey*, vol. 8, edited by Jo Ann Boydston, 98–103. Carbondale, IL: Southern Illinois University Press, 1979.

——. "Annual Address of the President to the American Association of University Professors." In *The Middle Works of John Dewey*, vol. 8, edited by Jo Ann Boydston, 104–108. Carbondale, IL: Southern Illinois University Press, 1979.

Dilthey, Wilhelm. "The Formation of the Historical World in the Human Sciences." In *Wilhelm Dilthey: Selected Works* Vol. III, edited by Rudolf Makkreel and Frithjof Rodi, 101–212. Princeton: Princeton University Press, 2000.

Doumani, Barbara. "Between Coercion and Privatization: Academic Freedom in the Twenty-First Century." In *Academic Freedom after September 11*, edited by Barbara Doumani, 11–60. New York: Zone Books, 2006.

Doumani, Barbara, ed., *Academic Freedom after September 11*. New York: Zone Books, 2006.

Finkin, Matthew and Robert Post. *For the Common Good: Principles of American Academic Freedom*. New Haven: Yale University Press, 2009.

Gadamer, Hans-Georg. *Truth and Method*. Second Edition. Translated by J. Weinsheimer and D. G. Marshall. New York: Crossroad, 2004.

Hegel, G. W. F. *Science of Logic*. Translated by A. V. Miller. Highlands, NJ: Humanities Press, 1969.

———. *Phenomenology of Spirit*. Translated by A. V. Miller. Oxford: Oxford University Press, 1977.

———. *Encyclopedia of the Philosophical Sciences in Outline: the Philosophy of Nature*. Translated by Steve Taubeneck. New York: Continuum, 1990.

Hutchins, Robert. *The Higher Learning in America*. New Haven: Yale University Press, 1936.

———. "Education for Freedom." *Christian Century* (November 15, 1944): 1315.

Menand, Louis. "The Limits of Academic Freedom." In *The Future of Academic Freedom*, edited by Louis Menand, 3–20. Chicago: the University of Chicago Press, 1996.

Nelson, Cary. *No University is an Island: Saving Academic Freedom*. New York: New York University Press, 2010.

Nussbaum, Martha. *Cultivating Humanity: A Classical Defense of Reform in Liberal Education*. Cambridge, MA: Harvard University Press, 1997.

———. "The Liberal Arts are not Elitist." *Chronicle of Higher Education*, February 28, 2010. Accessed February 12, 2012. https://chronicle.com/article/The-Liberal-Arts-Are-Not/64355/.

Ricoeur, Paul. *Freud and Philosophy: An Essay on Interpretation*. New Haven: Yale University Press, 1970.

Rorty, Richard. "Does Academic Freedom Have Philosophical Presuppositions?" In *The Future of Academic Freedom*, edited by Louis Menand, 21–42. Chicago: Chicago University Press, 1996.

Schroeder, William. *Continental Philosophy: A Critical Approach*. London: Blackwell, 2005.

Scott, Joan. "Academic Freedom as an Ethical Practice." In *The Future of Academic Freedom*, edited by Louis Menand, 163–186. Chicago: Chicago University Press, 1996.

Strum, Philippa. "Why Academic Freedom: the Theoretical and Constitutional Context." In *Academic Freedom after September 11*, edited by Barbara Doumani, 143–174. New York: Zone Books, 2006.

Veblen, Thorstein. *The Higher Learning in America*. New York: Hill and Wang, 1918.

III

Political Dimensions of Relevance

Chapter Seven

The University and the Polis in an Age of Relevance[1]

Bradley C. S. Watson

In this chapter, I suggest ways in which the American university should understand itself in relation to the polis, including the civic content and methodology of university teachings. Few would argue that civic education is irrelevant to higher education. Civic education is, after all, an education in matters of concern to every citizen qua citizen of a political community: the reasons, traditions, mores, and institutions by which a polis defines and defends itself. Most Americans share a sense that civic education is an essential component of liberal education, and that it is vital to the lives of the students who must—whichever career path they ultimately choose—become informed citizens.

But complicating the matter is the reality that a scholarship of civic education, to be worthy of the name, must also in some sense be patriotic: It must put into question what should be questioned as it reinforces what should not. So civic education cannot be an entirely liberating or liberal education— at least as liberal education is commonly conceived. Those interested in the relationship of the university to the polis must therefore arouse interest in and commitment to the idea of civic education, and then argue for its patriotic character in the context of a larger liberal arts framework.

However complex the relationship between liberal and civic education, there seems to be widespread concern nowadays that both are neglected, if not undermined, in many American institutions of higher learning. And indeed this intuition is borne out by national studies showing that a scholarship of civic education is sorely lacking in American universities.[2] Yet it is in the area of civic education that the university and the polis most obviously meet and (a reasonable citizen might hope) join forces. It is one of the areas—the other being the inculcation of productive knowledge and technique—where the university might most clearly claim that it is relevant to the polis, rather than to concepts largely internal to itself.

I want to begin by suggesting that it is not just ideological intransigence that causes civic and liberal education to be in a state of desuetude in the university. There is another problem that has manifested itself over the last two decades. Instead of, or in addition to, ideological antipathy—and often under the guise of relevance—the language, methodologies, and practices of education departments, both governmental and collegiate, are in a rather unsavory alliance with the language, methodologies, and practices of the business disciplines. All are being used to undergird the current emphasis on "assessment," that is, bottom line measurement in higher learning. Their alliance is aimed not primarily at the idea that the business or education disciplines should claim pride of place, exactly, in American institutions of higher learning, but rather at the idea that their understandings of "relevance" and how to measure it should exercise a hegemonic control over those who would pay serious attention to liberal and civic education. The language of "rubrics," "stakeholders," "accountability," "learning objectives," "learning outcomes," "assessment artifacts," and "institutional effectiveness" now vies for attention—and usually gets it—at the expense of the language of the liberal and civic arts.

As James Pontuso has noted, "A specter is haunting liberal arts institutions—the specter of assessment. All the powers of the educational establishment have entered into an unholy alliance to implement this specter: state and federal government agencies, the Department of Education, university and college administrators, and accrediting organizations."[3] Indeed, there is now something of a mania in American higher education for assessment of learning outcomes. These outcomes are usually associated with ill-defined, college-wide objectives such as, for example, "critical thinking skills," or "information literacy," or "ethical stewardship," or the like. Professors are increasingly tasked with devising ways to measure and refine their "outcomes," or in others words how what they do contributes to the various objectives of the institution—how, in short, they and their teachings relate to institutional goals: quite literally, how they are "relevant."

Assessment comes to sight as an unfunded mandate—originally, from the federal Department of Education, then through the accrediting agencies, down to the administrative bureaucracies of the colleges. Professors in the humanities and social sciences in particular find themselves under new pressures. These are not pressures to engage themselves and their students in critical inquiry of a Socratic sort, and occasionally to publish the results of such inquiry. Rather, they must now demonstrate quasi-empirically, to the satisfaction of various bureaucracies, that they are in fact teaching effectively, particularly when it comes to the amorphous goals that colleges these days set for themselves.

"Critical thinking skills" is a particularly *de rigueur* concept in the assessment maze. Such thinking skills are not necessarily, or even usually, understood to be a function of critical inquiry or what classicist Bruce Thornton calls "critical consciousness" in a philosophic sense—about which I will have something to say later. Critical thinking skills are rather a much more amorphous concept defined by the educational powers that be, usually at the institutional level (at least for now—though one can imagine governmental pressure to make uniform what is to be inculcated under this rubric). Most thoughtful teachers know there can be no thought when there is nothing to think about, and no critical thinking when there is neither thought nor knowledge of what one might seriously criticize. Assessment and what is being assessed are preponderantly concerned with a language alien to that of the serious classroom. They are alien to the substance of liberal and civic learning.

One byproduct of this alienation is that important books and ideas are—if not out—at least shunted aside in favor of assessing what is taught. And what is taught must of course be measurable, and measure up to the fashionable outcomes of the day. If one is pressured into becoming adept with a hammer and tracking one's use of it, there is an enormous incentive to concentrate one's attentions only on nails, and to count methodically all the nails driven home.

It is therefore likely that assessment is dangerous to serious liberal and civic education. And what is not dangerous is at the least useless. That is to say, the costs of its imposition far outweigh its benefits. At its best, the assessment fad results only in the wasting of precious time. Perhaps accrediting agencies could use fewer bad educational theorists and more good economists to remind them of a truism: time is a valuable commodity, and its misallocation imposes immense opportunity costs. One suspects that if a direct cost were assigned to assessment, in the form of payments by accrediting agencies to institutions, or by institutions to their faculty in the form of substantial course releases or higher pay for those tasked with the horrible work of assessment—the whole enterprise would cease forthwith.

Because faculty (especially at smaller colleges—those institutions most centrally concerned with liberal education) tend to be assigned the job of coming up with measuring instruments for their departments and courses, such instruments do not, to put it mildly, meet standards of scientific rigor. Faculty members—experts in their respective fields—have a strong sense of what is important. It is probably asking more than is humanly possible for them to come up with measuring instruments that avoid bias in their design and interpretation. Such design and interpretation are generally undertaken to "prove" that what faculty members are already doing is producing the results that they know, or think they know, the bureaucratic powers want to see. The only remedy for this is to take assessment out of faculty hands—in essence to turn over educational questions to committees of bureaucrats.

In short, it is unlikely that educational assessment can have scientific validity, as anyone with a PhD in the social sciences should know. But it is a recipe for control. It is a recipe for ensuring that everyone and everything in the university comes under the watchful eye of accrediting agencies and then . . . and then . . . who knows? And who knows how that control might be exercised, in terms of the degree of homogeneity that might be imposed over courses, professors, departments, and colleges. The nature of bureaucracy is to exercise control. Undoubtedly, control will first be exercised at the institutional level. But then, when that petty tyranny has exhausted itself, some version of "No College Student Left Behind" seems inevitable.

Good and experienced professors can spot critical consciousness when they see it, and they will know too—as did Plato—that some people will be capable of it, and others will not. Why this is the case is something of a mystery, but it is, alas, not demystified by spending countless faculty and administrative hours devising ways to measure outcomes that seem perilously divorced from the inputs so central to both liberal and civic education.

Most professors (and I suspect many administrators) engaged in the pretense of outcomes assessment see it for what it is: hoop-jumping. Without scientific validity, and without serious belief in such validity, assessment is unlikely to have much effect on individual or institutional practices. With belief, however—if such belief can be concocted—change will be demanded, albeit for spurious reasons. In fact, it seems an implicit premise of assessment is that change is generally better than its opposite, even if reasonable and gifted teachers of long experience are confident that the status quo, at least in their classroom, is as good as things can get. Such teachers share a kind of conservative disposition, if it may be called that. It's a disposition described by Michael Oakeshott as centering "upon a propensity to use and to enjoy what is available rather than to wish for or to look for something else; to delight in what is present rather than what was or what may be . . . [it is] appropriate to a man who is acutely aware of having something to lose which he has learned to care for; a man in some degree rich in opportunities for enjoyment, but not so rich that he can afford to be indifferent to loss."[4]

Finally, it is worth noting that questions as to the validity of the methodologies, costs, and benefits, if any, of assessment, demand answers—but from whom? And this raises another question: Who, exactly, is assessing assessment? For surely if assessment's premises are correct, such assessment must be undertaken.

So what is to be done? How might the American university at least begin to re-engage the theme of civic education in a coherent, scholarly way, that is also consummately relevant to what is, or should be, the university's mission, and to the wider society—particularly as universities, and especially public ones, come under increasing scrutiny and pressure, both political and economic. And this pressure pushes in two directions: encouraging the universities to educate students such that they become productive citizens—that is to say, both productive, and citizens. Sometimes there's a little too much emphasis on the "productive," at the expense of "citizens," so I will concentrate on the latter, while not denying the genuine concern of the polis for the former. If the universities choose to ignore or, in some cases, mock either productivity or citizenship, they are asking for a world of trouble in austere times. It is trouble they bring on themselves, by not defining their missions carefully and hiring professors who will take them seriously.

I began by suggesting that a scholarship of civic education is sorely lacking in most American universities, and that rebuilding it is complicated by the fact that civic education cannot be an entirely liberating or liberal education. So those interested in civic education have a couple of very tough nuts to crack.

In all cultures or civilizations, the passage of time invariably contributes to a certain amount of cultural amnesia—to a forgetfulness of one's civic identity. As Abraham Lincoln so eloquently said in his Lyceum Address, with America's founding generation having passed, and no one living having any direct contact with them, the silent artillery of time cannot help but erase their great contributions from our collective memory. The disturbing thing is not the reality of this erasing, but that in America, the great institutions we have created—particularly academic institutions—offer little or nothing to slow or halt this natural process of forgetting. Indeed, in many cases they try to accelerate it, telling us that our great civic achievements are nothing but the legacy of a dead, irrelevant past, or, worse still, something that should be actively shunned by us the living.

American universities might well be the envy of the world when it comes to the natural sciences, but when it comes to civic education—education in who we are as a people, an education in philosophy, politics, religion, history, literature, economic principles—our institutions are, as a group, in a doleful state. Our schools and universities have robbed American students of a sense of the immeasurable richness of their own heritage. And without this sense, American students—and those who will become national leaders—are unlikely to see or fully appreciate the manifold benefits their society has conferred on them, and consequently, I think, we can expect their civic and political choices to be poor.

The question of civic education is no longer (if it ever was) merely an academic concern. Students who know nothing of the American Revolution, the Civil War, or World War II cannot long be expected to remember, or draw intelligent lessons from, September 11, 2001. The lack of seriousness about civic education and civic assimilation has profound consequences, too, when we consider America's openness to immigrants who come—at the deepest level—precisely to share in the riches of our heritage, but are often taught nothing of them.

All of this is not to say that universities should engage in an uncritical celebration of, or education only in, things American. American civic education cannot be parochial, because America is not parochial. It is instead a political and cultural artifact of the West—the least parochial of all the civilizations of which we have record. And there is simply nothing quite like the power of the enduring ideas and Great Books of Western civilization to clarify contemporary questions, and once again make the university relevant in a comprehensive sense to the polis. In fact, I would suggest that we begin to rebuild our scholarship of civic education by concentrating once again on our Greek roots—in particular, by reconsidering not just our intellectual, but our *civic* origins in the Greek philosophical tradition. Considering our ancient origins of course does not exhaust who we are, but it is a beginning, and it does suggest the kinds of things that a real civic education ought to concern itself with—including a decidedly liberal component. It is one manner of approach to civic education.

The Greeks gave us something that makes us who we are. In a word, they gave us philosophy—not today's often dry academic discipline, prone to be as cut off from the rest of the modern university as it is from life itself, but philosophy as the love of wisdom, philosophy as *longing* for the highest things. It is in philosophy—the ceaseless questioning characteristic of Greek philosophic inquiry—that we find a major root of Western freedom, which is so nobly played out today in that form of life and government we know as liberal democracy.

Liberal democracy is a form of life and government in which the pursuit of the human good can arguably be made subject to more comprehensive rational reflection and choice than in any other form, or at any other time in the history of human civilization. And this is true whether we conceive that pursuit in terms of divine revelation, politics, aesthetics, scientific advancement, or otherwise. Rational reflection and choice—the exercise of these human possibilities is linked to the Greek achievement.

Why and how did the Greeks invent such a precious gift as philosophic inquiry, or critical consciousness? The answer is complex, but pursuing it—as few American college students are nowadays given the chance to do—is an intellectually exciting and uplifting experience in itself, and, for our purposes, it's also useful to understand who we are as a civilization and a nation.

There is a real story to be told here, which is far from an arid archaeological dig; it is a story that teaches us not merely about a distant past, but about ourselves and the kind of civic order we have created. It is a story about the intellectual gifts of our own civilization, and it is a story that can be told— must be told—without obvious condescension on the part of the instructor. (A common attitude, when such matters are taught nowadays.)

As an aside—a story I always like to tell—I distinctly recall being on a job search committee for a tenure-track social sciences position at my current institution, a self-described Catholic, Benedictine liberal arts college. One of the candidates was asked by one or two concerned committee members what the candidate thought of "Western civilization" (surely a question broad and interesting enough, one might think, to elicit a variety of broad and interesting responses). Instead, the candidate replied, incredulously, with a simple "what's *that*?"—with the emphasis on *that*. The question seemed, to this young PhD-bearing citizen, arrogant, irrelevant, or unanswerable—and perhaps all three. It was as if, as it were, we were speaking Greek.

We live in an era of academic specialization conjoined with condescension or ignorance (and often both) on the part of too many senior faculty members who produce the new humanists and social scientists—those who are to become the teachers and scholars of tomorrow. Ignorance and condescension have produced—*mirabile dictu*—amnesia, perhaps the ultimate weapon of mass destruction aimed at our country, culture, and civilization.

Considering the characteristics of this Greek enterprise we know as philosophy can help us overcome our cultural amnesia as it liberates us from the worst of our contemporary prejudices—for philosophy is not instrumental. It might be stimulated by some practical problem, or even by some apparent solution to a practical problem. For example, some might claim a materially prosperous society is good because people are comfortable and live a long time. To this, the philosopher will ask, as the Greeks asked, "live for what end? Are there more important things than material comfort? Or, in Christian terms, "What does it profit a man if he gain the whole world but lose his own soul?" Philosophy thus does not reduce to economics or health and welfare.

Philosophy is not a search for the best method—whether it be a method to hunt bison, grow crops, or travel through space. Philosophy is the search for the best, simply; or the true, simply. Further, philosophy is also not merely folk wisdom, or what people in a society customarily or conventionally believe. What we often call a society's "philosophy"—way of life—is not philosophy at all, properly understood. Rather, a society's philosophy, or way of life, is something that is subject to test, to rigorous inquiry, and to criticism by philosophy proper. Received wisdom and traditions are always subject to philosophical critique.

As children of the West, the philosophic *spirit*, if not philosophy itself, is something deeply rooted in our civic beings—we are rational, questioning, searching, reasoning people.

This is not to say that the contemporary West does not put many hindrances in the way of our quest to become rational and civically literate beings. One need only glance at the "philosophy" section in many bookstores to see that they are filled with many things not philosophical, and indeed most unhelpful to any inclination we might have to serve the civic or public world. In these sections, books in the "self-help" or pseudo-medicinal vein often crowd the shelves. These books tend to present "philosophies for life," which sometimes amount to little more than one author's assertions of the ten steps one can follow to true "self-actualization," or whatever the term *du jour* might be. (If there's an education section, the books will undoubtedly be on assessment.) In short, such books contain within them recommendations hardly worthy of our nature as political animals, and are hardly philosophical, for they do not question the terms of the debate over what it is to be fully human, or to be citizens of this land, or this civilization.

It is useful to consider the singularity of the Greek achievement by noting that it was the Greeks—not the Gauls, the Franks, the Saxons, the Africans, the Chinese, or Japanese—it was the Greeks—to whom we can best attribute our intellectual patrimony. They were the first in history to pursue the fundamental questions and not be content with merely traditional answers to them, or received wisdom. Ancient Greece was the first place in which entire competing schools of philosophy grew and flourished—schools whose goal was to put fundamental questions under searching scrutiny. They—or at least some among them—were the ones who put the terms of the debate into question. It was in ancient Greece that there developed schools of thought that did not to take the longevity or "success" of a practice or understanding as the measure of the truth or worthiness of that practice or understanding. The Greeks did this in a rational way that did not rely purely on custom or myth. Indeed, Greek philosophy put into question even its own all-encompassing, largely Homeric, mythic tradition.

But *why* the Greeks? This a more difficult question to answer, though I will suggest some answers. And even if readers (or the students in my classes) do not accept the answers I put forth, I still claim that an exploration of possible answers—plausible answers—will give them as much insight into our civilization, and therefore our civic inheritance, as any inquiry they might undertake.

The Greeks possessed unique attributes—some accidental, some chosen—that made them a civilization, and which give us some clue as to what we mean by "Western civilization." Some people offer reductionist explanations for the Greek achievement. For example, they might claim the Greeks invented philosophy because of their favorable climate, or location, though the Greek climate and location were not manifestly more hospitable than others of southern Europe or the Middle East or Asia.

Far more plausible than such reductionist or materialist explanations are several others. First is the nature of the Greek mythic and religious traditions and how they interacted with one another. To spend some time pondering these is, to repeat, not a game of Trivial Pursuit wherein all questions appear in the "history" category. It's a reflection on our own intellectual, cultural, and civic natures.

A characteristic of the Greek mythic tradition (particularly as it is handed down through the Homeric epics) is the principle of what I would call *individuation*. The human world for the Greeks was a world of individual beings with individual motivations and virtues—rage, jealousy, pride, fear, and the like. There is something deep *inside* the characters of Greek myth that animates them; not everything they do or think is reducible to impersonal, cosmic forces from the outside, or is even in some way referential to such outside forces. The characters might not be *free* in the sense of autonomously choosing their actions or situation, but Greek myth does disclose a deep subject-object distinction. And therefore the human *subject* becomes a locus of attention.

It is true that the passions and powers of some individuals are greater than those of others. Those whom we know as the heroic characters are the most full of life, passion, and vigor. The *Iliad* famously begins, "sing, o goddess, of the rage of Achilles, son of Peleus." The rage of a hero is, for Homer, characteristically human, and can be noble and justified; it is not something to be shunned, necessarily. When Homeric characters act and either succeed or fail, it is largely because of their own virtue, or their lack thereof—for example, their over-weaning pride. The gods might favor certain people, but those they favor are usually the virtuous ones, where virtue is something of a mean between extremes. For Homer and the Greeks, success or failure was not a consequence of an individual's failure to recognize his divinity, or the unity of the cosmos, as it might be, for example, in the Indian mythic texts such as the Upanishads.

And this raises the unrealized potential of taking our own civilization seriously, particularly in colleges and universities. Such an intellectual seriousness would inexorably lead us to a richer and truer multiculturalism, in the form of inquiry into non-Western cultures. We might again be inclined to take them seriously as objects of study, rather than as necessary and somehow purer alternatives to the West, or mere victim cultures without discernible characteristics, strengths, or weaknesses of their own. In an ideal educational world, we might, for example, expect that humanists would spend some time contrasting the Greek belief in individuation and the worldly human virtues of action, insight or argument, to other cultural or civilizational understandings.

They might for example consider further the Upanishads and the tradition that arose from them—surely another candidate for the origins of philosophic inquiry, being roughly contemporaneous with Homer. The Upanishads are the theoretical parts of the ancient Indian corpus of originally oral literature called the Vedas, and one can certainly find the seeds of critical reflection in them. They attempt to answer some of the large mysteries as to the nature of the cosmos and human life. In particular, they emphasize mythical explanations for basic ontological questions—what is there, and where does it come from? According to the Upanishads, the answers are to be found in *Brahman*—the universal or cosmic soul, the breath, the thing out of which everything is created; and *Atman*—the inner soul of each individual, which shares the eternal cosmic breath, and is therefore a microcosm, of *Brahman*.

In the Upanishadic tradition the individual is in some measure as one with the cosmos, for its animating principle is the same. There is no objectification of the cosmos as something apart from the human condition, as there is in Homer. But this very objectification is arguably a root of Western freedom—and a distinctly Western achievement—even where, as in Homer, the human subject is hardly acting freely in a modern sense. Lack of objectification, conversely, results in the lack of a strong sense of the subject—the *individual*—which is ever-present in Homer.

Suffice it to say that in other traditions, life's meaning and possibilities are given more comprehensively by myth, or hierarchical tradition (as for example in Confucianism) and less by individual insight and action. In this lack of a subject-object distinction, which we in the West take to be fundamental to our philosophical outlook, we see a building block of not just ours, but of other, civilizations.

A second and yet more obvious example of our civic natures embedded in the Greek achievement can be discerned by considering that in Homer and among the Greeks generally there is an assumption that human life, and the individual quest for meaning, happens within the context of a polis—a complete city or political community in our parlance. Man, as Aristotle said, is a by nature political animal. The "heartless, lawless, stateless man" is the least human and most miserable of all figures. When we act, we act individually, but also in a political context, for the sake of the good. What is good for us as individuals points the way toward what is beyond ourselves, what is good simply. Especially in the most compelling matters—those things for which human beings are willing to sacrifice their lives, we act for the sake of others, whether they be our immediate loved ones or our extended family that is the political community as a whole.

And we should note that there is a strong subject-object distinction embedded in and reinforced by the very notion of the polis. When we consider particular political communities, we realize there is us, and there is them. Americans, and Canadians; Americans, and Taliban—we have friends, and enemies. We fight for what is important to us—what our community thinks are the highest things. Ordinary patriotism is rooted in this impulse. In short, what we as individuals value often has little to do with us as individuals, strictly speaking, but us as moral and political actors concerned about people and principles outside of us and apart from our immediate circle.

In turn, the existence of a human community as a natural, intrinsic foundation of the human experience raises the question of justice, which is the question of how one ought to behave toward his fellow men. When we observe outsiders with different practices in this regard, we naturally ask who's right—us or them? If we are willing to die for our way of life, we must at some very deep level believe that we are right. But how do we know this? Should we be confident of it? All of this—implicit in Homer—prefigures Plato's and Aristotle's detailed and rigorous philosophic examinations of politics, including the good life for man qua man. So, the fact that we understand ourselves as political animals is key to this critical consciousness, which can lead to grounded patriotism.

A third inheritance from the Greeks stems from what they did *not* emphasize—which was all-encompassing mythic explanations for phenomena, human and non-human. Homer gives no comprehensive, cosmic answer to why things happen, whether they be minor events, or great tragic events like the Trojan War. Surely the will of the gods accounts for much, but so also do the failings and heroism of men. As well, accident and design each seem to play their part. In Homer, there is a genuine mystery to phenomena, and the limitations on our knowing are part of the tragedy of the human condition. Some things simply seem to happen for reasons that are not coherent, and cannot be well accounted for.

Beyond the limitations of these mythic accounts, the gods themselves are limited beings. They are, in fact, men and women—in many respects mere mortals—writ large. Oftentimes, they have even fathered mortals. True, the gods are immortal and powerful, but they are not without the full range of human emotions and failings. They are remarkably like us—flawed beings incapable of giving full answers to why *they* are like they are, much less why the cosmos is like it is. Indeed, they have their own problems to worry about, and are not comprehensively involved in much of what goes on in the human sphere. They are certainly not omnipotent, omniscient, or perfect as is, for example, the Christian God. Reason, philosophy—critical consciousness— must step up to the plate in this environment.

Fourth, even broader than the nature of the gods, is the fact that the entire religious tradition of the Greeks provides little in the way of dogma. The Greeks had no "state religion" that purported to give answers to what the best political practices were. Religious practice in ancient Greece reflected this fact. There were of course religious rituals, temples, and oracles, under the administration of priests. But when the gods spoke through the oracles, their voices were famously in the nature of prediction based on specific questions, rather than comprehensive pronouncements on such matters as the creation, or the rise and fall of man. The priests and oracles of the Greek world simply did not speak in these terms. Greek theology can be thought of as being indeterminate.

Greeks in short saw themselves as strangers in a strange land, without comprehensive answers to the great questions. Neither the gods nor the religious traditions and practices as a whole provided answers to moral, political, ontological, or epistemological questions. The lacunas in the Greek mythic tradition, and the fundamental inability of the gods to "take care" of metaphysics or ethics on behalf of humans, cry out for philosophy as an independent activity. The result was that, in Greece and in the West, philosophy and religion—Athens and Jerusalem—were never merged to the extent they were, for example, in the Upanishads. While there might be philosophical ideas in the Upanishads, they take symbolic or mythic form and are oriented—as are the religious notions themselves—to practical ends. They seek to free people from illusion, from false pursuits, and from human discontent by pointing them back to the true nature of the cosmos. By contrast, there is a strong sense of pursuing knowledge for its own sake in the unmerged—the bifurcated—Greek context.

Finally, we might say of the Greeks that they were a commercial and military people with wide-ranging contacts with other cultures throughout at least the Mediterranean rim. This led them, naturally, to comparisons—and again to have a strong sense of the subject-object, us-them distinction. It also led them to try to determine why other peoples do things as they do. And, given the diversity of human practices or conventions, it led them to ask which conventions are better, which are right? It even led them to ask, "Is it possible to answer such a question—is there a standard by which we can make such a judgment?"

In the end we must say of the Greeks that they did have a unique "climate" for philosophy, but it was largely a mythical, religious, and political climate rather than an atmospheric or geographic one. Outside of the Greek world then—and outside of the Western world today—there were relatively fewer grounds for skepticism, for intellectual restlessness, for passionate pursuit of intelligible, rational truth about the worldly and otherworldly phenomena. There were fewer grounds for human-centered inquiry into the human and non-human things, and therefore fewer grounds for the eventual development of Western individualistic notions of freedom as autonomy of the rational self.

The story of philosophy as a Greek and eventually Western enterprise still needs to be told if we are to understand not only our intellectual but our civic natures. As Christianity leavened the pagan world with its message of universalism and redemption, so the pagan world's great legacy leavened the Christian world's self-understanding and laid the foundation for the fruitful, healthy tension between reason and revelation which we still see being worked out in the West.

One thing is clear enough for anyone with eyes to see, in the post 9/11 world. The West—the great product of the synthesis of Judeo-Christian revelation and Greek rationalism—is not today the place of unrestrained fanaticism. But alas, this fact too is likely to go unnoticed by many college graduates thanks to the tendentiousness of American academics—many of whom, as I distinctly recall, were, in the days after 9/11, more righteously indignant over off-hand remarks by some American cultural and religious commentators than they were over the opening shot in what might be a catastrophic war of civilizations. Oftentimes the only pictures students are acquainted with are grotesque caricatures of "the West" (with America as its hideous apotheosis) as a place—*the* place—uniquely hegemonic and arrogant in the realms of ideas and action.

At the very least, one might think the relative lack of fanaticism on the part of the rationalist, humanist West might once again stimulate, in the halls of higher education higher, a real interest in just what kinds of lessons we teach our youth. These lessons cannot possibly reduce to the platitudes of tolerance and multiculturalism—themselves the by-products of the very civilization they are now used to attack.

One might think, in short, that in these perilous times we would be stimulated, as a culture, once again to study the Great Books of the Western canon—those that survive because they display deep critical consciousness—the impulse and willingness to stand back from humanity and nature, to make them objects of thought and criticism, and to search for their meaning and significance—"to see life steadily, and see it whole," as Matthew Arnold put it.

But those familiar with the American university will not hold their breath waiting for that to happen. While Socrates did not claim to have the answers to questions about the true and the beautiful, he did think he knew something of the important questions and therefore something of how to narrow the field of inquiry to direct our attention to the highest things. Large numbers of today's academics at once profess skepticism not only of "Western answers," but of the existence of important questions. Along with this two-fold skepticism comes a surprising hubris in proposing alternative, radical political, economic, and social arrangements for society outside the academy. These academics are at once more and less skeptical than Socrates. Perhaps the only thing one may say with confidence of their thought is that they do not know that they do not know.

I want to conclude with some caveats that go well beyond the fact that civic education of the sort I have suggested—that which would begin with and take seriously our Greek intellectual roots—is rarely practiced in the

American university, for both ideological and bureaucratic reasons. They are caveats that go back to the initial tension I posited between civic and liberal education, and how it might be worked out in the modern university.

If I am right, as Westerners our souls are philosophic—they are liberal, for the reasons I have elucidated. This is perhaps why we so often hear touted "liberal education," that is to say, an education befitting the free, and in fact promoting freedom of a certain sort: freedom from unthinking certitudes, freedom for the life of the mind to range over the full sweep of conceptions of the good life. But can a true liberal education, even if it were to exist, really be a civic education? For civic education, as I have suggested, requires piety and prejudice. That is to say, it must be something that attaches the pre-judgments of the people to their regime and their way of life. And what remains of liberal education today self-consciously shies away from doing this.

Indeed, academic cosmopolitans often see, and use, the phrase "liberal education" as fighting words, directed precisely against civic education. Yet each of three human goods—liberal education, civic education, and character formation—remain associated, to varying degrees, with the American academy. That is to say, they are goods that might, and we—citizens of the polis—tend to think should, be cultivated by the academy.

But what can be the status of any of these human goods in the American university which, as Peter Wood of the National Association of Scholars has put it, "has become too big, too administrative, too diffuse, too fractured, too pluralistic, too unaccountable, too corrupted, too legalistic, and withal too expensive to have a genuine idea of itself. It has instead a marketing plan."[5] In that view, the American university is not so much evil, or even derelict, as it is vulgar, simply uninterested in forming the souls of citizens, who in turn would support the regime, which in turn would support the university as we have come to know it. No, the American university has been reduced to an institution that simply gets the job done, whatever the job assigned to it might be, and by whomever assigned—federal bureaucrats, state legislators, ac-crediting agencies, feckless administrators, or politically tendentious faculty.

Certainly the heart and soul of the university—the professoriate—cannot be relied on to cultivate the civic virtues. Professors once believed that stu-dents needed models of human greatness—models who certainly were to be allowed to speak in their own words, but models that were to be put before the students, *ab initio*, by teachers who took their civic responsibility serious-ly.

Nowadays, many professors are perhaps more likely to believe, in the words of Peter Lawler, "that they're charged with liberating the student from 'the cave,'—traditional or religious or bourgeois conformity—to think for themselves. Yet, they must at least half-way know that their empty dogmas of non-conformism or self-creation or promiscuous libertarianism are a large part of the cave of any free and prosperous society."[6]

John Agresto, the former president of St. John's College, has noted that the increasingly common "understanding of the liberal arts as *naturally* the opponents and critics of whatever society they occupy is so narrow, so diminished, and, in many cases, so self-destructive a view of the liberal arts that . . . the whole enterprise of liberal education cannot again prosper without its significant re-thinking. The liberal arts have become so dogmatic in this view that they cannot even talk any longer of "thinking"—the rage is now "critical thinking"—their aim is not to wonder, not to understand, not to explain but, simply, *to be critical*. The questioning of all orthodoxies and the destruction of all idols has become, today, the liberal arts' true work."[7]

Hence the centrality, as a core goal of so many institutions, of the "critical thinking skills" I mentioned earlier. And then—as such skills are required to be bureaucratically assessed—the dog chases its tail every more rapidly, and vapidly. Teachings about the allegedly subversive nature of philosophy—or the liberal arts more generally—are usually not so cleverly masked as liberation. Yet they serve, of course, only to reinforce the very prejudices that many eighteen-year-olds bring with them to college in the first place. And so the false embrace of Socrates, or, better, the embrace of a false Socrates, has led us away from the idea that all philosophy begins in *wonder*.

But the liberal arts and civic education have in any case become a lesser and lesser part of the American academy. "Because of the emptiness . . . they promote, professors of humanities have just about put themselves out of business."[8] And so it is that American higher education—and the souls of American students—are torn between philosophical nihilism on the one hand, and modern business or science on the other, the latter promising relevant, measurable, tangible "outcomes." And increasingly they gravitate toward the latter. In the sciences and business disciplines at least, students are offered courses that stick to the "facts ma'am—just the facts." Furthermore, mastery of these facts does seem—unlike the liberal or civic arts—to ameliorate the human condition in concrete ways, not to mention offer the masters of the facts handsome livings for so doing.

So, we are left with important questions: Can liberal education be revived under such circumstances? And, perhaps more pressingly, should it be, if we wish it also to be civic education? I hope the answer is yes. But for those of us who hope for an education that is at once liberal and civic, we must be attentive to the truths of our regime. If and only if they are truths, as opposed to mere conventions, can liberal education and civic education be brought into harmony, because the truth is something from we cannot—ought not—be liberated.

And we must also teach of the institutions, habits, customs, and prejudgments that support those truths. So an education that is at once liberal and civic can start with Greece, but must move through the Bible, Aquinas, the common law of England, Locke, *The Federalist*, Lincoln, and the progressive revolt against any natural truth that transcends the mere processes of evolution. In short, liberal education must encourage certain kinds of characters—certain kinds of citizens, certain kinds of civic virtues—in order to support, or in some measure become, civic education. And the American university should embrace both.

It is my hope that we can once again try, at the institutional and individual levels, to encourage inquiry and critical consciousness—both patriotic and liberal—through the reading of the Great Books of Western civilization and the great writings of the American tradition. And it is also my hope that their power will be so manifest that no one will insist that we try to assess their relevance.

NOTES

1. Portions of this chapter have been adapted from my previous writings, including "Just as the Twig is Bent: Civic Education in an Age of Doubt," in *Civic Education and Culture,* ed. Bradley C. S. Watson (Wilmington, DE: ISI Books, 2005) and "The American University in Crisis," in *The Idea of the American University,* ed. Bradley C. S. Watson (Lanham, MD: Lexington Books, 2011).

2. See, for example, the annual reports on the state of civic learning in universities produced by the *Intercollegiate Studies Institute* from 2006-2011, accessed February 27, 2013: http://www.americancivicliteracy.org/.

3. James Pontuso, "The Assessment Waltz: How Outcomes Assessment is Hurting Liberal Arts Colleges," *First Principles,* April 9, 2008, accessed February 27, 2013, http://www.firstprinciplesjournal.com/print.aspx?article=578&loc=b&type=cbbp, 1. See also James Pontuso and Saranna R. Thornton, "Is Outcomes Assessment Hurting Higher Education," *Thought and Action* (Fall 2008): 61-69, accessed February 27, 2013, http://w.isea.org/assets/img/PubThoughtAndAction/TAA_08_08.pdf. I am grateful to Pontuso and Thornton for stimulating some of my thoughts here.

4. Michael Oakeshott, "On Being Conservative," in *Rationalism in Politics and Other Essays* (London: Methuen, 1962), 168–169.

5. Peter Wood, "Roller of Big Cigars: The American University as Cheerful Mortician," in *The Idea of the American University,* ed. Bradley C. S. Watson (Lanham, MD: Lexington Books, 2011), 56.

6. Peter Lawler, "Human Dignity and Higher Education Today," in *The Idea of the American University,* ed. Bradley C. S. Watson (Lanham, MD: Lexington Books, 2011), 99.

7. John Agresto, "Toward an American Liberal Education," in *The Idea of the American University,* ed. Bradley C. S. Watson (Lanham, MD: Lexington Books, 2011), 151.

8. Lawler, "Human Dignity and Higher Education Today," 109.

BIBLIOGRAPHY

Agresto, John. "Toward an American Liberal Education." In *The Idea of the American University,* edited by Bradley C. S. Watson, 141–153. Lanham, MD: Lexington Books, 2011.
Intercollegiate Studies Institute, "Civic Literacy Report." Accessed February 27, 2013. http://www.americancivicliteracy.org/.

Lawler, Peter. "Human Dignity and Higher Education Today." In *The Idea of the American University,* edited by Bradley C. S. Watson, 97–113. Lanham, MD: Lexington Books, 2011.

Oakeshott, Michael. "On Being Conservative." In *Rationalism in Politics and Other Essays,* 168–196. London: Methuen, 1962.

Pontuso, James. "The Assessment Waltz: How Outcomes Assessment is Hurting Liberal Arts Colleges." *First Principles,* April 9, 2008. Accessed February 27, 2013. http://www.firstprinciplesjournal.com/print.aspx?article=578&loc=b&type=cbbp.

Pontuso, James and Saranna R. Thornton. "Is Outcomes Assessment Hurting Higher Education." *Thought and Action* (Fall 2008): 61–69. Accessed February 27, 2013. http://w.isea.org/assets/img/PubThoughtAndAction/TAA_08_08.pdf.

Wood, Peter. "Roller of Big Cigars: The American University as Cheerful Mortician." In *The Idea of the American University,* edited by Bradley C. S. Watson, 55–66. Lanham, MD: Lexington Books, 2011.

Chapter Eight

Order and Educational Relevance

Crisis and Conservancy in Western Civilization

Michael Wayne Hail

The crisis of our civilization is coeval with the crisis of political philosophy. The relationship of the regimes of the West to the culture, the civilization, remains the most important connection to understanding the relevance of education to the most urgent of questions. This of course calls forth the old question of the relationship of man to the city, and of philosophy to the poetry of that city. Like all substantive enduring questions, the sage student of politics has recourse to the greatest teacher and founder of Western civilization, Plato. As A. N. Whitehead famously asserted, "The safest general characterization of the European philosophical tradition is that it consists of a series of footnotes to Plato."[1] Indeed Plato is the central figure that embodies the dimensions of the present crisis, as Friedrich Nietzsche so carefully discerned. Plato was an aristocrat, he was a man descended of a prominent family who understood politics of the regime and the connectivity of the gods of the city to the fate of philosophy. Plato was also the founder of the Academy, dedicated to teaching and conserving the knowledge of the highest things, the most essential things.

Moving from the question of teaching virtue in the *Meno*, to questions of teaching virtue, prudence, and ultimately statesmanship in the *Protagoras* (319a), Plato developed an intricate puzzle regarding the complexity of teaching the highest things while leaving little doubt that these are the things that must concern education and the regime of the city most centrally.[2] "There can be no doubt that this is the most important thing a man could teach, if it is really true that statesmanship can be taught. But Socrates feels a perplexity on the question on whether statesmanship is teachable."[3] The crisis of the West is concurrently the crisis of modernity and the central core in the resolution of these crises is education. The understanding of this reso-lution was first identified by Plato, who in the *Republic* and *Laws* clearly connects changes in cycles of regimes with the education of the citizenry. It is the centrality of the interdependence of the education system of the state with the regime of the state that is at the core of my analysis of the present crises and the values to sustain both Western government and Western civil-ization, which is to say the fate of Western political philosophy.

What forms a central question of this volume—"What is the relevance of higher education to society?"—is more fundamentally the question of the relationship of education to the state. And in addressing this foundational question we must recognize that we do not mean just any education or state. The "education" needs further clarification in that we mean education in the most important matters and the most important minds who studied them; we mean what Robert M. Hutchins called "the Great Books." "[The Great Books] are models of the fine and liberal arts. They hold before us what Whitehead called "the habitual vision of greatness." . . . Until very recently, these books have been central in education in the West."[4]

These Great Books are the compendia of the greatest minds of the West, and so education in our cultural context is education in our civilization. As Allan Bloom further noted, our civilization is not the only one, but it has a distinctiveness that makes it the most excellent among all in human history. "Only in Western nations, i.e., those influenced by Greek philosophy, is there some willingness to doubt the identification of the good with one's own way."[5] But the society in which we exist is losing its roots, its grounding; the very civilization that produced the regimes of the West is in a state of decline or collapse. "With the 1960s . . . any conception of Western civilization came under sustained assault, and the Western traditions have been on the defen-sive ever since. . . . [T]oday very few defenders of Western civilization can be found within the political, intellectual, and economic institutions of either America or Europe."[6]

WESTERN CIVILIZATION: REGIME AND LEGITIMACY

There has been a consensus for at least three centuries that the West is in a crisis that is destined for or descending into a decline. This decline has many dimensions and many manifestations, but a more central causality. Despite this consensus among the greatest minds of the social sciences, there have been many beginnings and endings in the assessment of the most thoughtful commentators. There have been since Plato those who understand the cycles of regime transformation, and those connected to population, education, and the exercise of political power. The political, and in turn, the educational, are connected through political philosophy. General historical assessments of these questions miss this point and are limited and usually follow a theoretical premise that hegemony is derivative of military and economic power, yet these are results rather than causes. There is great need for expanding our horizon of understanding to include that there are macro-political forces that created the circumstances for establishing military and economic dominance. And the relationship of these societal forces to underlying political culture, as transmitted by communities, families, and the institutions that govern them, is the essential network of values that requires careful analysis. The theoretical foundations of the political system, the structure of education, the capacity for innovation, and the cohesion of the public philosophy of the regime are all significant variables in the larger equation of the national interest. But of those, none is more important than the political philosophy.[7]

For the present study on education, Western Civilization is the societal-level question of concern and further, the specific Great Books foundation of Western education. Western Civilization begins in Athens, and from Greek and Roman civilization emerges the greater Western Civilization. At least since Spengler noted the significance of the events of the French Revolution for the "Crisis of the West," commentators have noted the importance of Enlightenment thought and the resultant crisis of modernity.[8] From political philosophy and historical experience, "the French Revolution is incontrovertibly the defining act of modern politics."[9] The seeds of the present crises are deeply and intrinsically sewn in the Enlightenment philosophy that informed the great revolutions of the modern era, and most significant among them the American and French Revolutions. As M.E. Bradford noted, "the culture of the English Enlightenment shared by the authors of our constitution was essentially antirationalistic, antimetaphysical."[10]

The essence of these revolutions was framed by the political philosophy of modernity, and in that fundamentally in the destruction of Western morality. As Allan Bloom remarked on the similarity with our situation in Dostoyevsky, "not referring essentially to the decay of the Czarist regime but of Western justice and morality, and that is what we are experiencing in all liberal society today."[11] The regime, and the legitimating philosophy for that government, is intricately connected to education and the place of political philosophy it the curriculum.

IDENTITY AND ORDER: DEFINING EDUCATION AND THE REGIME IN THE WEST

Western Civilization is the highest culture of the greatest of all civilizations in human history. Western Civilization, or the West, has alternately been termed Christendom, *Pax Britannia*, the Allies, the coalition of the willing, and the "free" world. The United States succeeded Great Britain at the end of the World Wars as the leader of this civilization. In terms of global dominance, as Leo Strauss noted, "In 1913, the West—in fact [the U.S.] together with Great Britain and Germany—could have laid down the law for the rest of the earth without firing a shot."[12] Politically, economically, and militarily, the West was at a zenith as the U.S. ascended into leadership. "Yet, the West was in crisis, resulting in a decline of culture and of faith, and at its core, the civilization was experiencing the decay of self-critique. The West was self-doubting, unsure of its future and with collective regret and angst over its past, and immersed in a present of materialism and Epicurean over-indulgence. It was in terms of internal forces that the West faced the most serious threat."[13] At the heart of this phenomenon, the West was experiencing a profound philosophical crisis, and with a concurrent crisis in education, and it was one it had faced for some period of time. In most respects, Allan Bloom documented this connectivity between the regime and education, and the consequences for our civilization from the crisis of modernity, definitively in *The Closing of the American Mind.*

When did the crisis of the West begin? What are its causes? Oswald Spengler diagnosed "the Decline of the West" as comprising "nothing less than the problem of Civilization [itself]," and this, he said, is "one of the fundamental questions of all higher history."[14] Spengler understood Western Civilization as the expression of culture, of the "soul-life." "THE standpoint from which to comprehend the economic history of the great Cultures is not to be looked for on economic ground. That which we call national economy today is built up on premises that are openly and specifically English."[15] English economics from Adam Smith and English philosophy from Hobbes lay the foundation for the modern framework of regime identity that circumscribes leadership for the West today. Yet as the British Empire declined and the American century ascended, the enduring features of the regime remained English political philosophy and Anglican political culture.[16] These were definitive at the time of the founding of the American republic, and as Gordon Wood noted, the Americans came "to believe that they alone among the peoples of the Western world understood the true principle of representation."[17] It was their Lockean natural right, their reclamation of their rights as Englishmen that was the basis of the American colonists' fight for independence, not a foundation built on some utopian theory. But it was a "right" still conceptualized and framed by Enlightenment political philosophy, even if manifest in this pragmatic American sense. The American founding was still founded in Enlightenment thought despite retaining the cultural continuity as Englishmen. The French Revolution was an entirely Enlightenment affair, and in limited time what had been a philosophical wave of change and crisis translated into political action that would come to threaten the prospect of philosophy itself and challenge education institutions as conservators of higher learning and civilization. The waves of modernity had presented a crisis of values that would transcend founding and regimes from these revolutions forward.

The American Revolution was soon followed by the French Revolution, and later by the Russian Revolution, and continental wars. The growing perils of extreme violence and mass destruction were again the consequences and results, but it was the spirit of radicalism that had been unleashed. This extreme radicalism was grounded in Enlightenment philosophy and various social utopian theories, but the results were mass political action and violence that transformed into ideology and political programs that demanded rights of all types that could be exploited for strategic advantage and ultimately to be utilized for internal self-destruction in the West.[18] The origins of the crisis are in Enlightenment philosophy but the debasement of that philosophy into ideologies, and then the radicalization of those ideologies, would form a perilous threat by the early twenty-first century.

These new mass cultural ideologies were the basis of what would transform into modern terrorist organization and extremist networks of the present. Edmund Burke, and other scholars of the West, recognized that civilization was threatened by the masses, the forces of mob rule, of what we later would call mass culture or popular culture. Western Civilization experienced a crisis of political philosophy, the crisis of modernity, just as it achieved global hegemony over other world civilizations.[19]

The era of decline the West has faced from at least the French Revolution to the multi-cultural wars of the "post-modern" present except through a return to the foundations of the West. As noted scholar Leo Strauss remarked, "However much the West may have declined, however great the dangers to the West may be, that decline, that danger, nay, the defeat, even the destruction of the West would not necessarily prove the West is in a crisis: the West could go down in honor, certain of its purpose. The crisis of the West consists in the West's having become uncertain of its purpose."[20] James Kurth concurs: "Post-modern ideologues have engaged in a compulsive anti-Western project both in Europe and America. They have been joined by their post-colonial counterparts in the non-Western world. Together, they have formed a grand alliance against Western civilization, and they seek to obliterate it everywhere around the world, and especially within the West itself."[21]

As these scholars have noted, the crisis of the West is fundamentally an internal crisis. "These forces are also not mutually exclusive; external forces and internal forces arrayed against the West are interdependent and mutually reinforcing."[22] Understanding the foundations of the West, particularly those of the U.S. founding and constitutional system, and their relationship to the values of the West is essential to contextualize the factors of decline in our culture and education systems.

RELEVANCE AND CONSERVANCY: THE NEGLECT OF DUTY
AND THE CRISIS OF IDENTITY

The question of relevance for the study of Western Civilization is one which has been de facto answered by higher education in America. As Allan Bloom so accurately commented, the college years are "civilization's only chance to get him."[23] Richard Weaver offers an assessment that underscores the crisis,

> It is not too much to say that in the past fifty years public education in the United States has been in the hands of revolutionaries. To grasp the nature of their attempted revolution, we need only realize that in the past every educational system has reflected to a great extent the social and political constitution of the society which supported it. This was assumed to be a natural and proper thing, since the young were to be trained to take places in the world that existed around them. . . . In the period just mentioned, however, we have witnessed something never before seen in the form of a systematic attempt to undermine a society's traditions and beliefs through the educational establishment which is usually employed to maintain them. There has been an extraordinary occurrence, a virtual educational *coup d'etat* carried out by a specially inclined minority. This minority has been in essence a cabal, with objectives radically different from those of the stat which employed them. An amazing feature of the situation has been how little they have cared to conceal these objectives. On more than one occasion they have issued a virtual call to arms to use publicly created facilities for the purpose of actualizing a concept of society not espoused by the people.[24]

One of the most important empirical studies that document the decline in the study of the West was done by the National Association of Scholars (NAS). They found "the decline and near extinction" of Western Civilization had been realized in forty-six years. The report stated,

> This course, covering classical antiquity to the present, was once part of the undergraduate curriculum's intellectual bedrock, not only because it was often a graduation requirement, but because it gave narrative coherence to everything else the university taught. In studying the rise of the West, students came to grips with how the arts and sciences encountered in other classes had been shaped. And because Western Civilization had "gone global," they also learned what made the world outside campus the place it had become. They usually finished with at least a partial recognition of their civilization as a grand monument to human achievement and something with which to identify.[25]

In 1964, NAS found twenty percent of the higher education institutions required courses in Western Civilization and the remaining eighty percent provided some form through electives and other courses. In 2010, "courses on the history of Western Civilization are not now required at any of them, and are available in some form at only 32 percent."[26] There is a collapse in the curriculum for not only courses on Western Civilization but of Western Civilization itself.

Western Civilization, understood through the Great Books tradition of Western Philosophy, is the central basis for evaluating relevance for the myriad scientific, technical, artistic, and humanist expansions in curriculum and knowledge. The decline in the place of Western Civilization as a coherent subject in the curriculum is a symbol of the greater decline in the place of the content of the highest things and forms a concurrent crisis for education in having a standard for understanding those matters which are of most relevance for the curriculum today and for civilization in the future.

CONCLUSIONS: THE FATE OF THE WEST

With the crisis of political philosophy and the decline of the West, we find mutually reinforcing factors of decay in the institutions that are the conservators of what Weaver called "the Permanent Things." Political leaders, poets, the family, churches, armies, all institutions of consequence in these matters, but it is the education institutions that are most central in the crisis. It remains an open question to what extent the highest things can be taught, whether virtue or statesmanship, to the many. But it is an institutional conservancy of these highest things in the curriculum of Western education institutions as well as the freedom afforded by Western regimes for free thought and inquiry, that remains a pivotal difference for the practical endurance of Western Civilization. Despite the clear importance of philosophy to regime and regime to civilization, Thatcher and Reagan are among the few leaders in the West to articulate this associational foundation. [27] Western leaders must recognize the importance of founding principles and the broader connection to civilization in governing.

"Nationalism, however inescapable, is simply no longer the historical force it was in the era between the French Revolution and the end of imperialist colonialism after World War II." [28] Without nationalism, without a public philosophy that honors the past and legitimates the future of the West, there can be only limited progress, and all that remains is the continuation of a rear guard action for defense of the philosophical foundations of Western Civilization.

In 1964 just as NAS was conducting its first study of Western Civilization in the curriculum, Leo Strauss published *The City and Man*, and he remarked of the present crisis, "as regards modern political philosophy, it has been replaced by ideology: what originally was a political philosophy has turned into an ideology. This fact may be said to form the core of the contemporary crisis of the West." [29] Leo Strauss goes on to note the East threatens the West unlike any epoch since earliest time.

> Today, so far from ruling the globe, the West's very survival is endangered by
> the East as it has not been since its beginning. From the Communist Manifesto
> it would appear that the victory of Communism would be the complete victory
> of the West—of the synthesis, transcending the national boundaries, of the
> British industry, the French Revolution, and German philosophy—over the
> East. We see that the victory of Communism would mean indeed the victory of
> originally Western natural science, but surely at the same time the victory of
> the most extreme form of Eastern despotism.[30]

The Eastern despotism Strauss refers to here is one of political theory reduced to political ideology. There remains an ever stronger threat to the West from Eastern ideologies and totalitarian regimes that foster them, from Chinese Communism to Islamic Jihad. "The war against extremist Islam is as much an ideological war as the cold war ever was. And despite all our successes on the battleground, the ideological struggle against extremist Islam is one we are losing—that is, when we bother to wage it at all."[31] If we are to win this battle, the West will need not only more unity within but also to be more persuasive abroad. Carnes Lord observes this point by stating, "At the end of the day, however, the terror war will not be won without creating—and sustaining—new friends and allies of the U.S."[32]

Allies require maintenance, just as the values of Western Civilization require the fiduciary conservation of the highest things, one that higher education has performed in the West at least since Plato founded the Academy. And among the distinctive and defining features of Western education has been the place of the Great Books at the core of Western Civilization, and its is the centrality of these matters to the evaluation of relevance for curriculum that higher education institutions must attend to if we are to meet the great challenges ahead.

The sage English philosopher Michael Oakeshott has remarked, "We consider education as a process in which we discover and begin to cultivate ourselves, we may regard it as learning to recognize ourselves in the mirror of this civilization. I do not claim universality for this image of education; it is merely the image (or part of it) which belongs to our civilization."[33] The crisis of modernity is a fundamentally philosophical one that has parallel crises in the foundations of the West, future and present—the education of future generations and the statesmanship capacity of current public leaders. The need for understanding the present forces of decline and their implications are of urgent importance. "If such is the most we can hope for, something toward that revival maybe prepared by acts of thought and violation in this waning day of the West."[34] The regimes of the West must face the crisis in the education of the next generation of leaders if the future of Western Civilization is to be as profound and glorious as its tradition and past accomplishments.

NOTES

1. Alfred North Whitehead, *Process and Reality* (New York: The Free Press, 1979), 39.

2. Plato, "Protagoras," In *The Collected Dialogues of Plato*, ed. Edith Hamilton and Hunt-ington Cairns, W. K. C. Guthrie trans., (Princeton, NJ: Princeton University Press, 1989), 308–353. For more on the relationship of education to the regime, see Allan Bloom's interpre-tive essay, Allan Bloom, *The Republic of Plato* (New York: Basic Books, 1968).

3. A. E. Taylor, *Plato: The Man and His Work* (New York: Meridian Books, 1959), 242.

4. Robert Maynard Hutchins, *The Great Conversation* (Chicago: Encyclopedia Britannica, 1952), 2.

5. Allan Bloom, *The Closing of the American Mind* (New York: Simon and Schuster, 1987), 36.

6. James Kurth, "Western Civilization, Our Tradition." *The Intercollegiate Review* 38 (Fall2003/Spring 2004): 8. See also, Samuel J. Huntington's "The Clash of Civilizations?" *Foreign Affairs* 72, no. 3 (Summer 1993): 22–49.

7. Michael Wayne Hail, "Factors of Destabilization and Collapse: A Comparative Study of the Roman and British Empires and the Consequences for Western Civilization," in *Advances in Cross-Cultural Decision Making*, ed. Dylan Schmorrow and Denise Nicholson (Boca Raton: CRC Press of Taylor and Francis, 2011), 132.

8. Leo Strauss, "Three Waves of Modernity," in *Political Philosophy: Six Essays*, ed. Hilail Gilden (Indianapolis, IN: Bobbs-Merrill, 1975), 81.

9. Gregory Claeys, *The French Revolution Debate in Britain—The Origins of Modern Politics* (Hampshire: Palgrave Macmillan, 2007), 1.

10. M. E. Bradford, *Remembering Who we Are* (Athens: University of Georgia Press, 1985), 36.

11. Allan Bloom, *Giants and Dwarfs* (New York: Simon and Schuster, 1990), 181.

12. Leo Strauss, *The City and Man* (Chicago: Rand McNally and Co, 1964), 2.

13. Hail, "Factors of Destabilization and Collapse," 135.

14. Oswald Spengler, *The Decline of the West*, trans. C. F. Atkinson (New York: Vintage Books, 2006), 24.

15. Spengler, *The Decline of the West*, 398.

16. Michael Wayne Hail and Stephen J. Lange, "Federalism and Representation in the Theory of the Founding Fathers: A Comparative Study of U.S. and Canadian Constitutional Thought," *Publius: The Journal of Federalism* 40, no. 3 (2010): 369.

17. Gordon Wood, *Representation in the American Revolution* (Charlottesville: University Press of Virginia, 1969), 1.

18. Hail, "Factors of Destabilization and Collapse," 136.

19. Hail, "Factors of Destabilization and Collapse," 137.

20. Strauss, *The City and Man*, 3.

21. Kurth,"Western Civilization, Our Tradition," 12.

22. Hail, "Factors of Destabilization and Collapse: A Comparative Study of the Roman and British Empires and the Consequences for Western Civilization," 132.

23. Bloom, *Closing of the American Mind*, 336.

24. Richard Weaver, *Ideas Have Consequences* (Chicago: University of Chicago, 1948), 114.

25. Glen Ricketts, Peter Wood, Stephen Balch, and Ashley Thorne, *The Vanishing West: 1964–2010* (Princeton: National Association of Scholars, 2011), v.

26. Rickets, et al., *The Vanishing West: 1964–2010*, 1.

27. Michael Wayne Hail, "New Federalism of Reagan," in *Federalism In America*, ed. Joseph R. Marchbach, Ellis Katz, and Troy E. Smith (Westport, CT: Greenwood Press, 2006), 451.

28. Eric J. Hobsbawm, *Nations and Nationalism Since 1870* (Cambridge: Cambridge Uni-versity Press, 1992), 169.

29. Leo Strauss, *The City and Man* (Chicago: Rand McNally and Co., 1964), 2.

30. Strauss, *The City and Man*, 3.

31. David Frum and Richard Perle, *An End to Evil* (New York: Random House, 2003), 147. Also see, Schmitt and Shulsky's work on Straussians and security studies as well as Shulsky's *Silent Warfare* for an understanding of how ideology is contrasted with philosophy in intelligence analysis.
32. Carnes Lord, *Losing Hearts and Minds?* (Westport, CT: Praeger Security International, 2006), 2.
33. Michael Oakeshott, *Rationalism in Politics and Other Essays* (Indianapolis: Liberty Fund, 1962), 188.
34. Weaver, *Ideas Have Consequences*, 187.

BIBLIOGRAPHY

Bloom, Allan. *The Republic of Plato*. New York: Basic Books, 1968.
——. *Closing of the American Mind*. New York: Simon and Schuster, 1987.
——. *Giants and Dwarves*. New York: Simon and Schuster, 1990.
Bradford, M. E. *Remembering Who we Are*. Athens: University of Georgia Press, 1985.
Claeys, Gregory. *The French Revolution Debate in Britain—The Origins of Modern Politics*. Hampshire: Palgrave Macmillan, 2007.
Frum, David and Richard Perle. *An End to Evil*. New York: Random House, 2003.
Hail, Michael Wayne. "New Federalism of Reagan." In *Federalism In America*, edited by Joseph R. Marchbach, Ellis Katz, and Troy E. Smith, 451–53. Westport, CT: Greenwood Press, 2006.
——. "Factors of Destabilization and Collapse: A Comparative Study of the Roman and British Empires and the Consequences for Western Civilization." In *Advances in Cross-Cultural Decision Making*, edited by Dylan Schmorrow and Denise Nicholson, 129–39. Boca Raton: CRC Press of Taylor and Francis, 2011.
Hail, Michael Wayne and Stephen J. Lange. "Federalism and Representation in the Theory of the Founding Fathers: A Comparative Study of U.S. and Canadian Constitutional Thought." *Publius: The Journal of Federalism* 40, no. 3 (2010): 366–88.
Hobsbawm, Eric J. *Nations and Nationalism Since 1870*. Cambridge: Cambridge University Press, 1992.
Huntington, Samuel P. "The Clash of Civilizations?" *Foreign Affairs* 72, no. 3 (Summer 1993): 22–49.
Hutchins, Robert Maynard. *The Great Conversation*. Chicago: Encyclopedia Britannica, 1952.
Kurth, James. "Western Civilization, Our Tradition." *The Intercollegiate Review* 38 (Fall 2003/ Spring 2004): 5–13.
Lord, Carnes. *Losing Hearts and Minds?* Westport, Connecticut: Praeger Security International, 2006.
Oakeshott, Michael. *Rationalism in Politics and Other Essays*. Indianapolis: Liberty Fund, 1962.
Plato. "Protagoras." In *The Collected Dialogues of Plato*, edited by Edith Hamilton and Huntington Cairns. Translated by W. K. C. Guthrie, 308–353. Princeton, NJ: Princeton University Press, 1989.
Ricketts, Glen, Peter Wood, Stephen Balch, and Ashley Thorne. *The Vanishing West: 1964–2010*. Princeton: National Association of Scholars, 2011.
Schmitt, Glen J. and Abram N. Shulsky. "Leo Strauss and the World of Intelligence (By Which We Do Not Mean Nous)." In *Leo Strauss, the Straussians, and the American Regime*, edited by Kenneth L. Deutsch and John A. Murley, 407–12. Lanham: Rowman & Littlefield, 1999.
Spengler, Oswald. *The Decline of the West*. Translated by C. F. Atkinson. New York: Vintage Books, 2006.
Strauss, Leo. *The City and Man*. Chicago: Rand McNally and Company, 1964.
——. "Three Waves of Modernity." In *Political Philosophy: Six Essays*, edited by Hilail Gilden, 81–98. Indianapolis, IN: Bobbs-Merrill, 1975.
Shulsky, Abram N. *Silent Warfare: Understanding the World of Intelligence*. Washington, DC: Potomac Books Inc., 2002.

Taylor, A. E. *Plato: The Man and His Work.* New York: Meridian Books, 1959.
Weaver, Richard. *Ideas Have Consequences.* Chicago: University of Chicago, 1948.
Whitehead, Alfred North. *Process and Reality.* New York: The Free Press, 1979.
Wood, Gordon. *Representation in the American Revolution.* Charlottesville: University Press of Virginia, 1969.

Chapter Nine

American Democracy and Liberal Education in an Era of "Relevance"

Jason R. Jividen

It is well understood that the focus of contemporary American higher education is increasingly geared toward the cultivation of skills necessary for individuals to gain employment and compete in the twenty-first-century global marketplace. For some, traditional efforts at a classical liberal education in our colleges and universities seem severely threatened by a more recent view that higher education ought to be offered, and undertaken, for the sake of utility, often framed in terms of economic utility. The notion that higher education should ultimately seek to enable students to consider well the perennial questions and competing answers about how one ought to live is seen as only marginally important, if not "irrelevant," to the demands of contemporary American society.

While we might tend to think such views are largely the result of the political and economic realities of the twentieth and twenty-first centuries, it has long been argued that there is an inherent and unremitting tension between liberal democracy and liberal education. This tension, some argue, is not so much the result of changing political and economic circumstances, but the result of something more fundamental. While the ultimate health of the American political and economic system may well require the presence of an enlightened, liberally educated citizenry with the moral and political virtues necessary to sustain a healthy polity, many elements characteristic of the American regime also paradoxically undermine the pursuit of these virtues. As Tocqueville once observed, the characteristic practicality and restlessness of a democratic people tend to undercut the appreciation of liberal learning for its own sake. According to Tocqueville, in American democracy, education is generally seen as useful insofar as it serves primarily vocational or

economic ends. Moreover, as some students of the history of political philosophy have argued, there might be something to the idea that the low but solid
ground of liberal modernity stands in tension with the pursuit of moral and
intellectual virtue characteristic of a truly liberal education.

In this chapter I will examine this seeming tension between liberal education and American democracy, broadly sketching its general outlines, especially as that tension is articulated in two seminal works on modern liberal
democracy and its effects upon American ideas, habits, and institutions:
Alexis de Tocqueville's *Democracy in America* and Allan Bloom's *The
Closing of the American Mind.*[1] I will then offer a few reflections on this
apparent tension in light of the present volume's theme of "relevance," arguing that there is (and always has been) not only room, but an urgent need,
for liberal education in American liberal democracy.

AMERICAN HIGHER EDUCATION, CULTURE, AND UTILITY

That higher education ought to be useful to individuals and society is hardly
a new idea. Indeed, the modern university has always defended its existence,
at least in part, through an appeal to the notion of "relevance." For some
defenders of liberal education, this emphasis on the relevance or utility of
knowledge undercuts the pursuit of knowledge for its own sake. Liberal
education, rightly understood, has traditionally been characterized as an education toward culture, that is, toward the cultivation of human reason and
what is highest in man. In being "liberal," this education has most often been
understood as an education worthy of a free, thinking, human being. Sometimes described as an education toward moral and intellectual virtue, it is an
education that seeks to form one's soul. Liberal education seeks to liberate
men from the prejudices or unexamined opinions of their own time, place, or
circumstance to arrive at examined opinions and potential answers to the
most fundamental questions of the human experience. It is not the education
of a slave, a wage earner, a producer, or consumer, but of a free man,
understood in the highest and most encompassing sense.[2]

Yet many proponents of liberal education regularly and reasonably suggest that an education in arts and letters, focusing on timeless questions of
human importance, is profoundly useful for individuals and society at large.
No less a defender of liberal education than John Henry Newman argued that
a traditional liberal education helped to cultivate skills and habits of mind
useful for enlightened citizenship and productivity in one's chosen trade or
occupation. But, for Newman, liberal education was above all a process in
which the intellect is "disciplined for its own sake, for the perception of its
own proper object, and for its own highest culture," rather than "formed or
sacrificed to some particular or accidental purpose, some specific trade or

profession." The incidental utility of a liberal education ought not to be conflated with the merits of liberal education understood on its own terms. Liberal education is first and foremost open to the pursuit of knowledge for its own sake, and it is, above all else, an education toward culture.[3]

Yet, as Cardinal Newman made clear, one can speak intelligently about the ends of college and university education in terms of both "utility" and "culture" and we need not immediately assume that an education toward one end necessarily destroys an education toward the other. In the modern American context, one particularly clear expression of this view can be found in the writings of Martin Luther King. Writing for the Morehouse College student newspaper, a young King suggested:

> It seems to me that education has a twofold function to perform in the life of man and in society: the one is utility and the other is culture. Education must enable a man to become more efficient, to achieve with increasing facility the legitimate goals of his life.

> Education must also train one for quick, resolute and effective thinking. To think incisively and to think for one's self is very difficult. We are prone to let our mental life become invaded by legions of half truths, prejudices, and propaganda. At this point, I often wonder whether or not education is fulfilling its purpose. A great majority of the so-called educated people do not think logically and scientifically. Even the press, the classroom, the platform, and the pulpit in many instances do not give us objective and unbiased truths. To save man from the morass of propaganda, in my opinion, is one of the chief aims of education. Education must enable one to sift and weigh evidence, to discern the true from the false, the real from the unreal, and the facts from the fiction.

> The function of education, therefore, is to teach one to think intensively and to think critically. But education which stops with efficiency may prove the greatest menace to society. The most dangerous criminal may be the man gifted with reason, but with no morals . . . [I]ntelligence is not enough. Intelligence plus character—that is the goal of true education. The complete education gives one not only power of concentration, but worthy objectives upon which to concentrate.[4]

For King, education ought to be aimed at serving both culture and utility, yet we see in his remarks that he questioned whether American higher education emphasized utility at the expense of culture or character. Thinking that stops only at providing efficiency or usefulness in achieving one's goals fails to provide individuals any defense against "half truths, prejudices, and propaganda." An education toward utility, even framed in terms of civic education, ought not to be divorced from an education toward culture or character. To use today's educational buzzwords, "higher order thinking," or "critical

thinking skills" are not enough. For King, students might be trained in critical thinking, but without anything worthy of thinking about, we perhaps do
more harm than good.

If American higher education tends to lean too far toward the notion of
utility, it seems to me that this utility is often understood as economic utility.[5] As noted in the introduction to this volume, recent higher education
policy is aimed explicitly (though not exclusively) at urging colleges and
universities to assist in stimulating sustainable economic development in
local and regional communities. Nearly anyone involved in higher education
today can readily recognize this tendency. Increasingly, it seems, higher
education must be marketed in terms of its ability to equip students with the
tools necessary to find and hold professional employment and compete in a
competitive and globalized marketplace. For those of us in the classroom, we
daily find not only that students expect this kind of education, but also that
college and university administrators increasingly speak this kind of language, if only because the realities of the business of higher education demand it. Responding to perceived demand, colleges and universities, if they
have not abandoned any principled support for traditional liberal education
for its own sake, they at least are forced to play the game and frame such
studies under the rubric of economic utility. We are familiar with the pitch:
an education in the "liberal arts" supplements one's primary, professional
education in some marketable set of skills. Simply put, learning to read,
write, and think is useful in getting a leg up on others in the marketplace. We
know the ubiquitous formulation: developing "critical thinking skills" are
essential for "problem-solving" in the real world.

With King, I would argue that all too often these skills are detached from
any serious, thoughtful consideration of whether the ends to which we are
devoted are really worthy of our choosing. King was concerned that, in
contemporary society, education toward utility, toward what we today might
refer to as "relevance," overshadows education toward culture. But we
should hesitate to assume that this elevation of utility over culture in
American education is somehow a wholly new development, or that it is
somehow necessitated by merely current trends or contemporary economic
circumstances. Rather, King was on to something that other observers have
considered fundamental to American democratic institutions. Among those
observers is Alexis de Tocqueville.

TOCQUEVILLE ON AMERICAN DEMOCRACY AND THE
AMERICAN INTELLECT

Tocqueville's *Democracy in America* clearly provides a rich, powerful, and
broad analysis of liberal democracy and the effect of equality of conditions

on American political development. For Tocqueville, the idea of equality in the modern world permeates nearly every aspect of American life in some respect, and *Democracy in America* examines the great merits and dangers of equality for American ideas, institutions, and culture. For our purposes, however, we will settle down on Tocqueville's account of the effects of equality of conditions on American intellectual habits. Tocqueville's observations on this head speak directly to theme of this volume, and it seems to me that they help us to better understand not only what we often mean when we refer to the contemporary "relevance" of higher education, but also the threat this pursuit of "relevance" might pose to traditional liberal education.[6]

Americans, Tocqueville observed, pay less attention to philosophy than any other country in the civilized world; they simply have little use for philosophy or theoretical concerns. This is, in part, due to America's relative youth. According to Tocqueville, nations only discover the taste for philosophy when they are growing old. In young regimes, there is simply not much incentive to ask the most important questions. A regime in its ascent, particularly one as restless and economically preoccupied as America, has neither the time nor the inclination toward contemplation. Rather, it is only with time, and if we take Hegel seriously, with decline, that individuals in a regime may be promoted toward reflection upon the most important and far-reaching questions of political and philosophic life.[7] But, importantly, this neglect of theory and philosophy is not simply due to America's youth. Rather, for Tocqueville, it is indicative of certain fundamental habits of the American mind. Equality of conditions, if it does not create certain habits of thinking, it at least reinforces and encourages these habits.

While Americans follow no philosophical school or tradition explicitly, it turns out that they do implicitly or rather unthinkingly embrace a kind of practical Cartesianism. The Americans, Tocqueville argued, "have a uniform method and rules for the conduct of intellectual inquiries . . . looking to results without getting entangled in the means toward them and looking through forms to the basis of things." Each American relies on individual effort and judgment in making decisions. Americans do not read or think much about Descartes; their busy commercial society distracts them from such things. Yet this same society leads them to adopt Cartesian principles in everyday practice. In all the countries of the world, Tocqueville claims, "America is the one in which the precepts of Descartes are least studied and best followed."[8]

Tocqueville's general argument here is that equality of conditions in America's commercial, democratic society weakens ties to the ancestral, contributing to an exaggerated confidence in human reason and Americans are skeptical of anything without immediate, first-hand experience. Men cannot fall back on class for the source of their beliefs, for in times of democratic equality, such class distinctions are obliterated. All citizens in American democracy are more or less similar in intellect and prudence, it is believed, and no one sees in another any "incontestable greatness or superiority." Individual men are thus continually "brought back to their own judgment as the most apparent and accessible test of truth." Americans are led to the idea that everything is accessible and explainable by unassisted human reason and they deny anything they cannot readily explain. Thus, Tocqueville suggested, Americans have "no need for books to teach them philosophical method, having found it themselves."[9]

This practical skepticism leads to what Tocqueville identifies as America's particularly democratic taste for general ideas. There are two very different kinds of generalizations, according to Tocqueville. One enlarges the sphere of human understanding, coming from the "slow, detailed, and conscientious labor of the mind." The other, "begets only very superficial and uncertain notions," and results from the "first and quick exercise of the wits." American democracy, Tocqueville explains, is prone to the latter. The American habit of generalization permits "human minds to pass judgment quickly on a great number of things, but the conceptions they convey are always incomplete, and what is gained in extent is always lacking in exactitude."[10] Americans learn how to get by with approximations and half-truths in pursuit of their material interests.

According to Tocqueville, in ages of democracy and equality of conditions, one often looks to great deterministic causes to explain the progress of human affairs. This both follows from, and reinforces, the democratic citizen's taste for general ideas. The American wants to find common rules for everything, filing a "great number of objects under the same formula," and tries to explain multiple facts by "one sole cause." In a society where each man looks to find truth for himself, the human spirit is directed—paradoxically perhaps—toward such generalizations. General ideas act as a kind of short-cut for assessing the situation before us, and serve the intensely practical concerns of citizenship in the commercial, democratic republic. According to Tocqueville, such habits are intimately related to the American taste for "easy success and immediate pleasures," something that is as true of intellectual pursuits as it is of any other endeavor. Men in democratic times, Tocqueville suggested, want immediate success without the trouble of working too hard for it. In American democracy, for most men, most of the time, equality of opportunity, careers open to talents, and the overwhelming desire to better one's condition without effort appear to boil ambition down to the restless and uneasy desire for material, economic gain.[11]

Equality of conditions in democratic society brings great benefits, Tocqueville claimed, but it also opens the human soul to an "inordinate love of material pleasure." Thankfully, for American democracy, its religious inheritance inspires "diametrically contrary urges." Religious dogma, according to Tocqueville, counters man's more selfish urges, and tends to raise men's sights from the material world.[12] Men are led to consider, if even briefly and incompletely, the realm of spirituality, virtue, and duty. Men are prompted to consider the notion that a tendency toward the inordinate love of material pleasure speaks to the enduring imperfection of human nature and stands in tension with our longing for higher things transcendent, beautiful, and good.

Importantly, Tocqueville argued that America's taste for practical pursuits and its denigration of deep thought need not lead us to believe that popular government as such is incompatible with the traditional domain of higher education: the serious study of science, literature, and the arts. Rather, there is something unique about American democracy that either turns citizens away from such pursuits, or at least prompts those who do pursue such things to place a particularly American stamp upon them. According to Tocqueville, America's Puritan religion at its point of departure was traditionally unfriendly to pomp and innovation, it was unfavorable to the fine arts, and it only reluctantly made room for literature. The Americans found themselves in a unique situation, occupying a new and wide open world, and every man suddenly enjoyed a new and unparalleled opportunity for making his fortune in that world. In such an environment a "breathless cupidity perpetually distracts the mind of man from the pleasures of the imagination and labors of the intellect and urges it on to nothing but the pursuit of wealth." All of America, in one way or another, was engaged in some form of productive industry and trade.[13]

The Americans, Tocqueville claimed, were in a truly exceptional situation. Connected to Europe, particularly through their English heritage, the Americans could borrow the fruits of intellectual pursuits in science, literature, and the arts, without having to produce them on their own. For Tocqueville, among other things, this made America different than any other democratic nation. The Americans' "strictly Puritan origin," their "exclusively commercial habits," the "country they inhabit," and their accessibility to Europe, all seem to "divert their minds from the study of science, literature and the arts . . ." According to Tocqueville, "[A] thousand special causes . . . have singularly concurred to fix the mind of the American on purely practical objects. His desires, needs, education, and circumstances all seem united to draw the American's mind earthward. Only religion from time to time makes him turn a transient and distracted glance toward heaven."[14]

In a condition of democratic and economic equality, with the breakdown of primogeniture, hereditary wealth, and privilege of birth, Tocqueville argued, every man derives his own strengths and successes from himself. A real chance at successful careers, successful innovations, and advances are open to all. Thus, it "becomes clear that the chief source of disparity between the fortunes of men lies in the mind. Whatever tends to invigorate, expand, or adorn the mind rises instantly to a high value." It turns out that, in Tocqueville's analysis, despite American democracy's distaste for higher thinking, despite its neglect of science, literature, and the arts, few Americans really allow themselves to be wholly confined to merely material concerns. Even the "humblest artisan" sometimes "casts an eager, fugitive glance at the higher regions of the mind." Democratic men quickly begin to see the utility of intellectual pursuits; they soon realize that some of these pursuits are "a powerful aid to the acquisition of fame, power, or wealth."[15]

We might ask whether we could find a better explanation of the contemporary idea of "relevance" in American higher education. On Tocqueville's view, such a quest for knowledge is not necessarily high or noble, but it does increase the number of those engaged in the study of science, literature, and the arts. But, there is a trade-off, for while the scope of individuals studying such things may widen, their results are often mediocre, low, or insignificant. Equality of conditions leads to a great many things, not the least of which is access to education, political opportunity, and wealth. But, as any student of Tocqueville knows, equality brings with it a middling effect that that pulls the high or excellent toward the center, just as it raises the low upward and expands equality of opportunity. One consequence of this middling effect for American intellectual habits, according to Tocqueville, is that Americans rarely bother with the "abstract and theoretical side of human knowledge." Rather, they turn almost immediately toward practical application, toward method. Ultimately, Tocqueville argued, men in democratic times are not necessarily indifferent to the study of science, literature, and the arts, but they "cultivate them in their own fashion and bring their own peculiar qualities and defects to the task." While democratic society doesn't necessarily "curb the vigor of the mind," it does push the mind in a particular direction.[16]

Tocqueville reminds us that the higher parts of the sciences require "meditation above everything else," but meditation requires leisure, something the average American citizen severely lacks. American democracy has no permanent, aristocratic leisure class. Every American citizen is on the move, in a continual and restless pursuit of self-interest and they have little time for using the higher realms of the intellect. Americans must make snap judgments to keep pace with the bustling commercial and political society around them and they cannot waste time in serious contemplation. Moreover, meditation is difficult, and Americans, Tocqueville argued, naturally attach little importance to it. American habits useful in action and pursuit of material improvement are not necessarily conducive to habits useful for deeper reflection. A "quick, superficial mind is at a premium" in American democracy. Here Tocqueville made a crucial distinction useful to our consideration of the "relevance" of American higher education, a distinction between the desire to seek knowledge for its *own sake*, and the desire to merely use knowledge for its *utility* in acquiring some perceived material good. The former is a passion that burns only in the hearts of the few. The latter evinces only a "selfish, commercial, banal taste for the discoveries of the mind."[17]

Most people in American democracy, Tocqueville asserted, are engaged in this lower pursuit of knowledge, eagerly pursuing material pleasures, and always seeking to better their position. When one studies science in America, he studies it in the "same spirit as one takes up a trade . . . only matters of immediate and recognized practical application receive attention."[18] According to Tocqueville:

> Most of the people in [democratic] nations are extremely eager in the pursuit of immediate material pleasures and are always discontented with the position they occupy and always free to leave it. They think about nothing but ways of changing their lot and bettering it. For people in this frame of mind every new way of getting wealth more quickly, every machine which lessens work, every means of diminishing the costs of production, every innovation which makes pleasures easier or greater, seems the most magnificent accomplishment of the human mind. It is chiefly from this line of approach that democratic peoples come to study sciences, to understand them, and to value them. In aristocratic ages the chief function of science is to give pleasure to the mind, but in democratic ages to the body.[19]

For Tocqueville, if we focus too heavily on the mere practice, utility, or relevance of scientific knowledge, we might easily lose sight of basic principles. When we denigrate theory in the sciences, we might apply methods poorly or misunderstand them, and at the same time we might rob ourselves of the tools with which can create new methods. According to Tocqueville, such habits are both natural and inevitable in democracies, and in such societies, the people will "look after the practical side of things for themselves." Thus, instead of "perpetually concentrating attention on the minute examination of secondary effects," Tocqueville urged, it is both necessary and desirable to lift our attention to "the contemplation of first causes." In our quest to discover the most efficient means to our desired ends, we ought not to lose sight of first principles. Reflecting on the American experience, Tocqueville warned that democracies must be sure not to lose their guidance. "If the lights that guide us ever go out," Tocqueville predicted, "they will fade little by little, as if of their own accord. . . . Some peoples may let the torch be snatched from their hands, but others stamp it out themselves."[20]

Following Tocqueville, we might apply this observation on learning and the higher realms of the sciences to liberal learning more generally. Insofar as the middling effect of equality of conditions turns men away from theory, it risks forgetting first principles and, in doing so, forgets the noble ends to which our studies are directed. Tocqueville continued to suggest that such a consequence is visible not only in the sciences, but in democratic literature and the arts, where superficiality and mere efficiency reign supreme. With the American study of science, American literature and arts bear the unfortunate mark of equality of conditions. While the scope of individuals engaged in such pursuits may be widened in democratic society, according to Tocqueville, the results are usually mediocre and rarely ascend from the production of the merely useful toward the contemplation of the good or beautiful as such. [21]

Yet one partial antidote to this democratic tendency toward neglecting first principles might reside in the study of ancient Greek and Latin literature. In ancient western literature, Tocqueville claims, nothing is "written hurriedly or casually." Rather, "it is always intended for connoisseurs and is always seeking an ideal beauty. No other literature puts in bolder relief those qualities democratic writers tend to lack, and therefore no other literature is better to be studied at such [democratic] times." Yet such literary education, Tocqueville suggested, is not for everyone. Indeed, in modern democracy, however much an education in classical literature might produce well-educated citizens it also might produce dangerous citizens. Those educated in classical literature, and not in scientific, industrial, and commercial pursuits, might want more than their highly theoretical education can provide. When their expectations exceed their capabilities, such individuals might "perturb the state, in the name of the Greeks and Romans, instead of enriching it by their industry." Thus, such things need not, and should not, be taught in all schools, but should be made available to those with a taste for it. According to Tocqueville, "a few excellent universities are a better means to this end than a multitude of bad schools in which the classics are an ill-taught extra, standing in the way of sound instruction in necessary studies." [22]

While an education in classical literature, part of what today would be considered part of an education in Great Books, might serve as an antidote to the failings of democratic literature, it does not seem that Tocqueville holds out hope for an American citizenry of classically trained gentlemen or philosophers pursuing knowledge for its own sake. Following Tocqueville, such things remain the privilege of the few. If we should lament the fact that equality of conditions turns most people, most of the time, toward intellectual pursuits merely for the sake of utility, we should nevertheless wonder whether, in expecting more than this in liberal democracy, we might ask for the impossible or even the undesirable.

This all-too-American tendency to view education through the lens of utility leads Tocqueville to examine briefly what he sees as a still more fundamental aspect of American democracy. According to Tocqueville, if democratic citizens are educated and free to pursue their individual interests as they see fit, they will daily make use of the world around them, improving techniques and methods to make life more secure, and more comfortable. For Tocqueville, democratic men take delight in this "proper and legitimate quest for prosperity," and there is no reason to expect it to stop. Yet, in the restless pursuit of self-improvement, the democratic citizen runs the risk of losing the "use of his sublimest faculties . . . [B]ent on improving everything around him, he may at length degrade himself. That, and nothing else, is the peril." Ever casting his eyes earthward toward physical comfort, democratic man may very well abandon a "taste for the infinite, an appreciation of greatness, and a love of spiritual pleasures."[23]

Tocqueville's concern here is with the modern tendency to embrace doctrines of materialism, that there is nothing in this word but matter and motion, and hence no objective, enduring standard by which to judge human action. So far, through their religion, Americans had been able to hold off a complete and far-reaching embrace of materialism; religion taught Americans about the existence and immortality of the soul, about things infinite, noble, high, and ordered. Nevertheless, Tocqueville explained:

> In all nations materialism is a dangerous malady of the human spirit, but one must be particularly on guard against it among a democratic people, because it combines most marvelously well with that vice which is most familiar to the heart in such circumstances. Democracy favors the taste for physical pleasures. This taste, if it becomes excessive, soon disposes men to believe that nothing but matter exists. Materialism, in its turn, spurs them on to such delights with man impetuosity. Such is the vicious circle into which democratic nations are driven.[24]

According to Tocqueville, theories which suggest that all things perish with the body are most pernicious in democracies and the men who profess them ought to be regarded as enemies of the people. Perhaps the greatest danger of an American education dedicated to knowledge and learning for the sake of mere utility is its tendency to exacerbate the modern predilection for materialism. In effect, such an education, if it does not already presume that human beings are without souls, it tends to foster this notion.

Following Tocqueville's analysis, then, it seems that liberal education, directed at the pursuit of knowledge for its own sake, is threatened by the effect that equality of conditions has upon American intellectual habits. For Tocqueville, should the doctrine of materialism take hold in American democracy, this problem is only made worse. For if liberal education, rightly understood, is meant to cultivate human souls, it assumes that human beings first have souls to cultivate.[25] If liberal education is meant to teach students how to consider fundamental and persistent questions about the right ordering of the soul, and to prompt them to weigh and evaluate the best competing answers to the question of how we ought to live together, then that education is threatened by the doctrine of materialism. In a universe (and thus in an America) where there is nothing but matter and motion, and nothing transcends the concerns of the body, higher education understandably focuses upon mere utility and the material concerns of self-preservation, bodily pleasure, and economic gain.

BLOOM ON AMERICAN DEMOCRACY AND THE AMERICAN UNIVERSITY

For those of us involved in higher education, Tocqueville's account of American intellectual habits and the focus on education for the sake of utility should seem all too familiar. But, for many perhaps, the most visible commentary on this phenomenon is not to be found in Tocqueville's seminal nineteenth-century analysis of American democracy. In more recent years, that honor likely belongs to Allan Bloom's controversial, and best-selling, twentieth-century critique of American higher education, *The Closing of the American Mind* (2012 marked the twenty-fifth anniversary of the book). Here Bloom situated the decline of liberal education in contemporary American colleges and universities within the long history of political philosophy. And Tocqueville's observations about the American mind loomed large in Bloom's analysis.[26]

Bloom explicitly identified Tocqueville as a major influence upon his own understanding of the defects of American intellectual culture and the purpose of the modern university in democratic society. According to Bloom, Tocqueville's account of American intellectual life serves as a "mirror in which we can see ourselves" today.[27] Among other things, Bloom argued, we learn from Tocqueville that the American preoccupation with the things merely useful, the things relevant to economic gain and physical comfort, makes the "theoretical distance" characteristic of liberal education for its own sake "seem not only useless, but immoral." For Bloom, the "for-its-own-sake is alien to the modern democratic spirit, particularly in matters intellectual." From the standpoint of American democracy, Bloom asked, what teacher or man of learning could claim the right to idly ask questions that have already been answered, engaged in the pursuit of knowledge merely for its own sake, when there are wars, disease, and poverty to confront? Can any man, in good conscience, engage in the leisurely pursuit of a true liberal education when there are far more immediate pressing problems to solve? In such times, Bloom asserted, "democratic men devoted to thought have a crisis of conscience," and they must "find a way to interpret their endeavors by the standard of utility, or otherwise tend to abandon or deform them."[28] While I hesitate to follow Bloom in going so far in psychologizing the motivations of all or most theoretically inclined men in American democracy, I think we can understand the tendency he described.

For Bloom, rightly understood, the true purpose of American higher education is to temper American democracy's tendency to elevate the body at the expense of the soul, the material at the expense of the transcendent, and the useful at the expense of the "for-its-own-sake." The university, Bloom contended, can do this. But it must resist the temptation to be all things to all people. On Bloom's analysis, it seems the university cannot serve two masters; it cannot serve the economic, vocational, or professional desires of most citizens, while at the same time providing the liberal education worthy of the few. It must resist the urge to do everything for American democracy. It must not serve society, at least not directly. For Bloom, the "university is only one interest among many and must always keep its eye on that interest for fear of compromising it in the desire to be more useful, more *relevant*, more popular" [emphasis added].[29]

The best way for the modern university to counter the tendencies of American intellectual life, Bloom claimed, is by keeping that life truly open to reason and reflection and, "in the first place, always to maintain the permanent questions front and center. This [the university] does primarily by preserving—by keeping alive—the works of those who best addressed these questions." In short, for the few, Bloom prescribes a liberal education that looks something like an education in the Great Books of western civilization, or at least an education that begins with such an approach. According to Bloom, in this we follow Tocqueville, for Tocqueville believed the ancient writers could "best make us aware of our own imperfections, which is what counts for us." Ultimately, for Bloom, there is but "one simple rule" for the university's activity in American liberal democracy. The university should "not concern itself with providing its students with experiences that are available in democratic society. They will have them in any event. It must provide them with experiences they cannot have there." According to Bloom, American universities have perhaps never performed this job well, but today it seems they have nearly abandoned the job altogether.[30]

Now, part of the task of this volume is to ask just what we mean when we say that American institutions of higher education ought to be "relevant" to the publics they serve. Both Tocqueville and Bloom show us that how we answer that question is perhaps very much influenced by the intellectual habits characteristic of American democracy. Both, it seems, would suggest that this relevance is usually framed in terms of utility, often economic utility. But they also would claim that the true sense in which we ought to understand the relevance of higher education consists, at least in part, in the tempering or moderating of this conventional notion of education toward the merely useful. American democratic society tends to describe the relevance of higher education in terms of economic utility. The friendly critics of American democratic society might describe the relevance of higher education in terms of the university's ability to counter that same utilitarian tendency.

We recall that Tocqueville had claimed that combating this American tendency to value things merely useful at the expense of knowledge for its own sake might require a frequent return to fundamental principles. We ought to make a conscious and serious effort to periodically cast our gaze back to first things, among them, fundamental ideas that combat the democratic affinity for materialism. Bloom too urged a return to first things, a return to the serious consideration of fundamental questions of human importance. Yet, as mentioned above, Bloom situated his critique of contemporary American higher education in the history of political philosophy. For Bloom, it turned out that, in a sense, the closing of the American mind did not begin with America. It began with the Enlightenment thought beneath the principles and institutions of American democracy.

According to Bloom, what distinguished the Enlightenment from classical political philosophy was its interest in extending knowledge to all men, allowing all men (rather than the few) the ability to live a life according to reason. Motivated by a new natural science and a corresponding new political science, Enlightenment thinkers sought to understand political life through a "mathematical science of the movement of bodies," and a new, improved understanding of human nature. Breaking sharply with ancient political philosophy, the modern Enlightenment thinkers began from the premise that men do not naturally belong together, inhabiting a universe comprised of nothing more than matter and motion. In the materialist language of Hobbes, there is no greatest good or final cause, no natural or cosmic teleology to which men might appeal to understand their fundamental ends or purposes. To believe otherwise was to cling to outmoded and false beliefs in spirits, ghosts, and things unseen.[31]

The Enlightenment, according to Bloom, claimed to offer a radical and "useful simplification of the human problem." The problem was no longer framed in terms of discovering the ends and means of human fulfillment or completion, human happiness, or a life lived in accordance with nature or virtue. Rather, the human problem consists in this: in the face of a nature hostile to man, man must seek his own comfortable self-preservation. "Since this is all men really want," Bloom explained, "whatever arrangements help [men] get food, shelter, health, and above all, protection from one another will, if they are properly educated, win their consent and their loyalty."[32]

With this lowering of the aims of political life, Bloom argued, it seemed to Enlightenment thinkers that the real political problem—the biggest threat to man's comfortable self-preservation—was scarcity of resources. Thus, the Baconian, Enlightenment conquest of nature became central to modern political thought. According to Bloom:

> The old commandment that we love our brothers made impossible demands on us, demands against nature, while doing nothing to provide for real needs. What is required is not brotherly love or faith, hope, and charity, but self-interested rational labor. The man who contributes most to relieving human misery is the one who produces the most, and the surest way of getting him to do so is not by exhorting him, but by rewarding him most handsomely to sacrifice present pleasure for the sake of future benefit, or to assure avoidance of pain through the power so gained. From the point of view of man's well-

being and security, what is needed is not men who practice the Christian virtues or those of Aristotle, but rational (capable of calculating their interest) and industrious men.[33]

On Bloom's reading then, Enlightenment thinkers sought to construct a political science that they believed would establish a lower, but more solid ground upon which to build a polity. They sought a political science that "could be used by Founders, *such as in America*, and a natural science that could master nature in order to satisfy men's needs" [emphasis added].[34]

These developments, Bloom asserted, helped lay the ground for American liberal democracy, providing the structure for the "key term of liberal democracy, the most successful and useful political notion of our world: rights." According to Bloom, the idea of natural and inalienable rights is new in modernity, initiated by Hobbes, and given its "greatest respectability" by Locke. And the idea begins from the notion that "man's most cherished passion" is "to live, and to live as painlessly as possible." For Bloom, rights are nothing more than "the fundamental passions, experienced by all men," liberated from (indeed, they are the opposite of) the concerns for justice, virtue, or duty characteristic of ancient and medieval political philosophy. According to Bloom, the Lockean (and American) teaching that all men are endowed with natural and inalienable rights, and that the purpose of government is to secure such rights is really just a way of giving legitimacy to the rule of human passions over human reason, turning Platonic political philosophy on its head. But we should wonder just what this has to do with Bloom's more specific account of the ills of the modern university. According to Bloom, the rights teaching, it turns out, "established the framework and the atmosphere for the modern university." From the right to self-preservation, and the right to be the judge of the means to that preservation, follows the "right to know," the very right that the modern American university holds above all else. The university's place in American democracy is necessarily tied to the philosophic grounds of American democracy.[35]

Thus, on Bloom's reading, if we are looking for the roots of the American preoccupation with utility (especially economic utility) in higher education, that preoccupation seems to be intimately related, and perhaps inseparable from, the first principles of American liberal democracy. For Bloom, all roads in America supposedly lead to the modern idea that individual selfishness, and the desire for material pleasure and comfortable self-preservation, can somehow be made the basis of a sound political order. The modern American university, Bloom suggests, merely follows suit. The ends of the university no longer have any reference to what is highest in man, and as such, the means of higher education increasingly cater merely to the tools necessary to satisfy the desires held by most men, most of the time. The consequences for liberal education should be clear enough. If we are persuaded by Bloom's account, American higher education did not enter an "era of relevance" in recent years; we've been living in that era all along.

CIVIC EDUCATION: FINDING A PLACE FOR LIBERAL EDUCATION IN AN "ERA OF RELEVANCE"

It is surely a matter of ongoing debate as to whether and how the American Founders were somehow complicit in Bloom's version of the decline of liberal education. Many of Bloom's critics have tirelessly argued that he is not so clear in nailing down the Founders' role in the eventual closing of the American mind. At the very least, on Bloom's reading, the Founders appear to have been duped by modern political philosophy and Hobbesian materialism smuggled into American thinking through their embrace of Lockean principles. A regime founded on the basis of rights teachings, Bloom argued, liberates man from all restraint, from all duty, from all but the very basest of his passions, chief among them the fear of violent death and its corresponding right to self-preservation. Surely this is a far cry from the view typical of the Founders themselves, perhaps most succinctly expressed in Hamilton's "The Farmer Refuted." Good and wise men in all ages, Hamilton claimed, have not embraced materialist, Hobbesian principles. Rather, such men have held that "the deity . . . has constituted an eternal and immutable law, which is, indispensably, obligatory upon all mankind, prior to any institution whatsoever." Hamilton suggested:

> Upon this law, depend the natural rights of mankind, the supreme being gave existence to man, together with the means of preserving and beatifying that existence. He endowed him with rational faculties, by the help of which, to discern and pursue such things, as were consistent with his duty and interest, and invested him with an inviolable right to personal liberty, and personal safety.[36]

We might also recall Jefferson's famous statement that the "only firm basis" of a nation's liberties is a conviction in the minds of the people that our liberties are the gift of God.[37] Here we find nothing resembling the notion that, by basing a regime on the principle of natural rights, the Founders somehow sought to release men from all duty, moderation, restraint, or reverence.

The Founders incorporated Lockean principles into a framework based on classical and Judeo-Christian traditions, and they did not read Locke as Strauss, or Bloom, read him, that is, as a closet Hobbesian.[38] As Charles Kesler has said, American political and intellectual history is not merely another chapter in the Strauss-Cropsey *History of Political Philosophy*.[39] This helps us to see one of the differences between Tocqueville and Bloom on the American mind. As Ralph Hancock has suggested, despite Bloom's attempt to take Tocqueville for his guide in understanding the purposes of the modern university, Bloom departs from Tocqueville's account of American Enlightenment. Bloom reads America as wholly the product of the materialist philosophy of the Enlightenment. Yet, as noted above, for Tocqueville, the American preference for practice over theory, and their religious heritage, constrain and temper their Enlightenment heritage. As Hancock suggests, a "lack of taste for pure theory may prevent Americans from reaching the greatest heights of the human soul, but it also saves them from rationalizing the soul away altogether."[40] For Tocqueville, this provides at least some window for openness to liberal education that seems to be lacking in Bloom's version of the American mind.

Many of Bloom's critics have also argued persuasively that in charting the decline of American liberal education in light of the history of political philosophy, he pays little attention to American politics. That is, Bloom does not attach much significance to the political thought, and actions, of prudential statesmen. In doing so, he robs us of the examples they provide, and the principles they sought to put into practice. A serious consideration of statesmanship, as an effort to prudentially apply abstract principles to concrete political circumstances provides an avenue toward American liberal education. But there is little room, and little need, for American civic education in the university for Bloom. For Bloom, America's founding principles and institutions are merely one more obstacle to overcome on the road to the philosophic life and, ultimately, the university is to serve the philosophic life, rather than the lives of citizens.[41]

With Tocqueville, I think it would be in vain to insist that American education should endeavor to cater only to the few philosophically inclined individuals possessing the desire and the ability to pursue Bloom's education for the few. We live in an era of "relevance" and there is no reason to expect that this will somehow change in the near future. However noble or high the first principles of American democracy might be, however much observers like Bloom ignore the things in the American experience worthy of our reflection and reverence, one would be hard pressed to insist that liberal education does not face many of the challenges both Bloom and Tocqueville identify. I do not expect that American institutions of higher education will soon have an overwhelming number of incoming freshmen eagerly seeking a liberal education. Nor do I expect that many state legislatures, boards of trustees, alumni, donors, or interested parents will soon be storming the universities in demand of liberal learning for its own sake. I suspect that the rhetoric of utility, economics, and vocational training will remain among the key marketing tools of American colleges and universities.

But I should also add that the prospects for contemporary liberal education might not be as bad as they appear.[42] American liberal democracy might indeed place burdens upon the possibility of liberal education, but at the same time it might be the modern regime most likely to tolerate the existence of that education. Other participants in this volume will speak on the Founders' understanding of liberal education, and its role in forming the civic virtue necessary to maintain healthy, republican government. One need only glance at Jefferson's plans for the ends and content of the education provided at the University of Virginia or Adams' recommendations for education in Massachusetts to see that the Founders did not neglect or undervalue the idea of liberal education.[43] My purpose here is to suggest that, in many respects, the prospects for American liberal education might reside, at least in part, in American civic education.

The path to a liberal education must ultimately begin from a critical examination of one's unexamined opinions, in one's own time and place. This includes our unexamined opinions about own regime. As Martin Diamond once argued, all of us have a natural inclination to love what is nearest to us and "the natural starting point for learning to love what is just and noble is the love of one's own." According to Diamond, the "ascent from opinion to philosophical knowledge—the final aim of liberal education—should begin with proper reflection on what in one's own is worthy of love. This means an inquiry into what is just and hence truly lovable in one's own country, an inquiry which points the student to the task of perfecting his own regime and, ultimately, the question of what is simply just."[44] And, there might really be something excellent, something noble, something about America worthy of our love. As Hancock suggests, the defense of the Great Books, and the defense of liberal education, *in America* "depends upon the defense of something great in America."[45]

In the study of American political thought, expressed primarily in the rhetoric of American statesmen, we encounter fundamental questions about the nature and purpose of American democracy, questions concerning what American democracy *is* and what it *ought* to be. We come closer to knowledge in weighing the alternative answers to such questions. Consider the fundamental questions of human importance raised by the serious and thoughtful study of the Declaration of Independence, *The Federalist Papers*, the Lincoln-Douglas debates, the writings of Woodrow Wilson, or the speeches of FDR and Martin Luther King, for example. Such questions often point us toward larger questions about human nature, the potentialities and limitations of human wisdom, and the nature and purpose of government as such.

If there is a place for liberal education in our "era of relevance," at least one avenue for that education resides in the study of American ideas and institutions. Such an education points us toward an arguably nobler version of the "utility" of higher education. While civic education might in one sense merely provide citizens with the tools necessary to pursue their interests in

American democracy, it can point far beyond this, revealing to us the choice-worthiness of civic duty and responsibility. Hopefully, such an education points beyond even this, toward the consideration of things true and good everywhere and always. Such an education helps one to begin to examine what it means to be both a citizen, and a human being. It seems to me there are few things higher education can offer that are more "relevant" than this.

NOTES

1. Alexis de Tocqueville, *Democracy in America*, trans. George Lawrence, ed. J. P. Mayer (New York: Harper and Row, 1969); Allan Bloom, *The Closing of the American Mind* (New York: Simon and Schuster, 1987).

2. See John Henry Cardinal Newman, *The Idea of a University: Defined and Illustrated* (1852; reprint, Westminster, MD: Christian Classics, 1973), 99–178; Leo Strauss, "What is Liberal Education," and "Liberal Education and Responsibility," in *Liberalism Ancient and Modern* (Chicago: University of Chicago Press, 1968), 3–8; 9–25.

3. Newman, *Idea of a University*, 152; cf. 101–02; 113–14.

4. Martin Luther King Jr., "The Purpose of Education," *The Maroon Tiger* (January–February, 1947): 10. I am indebted to Professor Gary Glenn of Northern Illinois University for bringing this passage to my attention.

5. It is worth noting that the *Making Place Matter* report, described in the introduction to this volume, was spearheaded by the American Association of State Colleges and Universities and the Alliance for Regional Stewardship. The latter organization is an affiliate of the American Chamber of Commerce Executives. See Kentucky Council on Postsecondary Education Resources Page, Regional Stewardship Overview, accessed April 1, 2012, http://cpe.ky.gov/policies/budget/resources+page.htm; American Chamber of Commerce Executives, Alliance for Regional Stewardship homepage, accessed April 1, 2012, http://www.acce.org/index.php?src=gendocs&ref=ARS&category=ARS&submenu=ARS.

6. While I hope my own account of Tocqueville's analysis of American mental habits and their relationship to American higher education contributes something to the conversation prompted by this volume, I am certainly not the first to tackle this subject. I refer the reader to the following works in particular: William Mathie, "Socrates in America," in *The Idea of the American University*, ed. Bradley C.S. Watson (Lanham, MD: Lexington Books, 2011), 83–95; Gary D. Glenn, "From Civilizational Memory and the Upward Lifting of Souls, to Upward Mobility, to Upending Social Mores: The Going Down of University Education in One Professor's Lifetime," in *The Idea of the American University*, 35–54; John Agresto, "The Liberal Arts Bubble," *Academic Questions* 24 (2011): 392-402; Ralph C. Hancock, "Tocqueville on Liberal Education and American Democracy" in *America, the West, and Liberal Education* (Lanham, MD: Rowman & Littlefield, 1999), 55–68.

7. Tocqueville, *Democracy in America*, 30. See G. W. F. Hegel, *Philosophy of Right*, trans. T. M. Knox (London: Oxford University Press, 1952), 12–13.

8. Tocqueville, *Democracy in America*, 429.

9. Ibid., 432.

10. Ibid., 432, 439.

11. Ibid., 440.

12. Ibid., 444.

13. Ibid., 454–55.

14. Ibid., 455–56.

15. Ibid., 457–58.

16. Ibid., 458, 459–60.

17. Ibid., 460, 461.

18. Ibid., 55.

19. Ibid., 462.

20. Ibid., 463, 464, 465.
21. See Tocqueville, *Democracy in America*, 465–68, 470–75. Against Tocqueville's characterization of American literature, see *Seers and Judges: American Literature as Political Philosophy*, ed. Christine Dunn Henderson (Lanham, MD: Lexington Books, 2002).
22. Tocqueville, *Democracy in America*, 476, 477.
23. Tocqueville, *Democracy in America*, 543.
24. Tocqueville, *Democracy in America*, 544.
25. Gary D. Glenn, "On the Future Possibility of Liberal Education," (invited lecture for Shimer College Fall Lecture Series, Shimer College, Chicago, Illinois, September 24, 2009, 2).
26. See Mathie, "Socrates in America," 87.
27. Bloom, *Closing of the American Mind*, 246.
28. Ibid., 250.
29. Ibid., 254.
30. Ibid., 252, 256.
31. Ibid., 164–65. See Thomas Hobbes, *Leviathan*, ed. Richard Tuck (Cambridge: Cambridge University Press), 9–11, 117–18.
32. Ibid., 164–65, cf. 286–93.
33. Ibid., 165.
34. Ibid., 258, cf. 287–88.
35. Ibid., 165–66.
36. Alexander Hamilton, "The Farmer Refuted," February 23, 1775, in *Selected Writings and Speeches of Alexander Hamilton*, ed. Morton J. Frisch (Washington, DC: AEI Press, 1985), 20.
37. Thomas Jefferson, *Notes on the State of Virginia*, Query XVIII, in *The Portable Thomas Jefferson*, ed. Merrill D. Peterson (New York: Penguin Books, 1975), 215.
38. Thomas G. West, "Allan Bloom and America," in *Essays on the Closing of the American Mind*, ed. Robert L. Stone (Chicago: Chicago Review Press, 1989), 169. See Leo Strauss, *Natural Right and History* (Chicago: University of Chicago Press, 1953), 202–51.
39. Cited in West, "Allan Bloom and America" 171.
40. Hancock, "Tocqueville on Liberal Education," 64.
41. Charles R. Kesler, "The Closing of the Allan Bloom's Mind: An Instant Classic Reconsidered," in *Essays on the Closing of the American Mind*, 179–80. Also see Harry V. Jaffa, "Humanizing Certitudes and Impoverishing Doubts: A Critique of the Closing of the American Mind," in *Essays on the Closing of the American Mind*, 129–57.
42. See Glenn, "On the Future Possibility of Liberal Education," 6–7.
43. See, for example, John Adams, "Thoughts on Government," in *The Political Writings of John Adams*, ed. George A. Peek Jr. (New York: Bobbs-Merrill, 1954), 83–92; Thomas Jefferson, "Report to the Commissioners of the University of Virginia," August 4, 1818, in *The Portable Jefferson*, 332–46.
44. Martin Diamond, "On the Study of Politics in a Liberal Education," in *As Far as Republican Principles Will Admit: Essays by Martin Diamond*, ed. William A. Schambra (Washington, DC: American Enterprise Institute Press, 1992), 278.
45. Hancock, "Tocqueville on Liberal Education," 66.

BIBLIOGRAPHY

Adams, John. "Thoughts on Government." In *The Political Writings of John Adams*, 83–92. Edited by George A. Peek Jr. New York: Bobbs-Merrill, 1954.
American Chamber of Commerce Executives. Alliance for Regional Stewardship (ARS) homepage. Accessed April 1, 2012. http://www.acce.org/index.php?src=gendocs&ref=ARS&category=ARS&submenu=ARS
Agresto, John. "The Liberal Arts Bubble." *Academic Questions* 24 (2011): 392–402.
Bloom, Allan. *The Closing of the American Mind*. New York: Simon and Schuster, 1987.

Diamond, Martin. "On the Study of Politics in a Liberal Education." In *As Far as Republican Principles Will Admit: Essays by Martin Diamond*, 276–84. Edited by William A. Schambra. Washington, DC: American Enterprise Institute Press, 1992.

Glenn, Gary D. "On the Future Possibility of Liberal Education." Invited lecture for Shimer College Fall Lecture Series, Shimer College. Chicago, Illinois, September 24, 2009.

———. "From Civilizational Memory and the Upward Lifting of Souls, to Upward Mobility, to Upending Social Mores: The Going Down of University Education in One Professor's Lifetime." In *The Idea of the American University*. Edited by Bradley C. S. Watson, 35–54. Lanham, MD: Lexington Books, 2011.

Hamilton, Alexander. "The Farmer Refuted." In *Selected Writings and Speeches of Alexander Hamilton*, 19–22. Edited by Morton J. Frisch. Washington, DC: AEI Press, 1985.

Hancock, Ralph C. "Tocqueville on Liberal Education and American Democracy." In *America, the West, and Liberal Education*, 55–68. Lanham, MD: Rowman & Littlefield, 1999.

Hegel, G. W. F. *Philosophy of Right*. Translated by T. M. Knox. London: Oxford University Press, 1952.

Henderson, Christine Dunn, ed. *Seers and Judges: American Literature as Political Philosophy*. Lanham, MD: Lexington Books, 2002.

Hobbes, Thomas. *Leviathan*. Edited by Richard Tuck. Cambridge: Cambridge University Press, 1991.

Jaffa, Harry V. "Humanizing Certitudes and Impoverishing Doubts: A Critique of the Closing of the American Mind." In *Essays on the Closing of the American Mind*, 129–57. Edited by Robert L. Stone. Chicago: Chicago Review Press, 1989.

Jefferson, Thomas. *Notes on the State of Virginia*, Query XVIII. In *The Portable Thomas Jefferson*, 214–15. Edited by Merrill D. Peterson New York: Penguin Books, 1975.

———. "Report to the Commissioners of the University of Virginia." In *The Portable Jefferson*, 332–46. Edited by Merrill D. Peterson. New York: Penguin Books, 1975.

Kentucky Council on Postsecondary Education Resources. Regional Stewardship Overview. Accessed April 1, 2012. http://cpe.ky.gov/policies/budget/resources+page.htm.

Kesler, Charles R. "The Closing of the Allan Bloom's Mind: An Instant Classic Reconsidered." In *Essays on the Closing of the American Mind*, 174–80. Edited by Robert L. Stone. Chicago: Chicago Review Press, 1989.

King Jr., Martin Luther. "The Purpose of Education." *The Maroon Tiger* (January-February, 1947): 10.

Mathie, William. "Socrates in America." In *The Idea of the American University*. Edited by Bradley C. S. Watson, 83–95. Lanham, MD: Lexington Books, 2011.

Newman, Cardinal John Henry. *The Idea of a University: Defined and Illustrated*. 1852; reprint, Westminster, MD: Christian Classics, 1973.

Strauss, Leo. *Natural Right and History*. Chicago: University of Chicago Press, 1953.

———. "What is Liberal Education?" In *Liberalism Ancient and Modern*, 3–8. Chicago: University of Chicago Press, 1968.

———. "Liberal Education and Responsibility." In *Liberalism Ancient and Modern*, 9–25. Chicago: University of Chicago Press, 1968.

Tocqueville, Alexis de. *Democracy in America*. Translated by George Lawrence. Edited by J. P. Mayer. New York: Harper and Row, 1969.

West, Thomas G. "Allan Bloom and America." In *Essays on the Closing of the American Mind*, 166–73. Edited by Robert L. Stone. Chicago: Chicago Review Press, 1989.

Chapter Ten

The Social Relevance of Egoism and Perfectionism

Nietzsche's Education for the Public Good

Mark E. Jonas

Colleges and universities are increasingly expected to be relevant to the communities in which they exist. As the *Alliance for Regional Stewardship*, the *American Association of State Colleges and Universities*, and the *National Center for Higher Education Management Systems* indicate in their report, "Tools and Insights for Universities Called to Regional Stewardship," to be relevant colleges and universities must integrate themselves in their local and regional economies.[1] According to the report colleges and universities must become "regional stewards" who produce and guide community growth and prosperity by helping to develop "knowledge economies," economies that are essential to the twenty-first-century democratic communal life.[2] As regional stewards, colleges and universities must conceive their mission as "working for the public good through education and engagement, thereby improving the lives of people in their communities, their regions and their states."[3] According to the report, the best way for colleges and universities to serve individuals is to serve the public by providing a solid intellectual and practical infrastructure for the community. If college and universities provide such an infrastructure, individuals within the community will have the opportunity to participate in the economic, social, and cultural benefits found therein. The question is whether working for the "public good" is the best way to improve the lives of the people in the community. It seems clear that in a democracy colleges and universities ought to serve communities, but it is not at all clear that the best way to do this is to focus on the public good in the hope the individual good will likewise be met. Colleges and universities would serve the community better if they focused primarily on cultivating individual goods in the hope that the public good will likewise be met. To make my case for this shift in priority, I turn to an unlikely source for political inspiration: Friedrich Nietzsche. Nietzsche offers an alternative conception of education that seemingly does away with concerns for the public good in favor of egoistic individualism and political perfectionism.

Nietzsche's radical individualism and political perfectionism have led most Anglo-American commentators to argue that his educational and political theory is incompatible with the public good. His seeming disdain for the masses and his insistence that education ought to promote the empowerment of the exemplary few at the expense of the many flies in the face of the American tendency to expect educational institutions to serve the welfare of the public. The question I examine in this chapter is whether Nietzsche's philosophy is as irrelevant to the public good as his commentators believe. I argue that it is not, and that, in fact, his ideas support the public good in important ways. Nietzsche believes that a focus on the flourishing of the individual is paradoxically the best way to serve the public good. Nietzsche offers us an alternative conception of how the university might support communities, a conception that may be more attractive to democratic flourishing than the one currently in fashion.

NIETZSCHE'S RECEPTION AMONG ANGLO-AMERICAN EDUCATIONAL AND POLITICAL THEORISTS

The majority of Anglo-American educational theorists argue that while Nietzsche's educational philosophy may be compatible with individual flourishing, it is decidedly incompatible with the flourishing of society. In this sense, Nietzsche's educational ideals may be relevant to the improvement of the individual but are irrelevant to the improvement of the rest of society. Eliyahu Rosenow and James Scott Johnston focus on Nietzsche's radical individualism and his insistence that the individual separate herself from her community and the norms and standards that make up the public good.[4] Kieth Jenkins, James Hillesheim, Aharon Aviram, and Jon Fennell go further, arguing that Nietzsche is not just individualistic but thoroughly elitist, advocating an education system that relegates the common masses to mediocrity, drudgery, and slavery, while empowering the elite few to become their masters.[5]

Nietzsche's reputation does not fare any better among political theorists. Alasdair MacIntyre, John Rawls, Bruce Detwiler, Thomas Hurka, and Leslie Theile, to name a few, argue that Nietzsche's philosophy is antithetical to the development of the public good.[6] Among these, MacIntyre and Theile argue that Nietzsche advocates a radical ethical egoism that rejects any common moral outlook upon which discussions of the public good could be based. Rawls, Detwiler, and Hurka argue that Nietzsche's perfectionism is elitist in that it denies the public good by recommending the unequal distribution of social capital between the few and the many.

The preponderance of individualistic and/or elitist readings among Nietzsche scholars does not mean that there have been no interpretations of Nietzsche's philosophy, which are more sympathetic to the public good. While remaining a minority, several interpreters, argue that Nietzsche's educational and political philosophy—especially in his early and middle works—is less hostile to democracy and the public good than it would seem.[7] These interpreters argue that while Nietzsche's rhetoric often seems at odds with the public good, a closer examination of that rhetoric reveals a different picture. This chapter utilizes a similar strategy by reexamining aspects of Nietzsche's early and middle period that seem to deny the public good—his egoism and perfectionism[8]—and argues that these aspects, far from denying the public good, actually promote it.[9] Nietzsche's philosophy offers a conception of education that is relevant to both the flourishing of individual and of society.

The chapter begins by highlighting Rawls's and MacIntyre's influential interpretations of Nietzsche's work—interpretations that rely exclusively on passages from Nietzsche's early and middle periods—and demonstrates the ways these interpretations miss the import of Nietzsche's egoism and perfectionism. The chapter then explores the central role education plays in Nietzsche's advocacy of his egoism and perfectionism,[10] and argues that while his ideas run counter to the contemporary rhetoric of relevance, they support a conception of relevance that may be more attractive than the contemporary one.

NIETZSCHE'S EGOISM

One of the ways Nietzsche promotes the public good is, paradoxically, to encourage *egoism*. It is Nietzsche's advocacy of egoism that has led MacIntyre and others to misinterpret Nietzsche as radically individualistic.[11] Paraphrasing aphorism 335 of the *The Gay Science*, MacIntyre argues that Nietzsche is an "emotivist" who believes that because modern humanity has lost a proper conception of order of rank, the only morality left which has any validity is that of willful, egoistic self-assertion.[12] According to MacIntyre, Nietzsche's ethical egoism requires that individuals make moral decisions based solely on their own desires, without regard for the impact these decisions will have on others. MacIntyre interprets Nietzsche thus: "If there is nothing to morality but expressions of will, my morality can only be what my will creates. There can be no place for such fictions as natural rights, utility, the greatest happiness for the greatest number. I myself must now bring into existence 'new tables of what is good.'"[13] While MacIntyre is correct that Nietzsche advocates egoism, he is incorrect when he suggests that individuals must therefore ignore the impact these decisions will have on others; on the contrary, Nietzsche insists the egoist must take into account the impact moral decisions will have on others—it is just that the accounting must avoid making moral decisions *solely* for the sake of others, which is what Nietzsche believes modern morality requires.

Nietzsche contrasts obeying the precepts of morality because custom demands it with choosing to act in accordance with a similar set of values because it makes one more powerful and whole. Nietzsche describes the detrimental effects morality, as custom, has on humankind: "The most moral man is he who *sacrifices* the most to custom. . . . Self-overcoming is [therefore] demanded, *not* on account of the useful consequences it may have for the individual, but so that the hegemony of custom, tradition, shall be made evident in spite of the private desires and advantages of the individual" (D, 9).[14] Nietzsche contrasts the detrimental self-overcoming found in the morality of custom with the beneficial self-overcoming found in the egoism of those individuals who obey laws they prescribe to themselves as means of their own advancement and elevation. "Those moralists, on the other hand, who, following the footsteps of Socrates, offer the *individual* a morality of self-control and temperance as a means to his own *advantage*, as his personal key to happiness, *are the exceptions.* . . . [in so doing] they cut themselves off from the community, as immoral men, and are in the profoundest sense evil" (ibid.). The distinction between the motivations behind this set of outwardly similar actions represents the point Nietzsche makes throughout his corpus. The fact that Nietzsche calls the second, beneficial kind of valuations "evil" is instructive. Whenever he refers to himself as an "immoralist" or promotes "immorality" he is *not* promoting anarchy and lawlessness, but only a refusal to "do what is right" *for the sake of custom*. Rather, one should "do what is right" only if it will actually be beneficial for herself and, as we shall see, humanity. However, doing what is beneficial for herself and humanity very often amounts to doing those things which western culture would also be inclined to call "moral."[15] As Nietzsche indicates in a line quoted above, many of the actions that we now do that are called moral should continue to be done, but only because they make us "happier."

Nietzsche's egoism must be qualified in a second way, however. Not only does it often share principles and actions that are also found in the edicts of morality, egoism is *not* purely self-interested. On the contrary, the egoism that Nietzsche seeks to confer benefits on others as well as oneself. This is a misunderstood aspect of Nietzsche's advocacy of egoism.[16] For Nietzsche, the importance of the health of the individual cannot be separated from the health of the community. The community is healthy only as the individual members of the community are healthy. To be healthy is to desire the health of others. Nietzsche asserts that having healthy and powerful community members (D, 449, 554; HH, I, 300;), friends (GS, 14) and even, in his late works, enemies (EH, "Why I am so Wise," 7) is essential to one's own sense of power and well-being. Nietzsche believes that the most powerful and healthy (the most egoistic) always desire power and health in others because (1) power and health are beautiful to behold (and beholding beautiful things makes us powerful through inspiration) and (2) desiring the power of others demonstrates a "spiritualization" of one's will to power. Instead of seeking to exercise our power by the domination of others, we exercise it by *dominating our need to dominate others*. The fully egoistic person never acts out of duty or self-sacrifice but out of a desire for health and power; and the fully egoistic person also desires to increase and support the health and power of his community—including both his friends and enemies. His advocacy of egoism is therefore meant to make the individual maximally healthy, but this occurs only when the community is maximally healthy. In other words, the egoism is valuable to the individual only insofar as it increases the health of the community. In contrast to Christianity, as he sees it, Nietzsche does not believe that humanity will be best served when individuals sacrifice their own happiness and well-being. He believes that humanity at large will be best served only when individuals seek their *own* happiness and well-being.

> It is in this *state of* consecration that one should live. . . . This is *ideal selfishness*: continually to watch over and care for and to keep our souls still, so that our fruitfulness shall *come to a happy fulfillment*! Thus, as intermediaries, we watch over and care for to the *benefit of all*; and the mood in which we live, this mood of pride and gentleness, is a balm which spreads far around us and on restless souls too (D, 554).

For Nietzsche, the egoism is meant for the benefit of the individual, and the "benefit of all."

Importantly, however, for Nietzsche, egoism is not a license to do whatever one wants, to whomever one wants, whenever one wants. On the contrary, Nietzsche's conception of egoism has nothing to do with selfishness as we might conventionally understand it. The egoism that Nietzsche recommends has to do with improving one's *health*, not gratifying one's *desires*. In fact, gratifying one's desires without consulting whether it would be healthful to do so is a sure sign of one's *unhealth*. In Nietzsche's mind, unreflectively gratifying one's desires is as unhealthy to the individual and her community as the "self-sacrifice" is.

The reason Nietzsche despises "self-sacrifice" is that he believes that those who promote it are intentionally sabotaging the moral, physical, intellectual, and spiritual strength of human beings. These individuals need human beings to be weak so that they can feel strong. Nietzsche will later call this nihilistic expression of the will to power: *ressentiment*. "Self-sacrifice" is the moralistic code word that attempts to disguise the real motivation for such concept: *ressentiment*.

The overweening need to exercise power over others in order to make them weak is for Nietzsche one of the highest form of weakness, whether exercised by the priests, or Parsifal, or Cesare Borgia. However, there is another sign of weakness which is important to understand with respect to Nietzsche's egoism. It is the weakness found in individuals who, seeking to feel powerful, attempt to gratify all their desires. Nietzsche asserts: "Be sure you mark the difference: he who wants to acquire the feeling of power resorts to any means and disdains nothing that will nourish it. He who has it, however, has become very fastidious and noble in his tastes; he now finds few things to satisfy him" (D, 348). A sure sign of a person who has power is that she has fastidious and noble tastes in what she does and desires. The actions and desires of the weak on the other hand will be multifarious and greedy. The question then is: what are the few actions and desires that the powerful seek? Interestingly, they are virtues rarely attributed to Nietzsche. Nietzsche calls them his good four: "*Honest* toward ourselves and whoever is a friend to us; *brave* toward the enemy; *magnanimous* toward the defeated; *polite*—always" (D, 556). These are the signs of strength and the kind of egoism Nietzsche is advocating. It is the healthy individuals who behave this way because they are strong enough to recognize the power and nobility of graciousness. They are so over-rich in power that they do not need to prove it by exercising it in the form of dominion over others or in any immediately gratifying form of their desires. Rather, part of what makes them so powerful is that they can overcome their own desire to dominate others by making them weaker and instead be "honest," and "magnanimous," and "polite" toward others, whether friends or enemies.[17]

Being, for instance, magnanimous toward the defeated does imply a type of domination over others. If an individual is defeated then clearly one has a certain power over her. But Nietzsche's emphasis on magnanimity demonstrates the kind of domination he is seeking—it is a domination which elevates. By suggesting that we be magnanimous with the defeated he is articulating a posture of graciousness rather than tyranny—graciousness is a sign of nobility and power, because it never revels in dominion even when that dominion exists. He reinforces this image in an aphorism where he paints a picture of an individual of superior intelligence and experience who offers his insight to others while making them feel as if they discovered the insights themselves. He describes the doctor "of the spirit aiding those whose head is *confused by opinions* without their being really aware of who has aided them! Not desiring to maintain his own opinion or celebrate a victory over them, but to address them in such a way that, after the slightest imperceptible hints or contradictions, they themselves arrive at the truth and go away proud" (D, 449). The fact that the individuals whom the doctor has treated go away proud is a metaphor for Nietzsche's concept of egoism. The doctor himself feels powerful because he has made his patients more powerful than they were. Later in the aphorism Nietzsche suggests that this is both a form of love and a form of selfishness; it is both self-serving and other serving. The doctor's job is to have "crept through the worm holes of errors of every kind, so as to be able to reach many hidden souls on their secret paths! For ever in a kind of love and for ever in a kind of selfishness and self-enjoyment!" (ibid.). The doctor in this metaphor is one who is powerful and even exercises a dominion over others; but it is a dominion that makes others powerful. In other words, the difference between this "doctor of the spirit" and a priest is that the doctor of the spirit augments the individual's power, increasing their knowledge and sense of well-being, while the priest decreases the individuals knowledge and demands the rejection of a sense of well being, thus making the individual weaker.

To summarize, for Nietzsche, egoism is paradoxically the only way to help others. To sacrifice oneself—to become smaller and weaker—will ultimately only make others weaker as well. The only hope to improve others is to choose a lifestyle that increases one's power. But to increase one's power one must not merely do whatever one wants and make others weaker. Rather, it is to develop "self-control and temperance" (D, 9) so that one has the strength to behave with nobility, magnanimity, and generosity, and thereby make others stronger.

NIETZSCHE'S PERFECTIONISM

With Nietzsche's conception of egoism in mind, we are now in a position to examine Nietzsche's *perfectionism*. Examining perfectionism is important because although a proper conception of Nietzsche's concept of egoism addresses the problem of Nietzsche's purported radical individualism, we have yet to repudiate the claim that he is elitist, working against the public good by favoring the advancement of exemplary few while enslaving the mediocre masses.

Rawls and others argue that Nietzsche's philosophy explicitly favors the good of the few over the good of the many.[18] Rawls claims: "The absolute weight Nietzsche sometimes gives the lives of great men such as Socrates and Goethe is unusual. At places he says that mankind must continually strive to produce great individuals. We give value to our lives by working for the good of the highest specimens."[19] To support his interpretation, Rawls offers a passage that is taken from *Schopenhauer as Educator* that he takes to be elitist. "Mankind must work continually to produce individual great human beings—this and nothing else is the task . . . for the question is this: how

can your life, the individual life, retain the highest value, the deepest significance: Only by your living for the good of the rarest and most valuable
specimens."[20] This short passage has been extremely influential in establishing Nietzsche as an *elitist* perfectionist.[21]

What is especially damning is the last line of Rawls's passage above,
where he paraphrases Nietzsche's passage by claiming that the lives of the
masses only gain value by "working for the good of the highest specimens."
As Cavell and Conant have effectively shown the German word *"Exemplare"*
is badly translated as 'specimen.'[22] *Specimen* connotes a biological organism
which has certain physical traits and qualities that are inherent to it. Because
the masses are supposed to live for the "rarest and most valuable specimens,"
the upshot is that the masses are not of the same class of specimens. But if
they are of a different biological makeup from the highest specimens, then
the masses can never achieve the status of the higher; they are fundamentally
different organisms and as such cannot exemplify the traits of the highest
specimens. As Conant states: "If one reads Nietzsche as presenting the great
human being to us as a specimen, then it becomes natural to assume that what
the great human being is a specimen of is a genus to which we do not
belong. . . . Specimens are characterized by their *traits*."[23] Conant then
contrasts this to the English word *exemplar*, which connotes not traits, but a
rare and high excellence which can be developed in other members of the
same genus, even if the development is rare.

> Specimens are characterized by their *traits*; exemplars (in Nietzsche's sense),
> by their *excellence*. One cannot serve as a specimen of a genus unless one
> exhibits traits all (nondeficient) members of the genus possess. But it is the
> whole point of an exemplar (in Nietzsche's sense) that other members of the
> genus do not share its excellence. A specimen exhibits what is essential in
> order to count as a member of a genus. An exemplar exemplifies one way of
> excelling *qua* members of a genus. A specimen is to be compared and
> contrasted with another specimen (that is one with different traits and hence
> belonging to a *different* genus). An exemplar (in Nietzsche's sense) is to be
> contrasted with members of its *own* genus (whom it surpasses in the relevant
> respect).[24]

Conant's point is that the word "specimen" implies an unsurpassable gulf
between the rare and high *Exlemplare* and average individuals; whereas, one
of the essential features of the relationship between an individual and her
exemplar is that it must not contain an unsurpassable gulf (HH, I, 114). The
exemplar is one who is fundamentally related to the individual and who by
virtue of the relation can guide the individual toward her higher self. The
goal of the exemplar is not to function as an impossible *other* who must be
served, but as a higher guide who helps the individual find her own way to
her higher self.

The word "specimens" helped to shape Rawls's interpretation, but the deeper problem stems from the idea that the average individual must find value in their lives only in "working for the good of the highest specimens." On the face of it, this seems like straightforward elitism. But, as Conant is correct to point out, the emphasis in the passage does not lie in working slavishly for the higher individual, doing all that she bids, but rather in *attaching* oneself to a higher individual so that she can lead the individual to become her highest self. Take for example a tennis coach. The coach serves herself in serving the tennis player. Her goal is not to sacrificially give herself in service to the player to promote the players' good alone, but to promote the end of winning tournaments, which is the tennis coach's ultimate personal goal. Achieving this necessitates helping the tennis player achieve her highest self, which may look as if the coach is sacrificially serving the tennis player, when in fact she is ultimately serving both the player and herself. The coach is, in other words, acting egoistically (in Nietzsche's sense) and not sacrificially when coaching the tennis player.

For Nietzsche, the reason that the average individual is supposed to "attach his heart to some great man" (as Nietzsche puts it a few lines after the passage Rawls quotes) is that it is only through these great human beings that the average individual is shown the way to his "higher self." The so-called "living for the good of the rarest and most valuable" is ultimately a living for one's self. As we have seen, Nietzsche believes that to sacrifice one's self for another is the height of stupidity, both for one's self and her culture. Rather, one should act *egoistically*, which, for Nietzsche, is acting only in such a way to increase one's power and the power of others. In living for the good of the highest and rarest, Nietzsche is paradoxically promoting radical egoism. It is only through helping to produce exemplary individuals that we can live for ourselves by increasing our power. As Nietzsche claims: one "profit[s] from a philosopher [exemplar] only insofar as he can be an example" (SE, 136). These higher individuals will help lead us to our own higher selves. Just as an athletic coach lives for his own joy, pleasure and power by "helping" his players to live for theirs, so too does every individual live for the good of herself by living for the good of her exemplars. Rawls's gloss ignores this fundamental aspect of Nietzsche's philosophy.

When Nietzsche claims that "The man who does not wish to belong to the mass needs only to cease taking himself easily; let him follow his conscience, which calls to him: 'Be your self! All that you are now doing, thinking, desiring, is not yourself'" (SE, 127), he is speaking quite literally in his egalitarianism. But in order for a person to "take himself easily" and find his true self, he needs to find an exemplar because it is only through her that he will learn how to maximize his power. In a concise summary of this position Nietzsche claims:

> [The exemplar] teaches us to distinguish between those things that really pro-
> mote human happiness and those that only appear to do so: how neither riches
> nor honours nor erudition can lift the individual out of the profound depression
> he feels at the valuelessness of his existence, and how the striving after these
> valued things acquires meaning only through an exalted and transfiguring
> overall goal: to acquire power so as to aid the evolution of the *physis* and to be
> for a while the corrector of its follies and ineptitudes. At first only for yourself,
> to be sure; but through yourself in the end for everyone (SE, 142).

This passage demonstrates Nietzsche's insistence that the majority is not
precluded from riches, honors, and erudition, as Rawls's interpretation implies. Rather, average individuals *and* the exemplars must learn to transform
the philistine desire for these social goods into meaningful approaches to
developing culture and thereby their own power. As a culture produces more
and more individuals of the higher type, the more each member of the culture
is elevated and can be drawn to the power of their higher and higher selves.

Finally, it is important to note that the distinction between the exceptional
and the average is not biologically determined for Nietzsche. Not only can
average individuals learn to become their highest selves from their exemplars, they may even be potential exemplars themselves. Nietzsche seeks to
demythologize the impassable gulf between the exemplars and the average
individual by focusing on the struggle and hard work exemplars must go
through to attain their exemplary status.

> Do not talk about giftedness, inborn talents! One can name great men of all
> kinds who were very little gifted. They *acquired* greatness, became "geniuses"
> (as we put it), through qualities the lack of which no one who knew what they
> were would boast of: they all possessed that seriousness of the efficient work-
> man which first learns to construct the parts properly before it ventures to
> fashion a great whole (HH, I, 163).

This passage is instructive because it collapses some of the distinction between the geniuses and the masses. Reflecting what he says earlier about the
relationship of the Greeks to their godly exemplars, geniuses are not some
sort of divinely superior or inspired group of people who are simply endowed
with profound gifts.

> The Greeks did not see the Homeric gods as set above them as masters, or
> themselves set beneath the gods as servants, as the Jews did. They saw as it
> were only the reflection of the most successful exemplars of their own caste,
> that is to say an ideal, not an antithesis to their own nature. They felt inter-
> related with them, there existed a mutual interest, a kind of symmetry. Man
> thinks of himself as noble when he bestows upon himself such gods, and
> places himself in a relationship to them such as exists between the lower
> aristocracy and the higher (HH, I, 114).

Exemplars, like average individuals, must work hard to cultivate the talents they have.

The fact that many geniuses must work hard to become what they are does not mean that they are not endowed with very fortunate dispositions, however. Nevertheless, the dispositions that are most important are not found in skills or talents themselves, but in the necessary character trait that allows for the expansive development of their talents: toughness, endurance and energy. Every person has individual skills and abilities that could be developed to an exemplary degree, but only certain individuals have an inborn talent for maximizing their skills and abilities. Nietzsche asserts: "Everyone *possesses inborn talent*, but few possess the degree of inborn and acquired toughness, endurance, and energy actually become a talent, that is to say *become* what he *is*: which means to discharge it in works and action" (HH, I, 263). The notion that we "must become who we are" is clearly evident as is the acknowledgment that every one possesses a higher self, even though becoming that higher self requires a rejection of the laziness and complacency. It is only when individuals overcome their laziness and complacency that the public good can flourish.

NIETZSCHE'S EDUCATION FOR THE PUBLIC GOOD

Nietzsche believes that the only solution to the problem of laziness and complacency is to inculcate strength of character through education. Because few individuals have the inborn toughness and self-mastery to maximize their talents, education must serve the purpose of forming this toughness in them. He argues that "in the case of the individual human being, the task of education is to imbue him with such firmness and certainty he can no longer as a whole be deflected from his path" (HH, I, 224). This applies to all students no matter whether they are average or exemplary. Some find firmness of character easier and some find it more difficult. But Nietzsche claims that they all share in common the fact that each finds "in himself some limitation, of his talent or his moral will, which fills him with melancholy and longing" (SE, 142). This universal longing is meant to function as a cohesive element between members of the student community. Each student must at this stage find an exemplar(s) who can guide them, through self-mastery, which is why they seek the production of the geniuses, artists and saints.

> By coming to this resolve [the young person] places himself within the circle of *culture*; for culture is the child of each individual's self-knowledge and dissatisfaction with himself. Anyone who believes in culture is thereby saying: I see above me something higher and more human than I am; let everyone help me to attain it, as I will help everyone who knows and suffers as I do . . . the

individual has to employ his own wrestling and longing as the alphabet by means of which he can now read off the aspirations of mankind as a whole. But he may not halt even here; from this stage he has to climb up to a higher one . . . that is to say a struggle on behalf of the culture and hostility toward those influences, habits, laws, institutions in which he fails to recognize his goal: which is the production of genius (SE, 162–63).

This passage captures the ever-expanding relationship between the individual and the community. For students to find their highest selves they must help cultivate the exemplars who can guide them to those selves. In so doing, the students play their own part in the creation of culture and the elevation of humankind.

Nietzsche's educational project is meant to initiate the above process by providing students with the necessary training to appreciate and approximate the power of others, and thereby to egoistically maximize their own power. This is accomplished by two broad educational strategies. The first is to train every individual, whether higher or lower, to recognize power in its highest forms (SE, 142; FE, 45). In order to be inspired by, or to become, an exemplar, one must be able to identify and appreciate artistic, intellectual, athletic, and moral genius (to name a few kinds of genius). The second is to train individuals to overcome the weakness of will that prevents them from maximizing their power (SE, 143; D, 195).

It is in this way that Nietzsche's philosophy advances the public good. He is a realist who understands that not all students will achieve the same level of success in their intellectual endeavors. Yet, he insists that every student should be given the opportunity to achieve at their highest potential. This means that every student must be given the same quality of education and should be expected to learn the self-mastery necessary to become higher individuals who all participate in the elevation of culture. In learning self-mastery students can avoid the temptation to resent those rare individuals— the artists, geniuses, and saints—who achieve at more advanced levels. Rather than experiencing *ressentiment*, which decreases one's self-respect and power, the average student will experience joy and inspiration as they behold the beauty of the achievements of others. That inspiration will then cause them to achieve even greater heights for themselves as they strive and strain to produce the highest quality of work in their own lives.

Far from opposing the public good Nietzsche promotes it determinedly. He wants every individual to become egoistic in the sense that they seek to make themselves more powerful. By doing this they will necessarily desire that others be as powerful as possible as well. Nietzsche believes this egoism must be inculcated in school. Students must be taught to be egoistical by training them to discriminate true power from false power. By providing the highest education to every student Nietzsche hopes to maximize power while simultaneously fostering the self-mastery necessary for students to overcome their desire to be equally talented. Each student has her own particular call to promote and expand culture and must egoistically focus on developing their own power while simultaneously receiving inspiration from the powerful expressions of others, thus promoting the public good.

THE FLOURISHING COMMUNITY

The fact that colleges and universities are rethinking their roles in the community is laudable. Too often, higher education institutions washed their hands of community involvement and saw their mission as nothing more than providing disinterested knowledge to their students. Nevertheless, the university's new mission—that is fast becoming dominant—to conceive of itself as an engine that helps drive the local and regional economy needs to be reexamined. It may serve the public by providing opportunities for economic flourishing, but in so doing may prove detrimental to individual cultural flourishing. The flourishing it describes is cached out almost exclusively in economic terms. The dominant conception of community engagement seems to assume that an economically flourishing community will necessarily lead to culturally flourishing community. The logic runs something like this: if a community has money then it will naturally support internal cultural and intellectual projects—opera houses, movie theaters, museums, and arboretums will be built; and if opera houses and the like are built then individuals within the community will have the opportunity to participate in culturally enriching activities; when individuals participate in such activities, the community itself is enriched. On the face of the logic is cogent. Opera houses, museums, arboretums, and the like do require local capital, and local capital requires a strong economy. But the question is whether this translates into a culturally flourishing community. It does not. It may, under favorable conditions, translate into a sub-community of flourishing *individuals*, but something more radical must take place if the entire community is to flourish. For cultural flourishing to happen within an entire community, the university must do more than integrate itself within the local economy; it must provide individuals within the community with an education that promotes individual cultural flourishing.

NOTES

1. Alliance for Regional Stewardship, American Association of State Colleges and Universities, and National Center for Higher Education Management Systems, *Making Place Matter: Tools and Insights for Universities Called to Regional Stewardship*, 2006, accessed on September 15, 2012, http://www.aascu.org/WorkArea/DownloadAsset.aspx?id=5459.

2. Alliance for Regional Stewardship, American Association of State Colleges and Universities, and National Center for Higher Education Management Systems, *Making Place Matter*, 1–2.

3. Alliance for Regional Stewardship, American Association of State Colleges and Universities, and National Center for Higher Education Management Systems, *Making Place Matter*, 1.

4. See Eliyahu Rosenow, "Nietzsche's educational dynamite," *Education Theory* 39, no. 4 (1989): 307–16 and James Scott Johnston, "Nietzsche as educator: A reexamination," *Education Theory* 48, no. 1 (1998): 67–83.

5. See Kieth Jenkins, "The dogma of Nietzsche's Zarathustra," *Educational Theory* 16, no. 2 (1982): 251–54; James Hillesheim, "Suffering and self-cultivation: The case of Nietzsche," *Educational Theory* 36, no. 2 (1986): 171–78; Aharon Aviram, "Nietzsche as educator?" *Journal of Philosophy of Education* 25, no. 2, (1991): 219–34; and Jon Fennell, "Nietzsche contra 'self-reformulation,'" *Studies in Philosophy and Education* 24 (2005): 85–111.

6. Alasdair MacIntyre, *After virtue* (Notre Dame, IN: Notre Dame University Press, 1981); John Rawls, *A Theory of Justice* (Cambridge, MA: Harvard University Press, 1971); Bruce Detweiler, *Nietzsche and the Politics of Aristocratic Radicalism* (Chicago: University of Chicago Press, 1990); Thomas Hurka, "Perfectionism," in *Encyclopedia of Ethics*, ed. Lawrence C. Becker and Charlotte B. Becker (New York: Garland Publishing, 1992); and Leslie Thiele, *Friedrich Nietzsche and the politics of the soul* (Princeton: Princeton University Press, 1990).

7. Jill Hargis, "(Dis)embracing the herd: A look at Nietzsche's shifting views of the people and the individual," *History of Political Thought* 31, no. 3 (2010): 475–507. Beyond Hargis, there are several other interpretations of Nietzsche's work that are sympathetic to democracy and the establishment of the public good. Jeffery Church, "Dreaming and the True Erotic: Nietzsche's Socrates and the Reform of Modern Education," *History of Political Thought* 27 (2006): 685–710; David Owen, *Nietzsche, Politics, and Modernity* (London: Sage Publications, 1995); Mark Warren, *Nietzsche and Political Thought* (Cambridge: Cambridge University Press, 1988); Dana Villa, "Democratizing the Agon," in *Why Nietzsche Still? Reflections on Drama, Culture and Politics* (Berkley: University of California Press, 2000), 224–245; Leslie Sassone, "Philosophy Across the Curriculum: A Democratic Nietzschean Pedagogy," *Educational Theory* 46, no. 4 (1996): 511–24; Charles Bingham, "What Nietzsche Cannot Stand About Education," *Educational Theory* 51, no. 3 (2001): 337–52; Mark Jonas, "A (r)evaluation of Nietzsche's anti-democratic pedagogy: The overman, perspectivism and self-overcoming," *Studies in Philosophy and Education* 28, no. 2 (2009): 153–69.

8. By "perfectionism" I mean the political and moral theory that asserts that some individuals and their ways of life are intrinsically superior to other individuals and their ways of life, and that political, educational, or social institutions ought to be arranged in such a way to maximize the flourishing, first and foremost, of these individuals and their ways of life. For various articulations of this definition of "perfectionism" see (Hurka, "Perfectionism," 946; Rawls, *A Theory of Justice*, 325; and W. Kymlicka, *Liberalism, Community and Culture* (Oxford: Clarendon Press, 1989), 31.

9. I focus only on the early and middle periods of Nietzsche's work because his later work presents complications that, while ultimately consistent with his early and middle works, require too much space to address. This paper is part of a larger project in which I ultimately argue that the ideas in Nietzsche's later period can also be reconciled with the public good.

10. For the sake of convenience, whenever I refer to Nietzsche's ideas in this chapter, I am only referring to Nietzsche in the early and middle period, unless otherwise indicated.

11. MacIntyre, *After Virtue*; Rosenow, "Nietzsche's educational dynamite;" Johnston, "Nietzsche as educator: A reexamination," Thiele, *Friedrich Nietzsche and the Politics of the Soul.*

12. Macintyre, *After Virtue*, 113–14.

13. Macintyre, *After Virtue*, 113–14.

14. References for all of Nietzsche's texts will be abbreviated according to the following: A (*The Antichrist*), D (*Daybreak*), EH (*Ecce Homo*), FE (*On the Future of our Educational Institutions*), GM (*On the Genealogy of Morals*), GS (*The Gay Science*), HH (*Human, all too*

Human), SE (*Schopenhauer as Educator*), TI (*Twilight of the Idols*). References for all passages will use section numbers rather than page numbers with the exception of SE and FE.

15. As Nietzsche asserts: "It goes without saying that I do not deny—unless I am a fool—that many actions called immoral ought to be avoided and resisted, or that many called moral ought to be done and encouraged—but I think the one should be encouraged and the other avoided *for other reasons than hitherto*" (D, 103).

16. Thus, while Mintz, for example, correctly identifies Nietzsche's criticism of morality's attempt to force every individual to "serve society rather his own selfish goals," he fails to appreciate the ambiguity in Nietzsche's concept of egoism. (See A. Mintz, "The disciplined schooling of the free spirit: Educational theory in Nietzsche's middle period," in *Philosophy of Education 2004*, ed. Chris Higgins [Urbana, Illinois: University of Illinois Press, 2004], 163. Accessed March 1, 2012, http://ojs.ed.uiuc.edu/index.php/pes/article/view/1652/386.) For Nietzsche, egoism is not an individual's insistence on serving "his own selfish goals," but rather his insistence on becoming a more powerful and more whole individual, which according to Nietzsche necessarily benefits the whole of culture and the individuals in that culture as well. Thus, the best way to serve society for Nietzsche is not to sacrifice one's self but to elevate one's self so that the entire community can benefit.

17. This is why Nietzsche continues to advocate self-mastery throughout his writings. Self-mastery is the only means by which a human can overcome their spiritually weak tendency to dominate others. For extended discussions this aspect of Nietzsche's conception of self-mastery see Walter Kaufmann, *Nietzsche: Philosopher, Psychologist, Antichrist* (Princeton, NJ: Princeton University Press, 1974); R. J. Hollingdale, *Nietzsche: The Man and His Philosophy* (Cambridge: Cambridge University Press, 1999) and Jonas, "A(r)evaluation of Nietzsche's anti-democratic pedagogy," 53–69.

18. Rawls, *A Theory of Justice*; Hurka, "Perfectionism;" Kymlicka, *Liberalism, Community and Culture;* Detwiler, *Nietzsche and the Politics of Aristocratic Radicalism;* K. Jenkins, "The dogma of Nietzsche's Zarathustra," *Educational Theory* 16, no. 2 (1982): 251–54; and Fennell, "Nietzsche contra "self-reformulation."

19. Rawls, *A Theory of Justice*, 325.

20. Ibid.

21. James Conant, "Nietzsche's perfectionism: A reading of Schopenhauer as educator," in *Nietzsche's Postmoralism: Essays on Nietzsche's Prelude to Philosophy's Future*, ed. Richard Schacht (Cambridge: Cambridge University Press, 2001), 181–239.

22. Stanely Cavell, *Conditions Handsome and Unhandsome*, (Chicago: University of Chicago Press, 1990) and Conant, *Nietzsche's Postmoralism*.

23. Conant, *Nietzsche's Postmoralism*, 194.

24. Ibid.

BIBLIOGRAPHY

Alliance for Regional Stewardship, American Association of State Colleges and Universities, and National Center for Higher Education Management Systems. *Making Place Matter: Tools and Insights for Universities Called to Regional Stewardship*. 2006. Accessed on September 15, 2012. http://www.aascu.org/WorkArea/DownloadAsset.aspx?id=5459.

Aviram, Aharon. "Nietzsche as Educator?" *Journal of Philosophy of Education* 25, no. 2 (1991): 219–34.

Bingham, Charles. "What Friedrich Nietzsche cannot stand about education: Toward a pedagogy of self-reformulation." *Educational Theory* 51, no. 3 (2001): 337–52.

Cavell, Stanley. *Conditions Handsome and Unhandsome*. Chicago: University of Chicago Press, 1990.

Jeffery Church. "Dreaming and the True Erotic: Nietzsche's Socrates and the Reform of Modern Education." *History of Political Thought* 27 (2006): 685–710.

Conant, James. "Nietzsche's perfectionism: A reading of Schopenhauer as educator." In *Nietzsche's Postmoralism: Essays on Nietzsche's Prelude to Philosophy's Future*, edited by Richard Schacht, 181–239. Cambridge: Cambridge University Press, 2001.

Du Bois, W. E. B. *Writings*. Edited by N. Huggins. New York: Library of America Press, 1986.
Detweiler. Bruce, *Nietzsche and the Politics of Aristocratic Radicalism*. Chicago: University of Chicago Press, 1990.
Emerson, Ralph Waldo. *The Portable Emerson*. Edited by C. Bode. New York: Viking Penguin Press, 1981.
Fennell, Jon. "Nietzsche contra "self-reformulation." *Studies in Philosophy and Education* 24 (2005): 85–111.
Hargis, Jill. "(Dis)embracing the herd: A look at Nietzsche's shifting views of the people and the individual." *History of Political Thought* 31, no. 3 (2010): 475–507.
Hillesheim, James. "Suffering and self-cultivation: The case of Nietzsche." *Educational Theory* 36, no. 2 (1986): 171–78.
Hollingdale, R. J. *Nietzsche: The Man and His Philosophy*. Cambridge: Cambridge University Press, 1999.
Hurka, Thomas. "Perfectionism." In *Encyclopedia of Ethics*, edited by Lawrence C. Becker and Charlotte B. Becker. New York: Garland Publishing, 1992.
Jenkins, Kieth. "The dogma of Nietzsche's Zarathustra." *Journal of the Philosophy of Education* 16, no. 2 (1982): 251–54.
Johnston, James Scott. "Nietzsche as educator: A reexamination." *Education Theory* 48, no. 1 (1998): 67–83.
Jonas, Mark and Nakazawa Yoshiaki. "Finding truth in 'lies': Nietzsche's perspectivism and its relation to education." *Journal of Philosophy of Education* 42, no. 2 (2008): 270–85.
Jonas, Mark. "A (r)evaluation of Nietzsche's anti-democratic pedagogy: The overman, perspectivism and self-overcoming." *Studies in Philosophy and Education* 28, no. 2 (2009): 153–69.
Kaufmann, Walter. *Basic Writings of Nietzsche*. New York: The Modern Library, 2000.
Kaufmann, Walter. *Nietzsche: Philosopher, Psychologist, Antichrist*. Princeton, NJ: Princeton University Press, 1974.
Kymlicka, Will. *Liberalism, Community and Culture*. Oxford: Clarendon Press, 1989.
MacIntyre, Alastair. *After Virtue*. Notre Dame, IN: Notre Dame University Press 1981.
Mintz, Avi. "The disciplined schooling of the free spirit: Educational theory in Nietzsche's middle period." In *Philosophy of Education* 2004, edited by Chris Higgins, 163-70. Urbana, Illinois: University of Illinois Press, 2004.
Nietzsche, Friedrich. "Ecce homo." In *The Basic Writings of Nietzsche,* edited by Walter Kaufmann, 657–791. New York: Random House, 2000.
——. "On the genealogy of morals." In *The Basic Writings of Nietzsche,* edited by Walter Kaufmann, 439–599, New York: Random House, 2000.
——. "The antichrist." In *The Portable Nietzsche,* edited by Walter Kaufmann, 565–656. New York: Viking, 1968.
——. "Twilight of the idols." In *The Portable Nietzsche,* edited by Walter Kaufmann, 463–563. New York: Viking, 1968.
——. *Human, all to human*. Translated by R. J. Hollingdale. Cambridge: Cambridge University Press, 1996.
——. "Schopenhauer as educator." In *Untimely Meditations*. Translated by R. J. Hollingdale, 217–194. Cambridge: Cambridge University Press, 1997.
——. *Daybreak*. Translated by R. J. Hollingdale. Cambridge: Cambridge University Press, 1997.
——. *The Gay Science*. Translated J. Nauckhoff. Cambridge: Cambridge University Press, 2001.
——. *On the future of our educational institutions*. South Bend, IN: St. Augustine's Press, 2004.
Owen, David. *Nietzsche, Politics, and Modernity*. London: Sage Publications, 1995.
Rawls, John. *A Theory of Justice*. Cambridge, MA: Harvard University Press, 1971.
Rosenow, Eliyahu. "Nietzsche's educational dynamite." *Educational Theory* 39, no. 4 (1989): 307–16.
Thiele, Leslie. *Friedrich Nietzsche and the Politics of the Soul*. Princeton: Princeton University Press, 1990.

Villa, Dana. "Democratizing the Agon." In *Why Nietzsche Still? Reflections on Drama, Culture and Politics*, 224–245. Berkley: University of California Press, 2000.

Warren, Mark. *Nietzsche and Political Thought*. Cambridge: Cambridge University Press, 1988.

IV

Socio-economic Dimensions of Relevance

Chapter Eleven

Irrelevance is Not an Option

*Higher Education and the American
Socio-economic System*

Stephen Clements

ACADEMIC IDEALISM WITHIN THE CONTEXT
OF AMERICAN SOCIETY

Long has it been fashionable, especially among faculty in the humanities and social sciences, to think of their academic work as somehow beyond the realm of practicality. Such professors may occasionally meet prospective students or their parents and find themselves, willy nilly, discussing job options or career tracks. But as part of their personal and professional narratives, faculty members in traditional arts and sciences disciplines, from history to philosophy, literature, sociology, religion, art, mathematics, and other fields, exult in following their own intellectual interests, in seeking truth (or at least its latest incarnation) within the context of developments in their scholarly fields and without external encumbrances. Some version of this academic ideal, of course, is promoted in virtually every masters and doctoral program in the land, as graduate students are invited to join the quest for knowledge within each discipline. Such optimistic thinking doubtless helps compel many thousands of academically talented young adults to enroll each year in graduate school, even though the academic job prospects for full-time tenure track positions in many fields have been slim for years. But academic organizational imperatives also drive faculty members away from relevance as much as does this scholarly idealism. As faculty members seek publishing opportunities to earn tenure and promotion, they are compelled to identify gaps in the theoretical and research literatures to address in their own work.

Unfortunately, these gaps seldom correspond to the immediate needs in society, or even to the many arenas of policy or practice. Any overt effort by a provost or dean to oblige researchers and teachers to be relevant, moreover, would be perceived by most faculty members as an attempt to distort their efforts, distract their attention, and derail their attempts to make scholarly contributions. For a variety of reasons, therefore, academics typically eschew the notion that they should pursue their work with specific applications in mind.

Indeed, the larger argument about shielding faculty from the need to be relevant is quite compelling, and can be defended on grounds of both epistemology and practice. If academics were not free to roam intellectually, but instead tied to the most urgent (and fundable) needs of government, the professions, private corporations, and social communities, then it is unclear how and when new lines of thought, new theoretical perspectives, new research methodologies, or even new disciplines, might emerge from the highly bounded explorations that would likely take place under the requirement of "relevance." One line of criticism of the modern academy is that the natural sciences have already allied themselves too closely with corporate interests and their funding of research that can be turned into profits.[1] Though many of us are pleased to live in a market-based economy, and to enjoy the fruits of our wealth production system, we also recoil at the notion that academia might ever be organized so as to be the direct handmaiden of AT&T, Merck, ExxonMobil, Google, NBC, a state legislature, or any entity of the U.S. federal government. Beyond the distortions of inquiry that would likely result from such a shift, merely responding to these and other corporate clients would require an entirely new layer of administrative personnel in academia, to help manage and monitor the pursuit of relevance. Faculty members themselves usually have enough on their minds in preparing for classes, grading assignments, participating on committees, and attempting to keep up with scholarship in their field such that vigorously pursuing relevance of their work as external constituents define it is often beyond their time and energy. And given increasing fiscal constraints on academic institutions, it is unclear how an infrastructure for a "vice-president for relevance" would be funded.

As a pertinent aside, we often employ a version of this non-relevance argument in promoting an undergraduate education in the liberal arts, which a great many faculty members in the arts and sciences usually support whether or not they work at an explicitly liberal arts institution. As students are brought into the intellectual life of the disciplines on ivy-draped campuses, rather than directly into the hustle and bustle of a work enviornment or corporate center, we claim they will acquire cognitive capabilities and analytic skills that will enable them to thrive in an array of professional and social settings later in life. Even for those of us who bring current events and contemporary case studies into the classroom, or who send students out for internships, our university programs and activities embody the notion that young adults need a space to gather that is separate from practical affairs, wherein faculty and students together can consider with detachment the claims of theory, research, and practice. Some of us further assert that only a broad education in the humanities, social sciences, natural sciences, and in my institution's case religious studies, prepares students to live as truly autonomous beings, engaged in culture and society but fully capable of recognizing with cognitive rigor their position relative to their own historical and philosophical context. In this framework, we believe, students can best develop competencies necessary to thrive in a post-industrial, knowledge-based society even while pursuing seemingly "irrelevant" academic work.

Readers conversant in the discourse of liberal education will recognize this vision as reflective of Cardinal Newman's perspective on higher education from the nineteenth century, wherein knowledge is to be pursued for its own sake, and all members of the collegiate community are urged to gain knowledge and wisdom without reference to professional or vocational purposes. In terms of my own academic background, I embraced a version of Newman's orientation in my undergraduate days, having disavowed an initial interest in architecture and engineering for a focus on history, philosophy, literature, and classical languages. I then pursued graduate work in classics, and can assure readers that the study of Greek and Roman history, language, mythology, and archaeology lacks relevance to most elements of contemporary American society. As I began working in the policy and political arenas, first in Washington, DC, and later in Chicago and Kentucky, I became convinced that liberal learning should be purposefully linked to relevant preparation for jobs and careers, and not left untethered from the particular concerns of economic and political decision-makers. Having worked for over a decade in undergraduate and graduate education in multiple institutions, and having thought about the uses to which a liberal education can be put in the twenty-first-century economic landscape, I am increasingly convinced that relevance should be a greater part of the DNA of a liberal education than in the past. This personal and professional concern has spurred my involvement in this volume.

What I will argue in the pages that follow is the result of these reflections and experiences. I maintain that while there is significant merit in the contention that university education and scholarship should be pursued without regard to relevance, it is nevertheless politically and functionally hazardous for American universities to embrace such an approach, for a variety of reasons. My first and foremost argument is that academia is too expensive an enterprise in the United States, and has become too much a part of our larger economy, not to be linked to concerns about relevance. Here I am not addressing so much the issue of tuition costs, but rather the overall swath of our

national economic resources devoted to higher education that renders irrelevant, one might say, our yen for irrelevance. To this I add two secondary
arguments. One is that academia is already heavily intertwined with credentialing and certification functions across a range of professions and lines of
work, so it is closely linked to the American economy already and therefore
of necessity "relevant," whether idealistic faculty members wish it to be or
not. This is actually fortuitous, I contend, because university-based credentialing, while relatively inefficient and peripheral to the mission of many
institutions, nevertheless links many members of the workforce with theory,
research, and critical thought that would be ignored if universities handed
this credentialing role to the private sector alone. My final argument is that
higher education in the United States leads the world in part because it was
designed from the ground up to be relevant, to embody and promote the
scientific, agricultural, and mechanical aspirations of the American people.
As Clark Kerr put it some years ago, the American university represents a
new and hybrid institution that cuts a middle path between Newman's undergraduate pursuit of knowledge for its own sake, and the nation's own adapta-
tion of the Berlin model of graduate and research education established in
Prussia in the early nineteenth century. I conclude the chapter with a few
comments on the implications of these three arguments for our thinking
about relevance and the university setting. I have come to believe that all
proponents of liberal learning should keep strongly in mind the unique and
relevant nature of American higher education, and that we should celebrate it
and allow it to animate us, even if we are otherwise tempted to eschew it as a
distraction.

THE COSTS OF HIGHER EDUCATION
AND THE BURDENS OF ACCOUNTABILITY

Throughout much of the nation's history, higher education was a peripheral
activity, affecting only a small percentage of the population. Around 1910,
for example, only about 355,000 students enrolled in the 951 colleges and
universities then in existence,[2] much less than one percent of the U.S. population that year of 92 million.[3] But since World War II, and especially in the
last three decades, the reach of higher education has expanded vastly, and its
costs to the economy have burgeoned as well. In terms of enrollments, in
1949, and bulging with GI Bill participants, just shy of 2.5 million students
were in degree granting programs in the nation's institutions. By 1980 total
enrollment across U.S. higher education had risen to 12 million, and by 2010
the total had risen to 21 million, or about 7 percent of that years' total
American population of 308 million.[4] One significant source of this increase
during this latter three decade era has been adult students over twenty-five

years of age. According to U.S. Department of Education projections, by 2019 about 10 million adults twenty-five or older will be enrolled in postsecondary programs, at a time when the traditional 18–25 year old population sector will only supply about 13.4 million students to academic programs.[5]

As ever greater percentages of students across the age range have chosen to take part in college and university programs, the personal, familial, institutional, state, and national investment of resources has increased. My argument here is about the overall costs to the nation of the higher education enterprise, within the context of the larger economy, not the related issues of rapidly rising tuition costs and increasing student loan debt, though these latter concerns most often makes headlines. The costs to individuals of attending college are indeed an important problem of policy, finance, and social equity. Over roughly the past thirty years, while the consumer price index has increased about 115 percent, the college cost index, made up mostly of the price of tuition and room and board at four-year institutions, has increased by around 400 percent.[6] As a result, full freight costs at the most competitive private institutions are now nearly $55,000 per year. Middle range private institutions in Kentucky, such as Asbury University, Georgetown College, and Campbellsville University, cost from $30,000 to $33,000 per year or so for tuition and room and board—such costs represent heavy burdens on the middle class families that feed them students. And tuition increases at public universities, prompted in part by shrinking state funding, have elevated total annual tuition and board costs at flagship public universities in many states to $20,000 or more. Even costs at community colleges, generally the cheapest and most heavily subsidized campuses, have increased across the country in recent years, as state budgets have been squeezed by increases in pension costs, health care costs, and other budget priorities. Perhaps the best summary of the tuition increase problem is as follows: In 1980–81, average tuition and room and board costs across all four year institutions was $8,672 in constant, 2008–09 dollars. In 2010, that same education cost nearly $21,000, again in constant 2008–09 dollars.[7] In other words, persistently growing numbers of Americans over time have become involved in an activity—postsecondary education—that is becoming ever more expensive.

An issue connected to soaring tuition rates has been the explosion of student loan debt, and it too is an important political concern. Indeed, increasing tuition combined with a federal policy shift in the 1980s away from grants and toward loans have yielded a heavily debt-burdened cadre of students, mostly from lower and middle class families. A recent study revealed that the average student who graduated college in 2010 carried some $25,250 of loans, and of course that is an average, so some students may walk away with $40,000 or $50,000 or more of debt.[8] In all, the total of such debt recently passed $1 trillion, which surpasses outstanding credit card debt in the United States. This is also a critical problem, and when combined with increases in college costs overall should concern us deeply, if for no other reason than for the impact of these costs on social mobility and social inequality in the United States. Given that wage income has stagnated over the past decade or so among adults with the lowest levels of formal education, the relentlessly rising costs of higher education have priced many lower SES students completely out of the college market, or obliged them to enter that market with the expectation of emerging after four years with tens of thousands of dollars worth of debt. This will limit the ability of individuals from the lower and lower-middle strata of our society to move into the middle class, and will burden many middle class children such that they have ever more difficulty competing with their upper class peers, who already bring to the market an array of social capital advantages.

The argument at hand, however, is about the costs of the higher education sector in the aggregate to the economy, not about the impact of these costs on students and théir families. The numbers here are really quite staggering, and help provide a picture of what can be referred to as the higher education industry. Though individual faculty members would doubtless take umbrage at the notion that they are but widgets in a vast economic enterprise, they should bear in mind the level of student engagement in this sector of the economy, and the devotion of resources to that sector. The federal count of postsecondary students in the Fall of 2009 identified some 20.4 million students enrolled across the range of institutions, including community colleges, public and private undergraduate and research universities, and for-profit institutions.[9] As many readers might anticipate, the fastest growth during the past few recessionary years has been in community colleges, the least expensive institutions, and the for-profit colleges, many of which are operating online and across state lines, and are employing marketing techniques that traditional institutions have only just begun to consider.

These 20.4 million students in 2009–10 were spread across some 1,672 public institutions, 1,624 private not-for-profit institutions, and 1,199 private for-profit institutions, which totals just about 4,500 postsecondary institutions. Here is where the numbers begin to add up. These institutions collectively employ some 3.7 million full time faculty, staff, and administrators,[10] and if the network of part-time instructors on the periphery of these institutions were added in the total number of people involved in higher education would be higher still. And in 2010, according to estimates compiled by the U.S. Department of Commerce, these colleges and universities in the United States had operating and capital expenditures of about $461 billion, divided up between public institutions ($299 billion) and private institutions ($172 billion). While $461 billion only represents about 3.2 percent of our nation's $14.4 Trillion GDP for 2010,[11] this still represents a very substantial sector of our economy. Compare the 3.7 million full time employees in academia, for example, to the 2.5 to 3 million employees nationwide who were estimated to involved at all levels in the production of automobiles for America's big-three auto manufacturers around this same year.[12] Higher education's $461 billion for 2010 is less than the $650 billion our nation spent that year on K-12 education in 2010. But the K-12 system includes almost twice as many students as are involved in higher education. In addition, the K-12 education system is more directly dependent upon local and state government funding, whereas the higher education system obtains its fiscal support from a broader array of sources.

A look beyond annual operating expenditures of the 4,500 colleges and universities reveals even more accumulated resources in endowments and campus properties. Most educated citizens know that higher education institutions hold investments across the economy as part of their endowments, and these numbers are worthy of note. In 2009, after the drop in the stock market had bitten deeply into endowment portfolios, university endowments for U.S. academic institutions were still worth an estimated $326 billion (an amount that has presumably bounced back with the stock market). Unfortunately for most institutions, the distribution of these resources across institutions is anything but equitable. Indeed, the five wealthiest institutions of 2009—Harvard, Yale, Princeton, Stanford, and the University of Texas—accounted for $243 billion, or about three-fourths of the total endowment wealth.[13] In addition, lower interest rates and lower return rates on investments in general since 2008 have reduced the revenue many institutions receive from their endowments. This has in turn contributed to the aforementioned tuition cost increase problem, as low return rates on modest endowments oblige institutions to pass on rising costs to customers through hikes in tuition and fees. Finally, the property and buildings belonging to these 4,500 institutions represent many hundreds of billions of dollars of value, although no organization collects data on the property values across the academic landscape into one repository. The College Planning and Management association estimated, for example, that higher education institutions spent about $11 billion in construction expenses in 2010 alone for new and remodeled buildings. But the amount spent annually on new construction and renovation work at 4,500 institutions provides little help in determining overall campus wealth across all U.S. higher education physical facilities. The general point, rather, is simply that American colleges and universities have built themselves into a formidable sector of the economy, especially since World War II.

If higher education accounts for at least $460 billion in annual operating expenses, another $350 billion or so in endowment wealth, and several hundred billion more in campus property values, then this sector should certainly be deemed "relevant" to the U.S. economy by size alone. But exploration of the *sources* of revenue supporting U.S. higher education increases substantially the impact of these numbers. As most higher education watchers know, many of the resources to support the nation's higher education industry come from federal and state coffers—and this accounts for the rising entanglement of government with higher education. Federal support for college students alone has risen from about $35 billion per year in 1995 to an estimated $155 billion for 2011, with that aid provided to some 4.3 million students.[14] The Pell Grant program itself has grown during this period from $5.4 billion in 1995 to $35.8 billion, but the largest increase has come in the form of federal support for loans to students and their families.[15] Another significant source of college and university support comes from federal higher education support provided to veterans, through the GI Bill and various related programs—this represented in 2010 about another $8 billion.[16] Finally, state governments themselves provide considerable resources to underwrite higher education, through direct annual subsidies to state institutions and indirectly to private institutions through state scholarship or supplemental grant programs, such as KEES here in Kentucky and the HOPE scholarship in Georgia. In the 2008–09 academic year, for example, states contributed another $65.5 billion to higher education, and local governments an additional nearly $10 billion.[17]

Totaling all of these numbers reveals, interestingly, that federal, state, and local governments contributed directly or indirectly approximately *half* of the amount of operating revenue consumed by the higher education industry in the United States last year. Much of this revenue takes the form of loan and grant subsidies to students and their families, and another portion involved direct subsidies to state institutions. Given this level of resource commitment by governments at all levels, it should be no surprise that politicians and even average taxpayers are concerned about institutional accountability for these expenditures. The most recent expression of the concern for postsecondary accountability at the federal level came in 2006, with publication of the Spellings Commission report, a Bush administration-appointed task force that called for development of an accountability approach in higher education to ensure that federal, state, and local funds were not being squandered by lazy or unscrupulous institutions.[18] Though higher education has for the moment dodged the bullet of standardized testing requirements ala No Child Left Behind, regional accreditation bodies, operating under the aegis of the Council for Higher Education Accreditation (CHEA), have been brokering the development of new and varied assessment mechanisms at colleges and universities across the land, to enhance institutional accountability. It remains to be seen as to whether this experiment in accountability-through-accreditation will satisfy government authorities that universities are adequately attentive to student learning and institutional performance. Though academics may complain about this level of intrusion into academic affairs, they arguably have little real room to complain—the sheer magnitude of public investment in higher education explains both the demand for greater accountability for results, and also explains why institutions must continue to find ways to be relevant to the economy and society. Put differently, if higher education institutions refuse to play a direct, relevant role in the U.S. economy and society, they could reasonably expect policy makers to respond by redirecting many billions of dollars per year of educational investments by governments elsewhere.

HIGHER EDUCATION AND THE U.S. CREDENTIALING SYSTEM

Another reason why universities are obliged to be relevant is their intricate involvement with most of the professions in the nation. While most Americans think about colleges and universities in terms of undergraduate degree production—and the 4,500 institutions did grant 1.6 million bachelor's degrees and just over 787,000 associate's degrees in 2009[19]—higher education is also responsible for preparing and credentialing a great many of the professionals who play key roles in our economy and our social system. During 2009, for example, American universities awarded some 657,000 masters degrees, and nearly 68,000 doctoral degrees, thus providing post-baccalaureate preparation to individuals destined to serve in many professional and management positions in the economy. In other words, nearly a quarter of the 3,112,000 degrees granted by academic institutions in 2009 were graduate and professional degrees, the vast majority of which were designed for an explicitly vocational or professional purpose within our economy. The largest batch of master's degrees awarded are in education, and American institutions have long provided the training necessary for K-12 teachers, counselors, and administrators. The relationship between K-12 and higher education therefore continues to be co-mingled, even if the two are formally separated in our policy governance approach.

But academia produces far more than elementary and secondary teachers. It produced nearly as many MBAs as education masters degrees. Arguably the nation's dramatic advances in gross domestic product over the last thirty or forty years, plus its involvement in globalized industry since the end of the Cold War, have been greatly facilitated by the growing presence of women and men in the workforce with professional training in finance, management, accounting, logistics, marketing, and the other areas of study offered within business programs. In addition, the fastest growth of master's degrees since 1980 has occurred in the health professions, which makes sense given the explosion of growth in this sector—which now unfortunately consumes 17 percent of our GDP. Academic institutions also continue to produce tens of thousands of credentialed engineers, scientists, statisticians, psychologists, lawyers, social workers, computer scientists, and public administrators, as well as individuals trained in religious vocations and the performing arts. While it is true that some American graduate programs are dominated by foreign students who will take their knowledge and expertise out of the country, as of 2008–09 only about 12 percent of these masters and doctoral degrees are typically awarded to international (or "non-resident alien") students, and some portion of them will end up remaining in the United States. [20]

If a quarter of the graduates every year of the nation's higher education institutions are destined for a broad array of professions, and for refreshing the ranks of academia itself, then arguably this sector of the economy is linked inexorably to the national economy and the broader professional and social systems in ways not perceived by many faculty members. Indeed, inquiry into the history of nearly every profession in the nation, from education to medicine to law to engineering to social work to the ministry, will reveal significant linkages to academic institutions that go back decades or even well over a century. The development of the K-12 teacher workforce offers a first-rate example. One reason for the establishment of high schools in the late nineteenth century was to prepare individuals to teach in the elementary grades—initially the only requirement in most states to teach in a primary school was education at the high school level. As opinion leaders recognized the need for teachers to have college level training, states established "normal schools" in the early twentieth century, essentially community colleges, to provide associate's level education, again primarily to provide K-12 teachers for schools in the regions of the normal schools. When states sought to establish full-fledged university systems in the subsequent decades, they typically did so by transforming normal schools into four-year institutions, and then expanded those institutions after WWII into comprehensive universities. [21] Eventually teachers were obliged to have baccalaureate degrees to teach at the K-12 level, and in most states now a master's degree is either required or simply rewarded as part of the teacher career advancement process. Similarly, the field of educational leadership has blossomed over the past several decades as principals, superintendents, and other school administrators have had their educational needs addressed by academic leadership departments at universities. [22]

Throughout this long development process colleges and universities have been the only entities in society with the credentialed faculty and organizational capacity to take on the increasing requirements of teacher education. Similar developments have taken place in the other professions as well. Hence, most schools of medicine and law, schools of architecture and engineering, and schools of social work and public policy, nearly all of these are attached to universities across the country. The argument here is not that, because most professionals are prepared in universities that such training or credentialing in the United States is perfect or cannot be improved, or that academic institutions are always the best locus for preparation of professionals. In fact, a powerful ongoing critique of professional education today is that academicians with the right credentials have often been out of the front-lines of education or business or law for years (or decades), and therefore not well acquainted with current problems of practice. Rather, the point is that from an organizational capacity and location standpoint, the nation's higher education industry has expanded and developed itself in part as a response to the growing needs of the professions, and their credentialing and on-going professional development demands. If the United States sought to replace the current professional preparation system with something else, the costs to society and the private sector would be staggering, and there is no obvious model at hand for what a different system might look like that would be as effective as the current approach, inefficient as it may be in some ways.

American Universities and their Relationship to the Scientific Enterprise

This chapter has argued so far that U.S. universities must be relevant because much of their operating revenue comes from government sources, and because they are an integral part of credentialing the nation's profession-als. The third and related argument about the relevance of universities is based on a historical feature about the origins of these institutions that many in this nation—and in universities themselves—have forgotten or indeed never knew. Namely, American universities have become the envy of the world today not due to faculty detachment, to their ability to pursue inquiry without regard to relevance, but *because* most such institutions were estab-lished in the late nineteenth century, and then expanded at various points over time, to be explicitly relevant to the practical needs of American soci-ety. It is useful to remind U.S. voters of this history when they lament the use of tax dollars to support higher education, and to remind academics of this when they claim to have no obligation to be relevant or owe nothing to society at large.

Unlike those who promote academic detachment, generations of federal and state lawmakers have sought diligently to build academic institutions across the nation to raise the levels of general, scientific, agricultural, and mechanical knowledge of citizens, and thereby feed economic growth and social infrastructure in even remote parts of the country. Though lawmakers have not been opposed to the open-ended pursuit of knowledge, or to devel-opment of liberally educated individuals, these have not been their primary motivations (even if such views did characterize the antebellum movement to establish liberal arts and theologically connected colleges on the nation's frontiers). But in the post-Civil War era, when industrialization became even more prominent, then the attention of political and corporate leaders clearly turned to the establishment of higher education institutions that would be engines of economic and commercial development, especially by the promo-tion of the sciences.

Versions of this story have been told by many scholars over the years. Perhaps the most famous has been offered by Clark Kerr, the progenitor of the California State University system in 1960, who provided an influential interpretive spin on this topic in the 1960s.[23] Perhaps the most noteworthy recent iteration has come from the University of Kentucky's John Thelin, a nationally recognized historian of higher education.[24] Interestingly, there are books, articles, and dissertations within most disciplines that describe these developments from the perspective of a particular field. In the mid-1970s, for example, the political scientist David Ricci narrated the evolution of my own academic discipline, and situated it within the creation of universities in the United States in the late nineteenth century.[25] Before the Civil War, Ricci notes, some 200 largely sectarian colleges had been founded across the land, primarily to mold the character of students—destined for the ministry or what passed for law or medicine at the time—through discipline and exposure to the classical curriculum. In 1862, Congress passed the Morrill Act, which granted federally owned land to states, which would in turn sell the land to raise funds for the establishment of agricultural and mechanical colleges and universities. In the three decades following the war, as states sought to establish A&M institutions, philanthropists also began establishing new private institutions, such as Johns Hopkins, Cornell, Chicago, and Stanford, all founded to promote graduate education and research (based on a version of the German university model), and dedicated to the scientific enterprise, rather than to shaping the character and theological predispositions of young men. The influence of this new approach to higher education was overwhelming by the dawn of the twentieth century, such that state universities in places like Wisconsin and Michigan were established on this model as well, while older private colleges like Harvard, Yale, and Princeton also adapted themselves into versions of this image. According to Ricci, "Thus universities actually became a more independent force in America than the old colleges because they grew into the leading producers and custodians of scientific knowledge, a new fund of wisdom that was generated mainly in the universities rather than outside, and which was both constantly growing and commonly judged indispensable to the nation's well-being."[26]

The transformation of American higher education that took place over the decades that followed has produced much of the infrastructure in which we operate today. In 1860, for example, some 39 percent of college trustees were clergymen—that number had shrunk to 7 percent by 1930, and of course today most university boards are dominated by business executives, entrepreneurs, civic notables, and policymakers, most of whom are firmly linked to the economy and the social and political order.[27] Expansion of new fields of study and new academic disciplines over time reduced undergraduate exposure to the classical curriculum, and also led to the reorganization of institutions into the current academic department and school/college model within a broader university, and a far cry from the interdisciplinary approach that characterized earlier era colleges. The rise of both the professions and of the middle class in the United States has tracked fairly closely with the growth and expansion of academia, as professions have sought credibility and prestige by grounding themselves in the scientific and systematic studies embodied in American universities, which employ the vast majority of experts across most fields of human endeavor.

But the story here is not simply one of numbers of credentialed professionals sent forth into the nation's increasingly complicated economic landscape, or of business imposing itself on academic institutions through donations or partnerships. As the recent and growing literature on business-university linkages demonstrates, university-based professional education, whether in management, engineering, law, teaching, or medicine, has strongly shaped the culture and practices of the for-profit and non-profit sectors of the economy over the decades, especially during the twentieth century, through systematic instruction of the young men and women who go forth to inhabit these professional fields. In other words, as scholars in the professions developed and systematized new knowledge and skills in these areas, and taught this material to successive generations of students, they helped create and extend the structure of the professions. And in turn, the revolution in industrial management at the dawn of the twentieth century, most frequently associated with Frederic Taylor, prompted higher education institutions themselves to come to be operated along the same managerial lines as their students were learning in their professional preparation programs. Hence, this progression helps explain the evolution within universities of different categories of employees, from administrators—presidents, provosts, vice presidents, deans, and so forth—who make high level management decisions about operations and resource allocation decisions, to faculty, who are primarily concerned with instruction, curriculum, academic programs, and scholarship, to staff, who are engaged in the bureaucratic work of the institution, to graduate students and part-time faculty (these latter persons tend to be the least well remunerated and therefore most exploited members of the organization).

This is essentially the argument laid out by Christopher Newfield in his excellent 2003 volume entitled *Ivy and Industry: Business and the Making of the American University, 1880–1980*. According to Newfield, though instruction in fields such as business management contributed heavily to the organizational practices in the contemporary American economy, the locus of professional education within the broader university umbrella also enabled humanists to have a salutary impact on development of corporate practices, such that solid middle class virtues could be developed across broad swaths of society. For Newfield, humanism in the university, embodied by faculty in the arts and sciences, ". . . provided some of the crucial elements that allowed managerialism to work as a consent-based, ostensibly liberating middle-class ideology. Freedom, concrete personal experience, and the right to self-development were all essential to the humanization of management in a sense that mixed manipulation with genuine progress toward better work for managers."[28] The organization of the university, with its clusters of discipline-based, autonomous faculty experts who provided instruction in their fields to the uninitiated, provides a model of adult life to students. Students educated in this environment, according to Newfield, typically possess ". . . a deep comfort with nondemocratic group life, if not an active belief in it . . . [as well as] a willingness to preserve craft labor ideals while directing them toward market production."[29]

Whatever the merits of Newfield's argument, it is certainly true that scholars of the American academic environment enjoy pointing out the parallels between management structures, personnel evaluation mechanisms, and planning systems in large corporations and those that have been in operation in universities since the early 1900s. One of the most influential higher education books of the 1980s, for example, was George Keller's *Academic Strategy: The Management Revolution in American Higher Education,* essentially a case study of numerous universities that had revitalized themselves during the previous decade or so by adopting strategic planning approaches pioneered earlier in large U.S. corporations. A related line of literature moves even further in showing the strong connections between higher education institutions and private sector businesses. According to *Academic Capitalism and the New Economy: Markets, State, and Higher Education,* by Sheila Slaughter and Gary Roades, for example, universities do not merely adopt management practices adopted first by corporations. Rather, these authors argue that contemporary universities typically employ an array of means to integrate themselves into regional economic systems. Students are not merely treated as consumers of university goods, but are deemed to embody the traits of their alma mater. Students then carry these traits with them into the workplace, and their success in companies helps establish links back to their university. These links in turn enable ideas, personnel, and capital to flow back and forth between institutions and firms that are part of the area or regional economy. Though individual faculty members might fail to apprehend these connections, the literature produced by Slaughter and Roades and others working in this field helps show ". . . the blurring of boundaries among markets, states, and higher education."[30]

From the historical perspective of roughly the past 150 years, then, the creation of the modern American economic and social order—arguably the largest wealth-production system in the history of mankind—has been closely tied to the growth of the nation's higher education system, with its undergraduates produced and fed into an ever-growing array of graduate, research, and professional enterprises. Hence, the nation's ability to produce food on a vast scale, and feed Americans cheaply and sell surplus food products around the world, is due to university-educated—and in many cases university-based—scientists and engineers working closely with farmers and agribusiness personnel. The development of modern medicine, with its ability to conquer diseases and extend life, grew out of university-based medical schools and research centers. The amelioration of social problems, from housing shortages to transportation difficulties to learning disabilities, have often been driven by the interplay between academics studying these issues and government and private sector workers who are seeking regularly to resolve such problems. Similarly, the stories of technological developments associated with the allied victory in World War II, the race to the moon in the 1960s, and the computer revolution of the last few decades have all been driven by American universities. From this perspective, then, American universities have not only been relevant, but have been key drivers of development of the American colossus, to invoke historian Niall Ferguson's recent description of our global empire.

FINAL REFLECTIONS ON RELEVANCE AND THE POLITICS OF HIGHER EDUCATION IN THE UNITED STATES

The argument of this chapter has been one offered from a macro level, and has been based on fiscal, policy, historical, functional, and even institutional considerations. The foremost point here, to reiterate, is that higher education has grown over the last 150 years into a vast industry, with roughly 4,500 public and private institutions spending nearly a half trillion dollars per year on operating costs and capital investments, with many additional hundreds of billions of dollars included in endowments and institutional properties, millions of employees, and tens of millions of students. Significantly, nearly half of operating expenditures of the industry come from federal, state, and local sources, and these resources inextricably oblige higher education to seek relevance to the economy and social order. In addition, colleges and universities are critically involved with the production and credentialing of professionals and experts, whose knowledge and skills both undergirds our economic system and drives much of the entrepreneurship our economic growth depends upon. Indeed, the modern American nation-state has grown and expanded over the past century and a half in concert with the founding and proliferation of the research university model, with its natural and social science units, engineering schools, agricultural schools, extension units, law schools, medical research schools, business schools, social work units, and so forth providing knowledge and operating acumen to our economic and social order via graduates and credentialed specialists embedded in firms and organizations. Universities have thus been the quintessentially "relevant" institutions in our national life, both driving change and improvement in society, and in turn being modified themselves by economic, social, and political forces.

An extension of this argument would be as follows. If universities' attempt to define themselves is "irrelevant" to the economy and society, they will risk alienating taxpayers, philanthropists, corporate supporters, and parents—and this could have catastrophic results for academicians of all stripes. How might this play itself out? First, if universities were no longer perceived as making positive contributions to society, then policymakers would likely move to truncate the public investment in these institutions, or would increase dramatically the accountability and outcome requirements for institutions, or would pursue some combination of these two things simultaneously. Given the precarious fiscal condition of many institutions, curtailment of student grant and loan support would lead to the shuttering of a great many private, and even some public institutions. Similarly, greatly increased accountability requirements would turn higher education into a regimented environment that would squelch creativity and innovation.

In addition, a flight from relevance would also prompt the broader American marketplace to punish these institutions for such moves. Arguably corporate and philanthropic dollars find their way to support colleges and universities not primarily for industrial or scientific results, or simply out of altruistic motives, but because donors and corporate partners believe that these institutions not only make important contributions to learning and character of individuals, but also because they contribute both directly and indirectly to the stock of social and economic capital across the nation. This is especially important with regard to the credentialing and knowledge- and cultural-diffusion role colleges and universities play everywhere, and especially in the rural parts of the nation. It is also important with regard to the theoretical and historical consciousness that universities can bring to the professions and indeed all citizens. Hence, the decline of support for colleges and universities would have particularly baleful effects outside of the metropolitan areas of the nation. Though faculty can argue about just what relevance looks like in a modern university, they should keep in mind how politically harmful it could be to universities if they sought to redefine their role away from relevance.

Though this chapter has connected universities and the nation's economy and society in fiscal, practical, and historical terms, a final caveat is in order with regard to the future. Many prognosticators are arguing that higher education is an industry ripe for disruption, as the combination of broadly available distance learning technologies, possible diminution of federal and state funding, and cultural shifts away from borrowing money for students to study in residential undergraduate and graduate settings drives students away from traditional, campus-based university involvement.[31] If there is indeed a higher education bubble that bursts, the resulting financially and technologically induced chaos could oblige a redefinition of university operations and "relevance" that could take these institutions in a direction not anticipated by what has transpired over the previous 150 years. Such a shift might induce every faculty member at every higher education institution to reconsider the nature of his or her participation in the knowledge production industry.

NOTES

1. See, for example, Jennifer Washburn, *University Inc.: The Corporate Corruption of American Higher Education* (New York: Basic Books, 2006), or Daniel S. Greenberg, *Science for Sale: The Perils, Rewards, and Delusions of Campus Capitalism* (Chicago: The University of Chicago Press, 2007).

2. U.S. Department of Education. Institute of Education Sciences, National Center for Education Statistics, 2011, Table 197, accessed February 13, 2013, http://nces.ed.gov/programs/digest/2011menu_tables.asp.

3. The 2012 Statistical Abstract, Historical Statistics, U.S. Census Bureau, Table HS-1 Population 1900 to 2002, accessed February 12, 2013 http://www.census.gov/statab/hist/HS-01.pdf.

4. U.S. Department of Education. Institute of Education Sciences, National Center for Education Statistics, 2010, Table 198, accessed April 7, 2013, http://nces.ed.gov/programs/digest/d10/tables/dt10_198.asp.

5. Ibid., Figure 14: "Enrollment in Degree Granting Institutions, by Age: Fall 1970 through Fall 2019," accessed April 7, 2013, http://nces.ed.gov/programs/digest/d10/tables/dt10_199.asp.

6. Timothy McMahon, "College Tuition and Fees vs. Overall Inflation," analysis prepared for http://www.inflationdata.com, 2011, accessed February 1, 2013. For a slightly different set of cost increase comparisons that is less up to date, see Patrick Callen, *Measuring Up 2006: The National Report Card on Higher Education*, accessed February 1, 2013, http://www.highereducation.org/reports/reports_center_2006.shtml.

7. U.S. Department of Education. Institute of Education Sciences, National Center for Education Statistics, "Fast Facts: Tuition Costs of Colleges and Universities." Source cited is the "Digest of Education Statistics," 2010 (NCES 2011-015), chapter 3, accessed February 13, 2013, http://nces.ed.gov/programs/digest/d10/ch_3.asp.

8. Tamar Lewin, "College Graduates' Debt Burden Grew, Yet Again, in 2010," *New York Times*, November 2, 2011, accessed February 13, 2013, http://www.nytimes.com/2011/11/03/education/average-student-loan-debt-grew-by-5-percent-in-2010.html?ref=tamarlewin&_r=0.

9. U.S. Census Bureau, Statistical Abstract of the U.S., 2012, "Table 278—Higher Education: Institutions and Enrollment, 1980–2009." This count does not include students in less-than-two-year institutions. Accessed April 7, 2013, http://www.census.gov/compendia/statab/2012/tables/12s0278.pdf.

10. U.S. Census Bureau, Statistical Abstract of the U.S., 2012, "Table 296—Employees in Higher Education Institutions by Sex and Occupation: 1995-2009," accessed April 7, 2013," http://www.census.gov/compendia/statab/2012/tables/12s0296.pdf.

11. World Development Indicators Database, World Bank, 1 July 2012, accessed February, 13, 2013, http://data.worldbank.org/indicator/NY.GDP.MKTP.CD.

12. According to an auto industry source, the "big three" auto companies plus the international producers employed just over 900,000 individuals directly in 2009, and a "full contraction" of the auto industry could result in an estimated job losses of 2.5 to 3.0 million. Sean P. McAlinden, Debra Maranger Menk, and Adam Cooper, "CAR Research Memorandum: The Impact on the U.S. Economy of Successful versus Unsuccessful Automaker Bankruptcies," *Center for Automotive Research*, May 26, 2009, 1.

13. U.S. Department of Education. Institute of Education Sciences, National Center for Education Statistics, "Fast Facts: Tuition Costs of Colleges and Universities," chapter 3, accessed February 13, 2013, http://nces.ed.gov/programs/digest/d10/ch_3.asp.

14. U.S. Census Bureau, Statistical Abstract of the U.S.: 2012, "Table 291—Federal Student Financial Assistance: 1995–2011," accessed April 7, 2013, http://www.census.gov/compendia/statab/2012/tables/12s0291.pdf.

15. Ibid.

16. U.S. Department of Education, National Center for Education Statistics, Digest of Education Statistics 2011, Table 382, "Federal on-budget funds for education, by level/educational purpose, agency, and program: Selected fiscal years, 1970–2010," 556, accessed April 7, 2013, http://nces.ed.gov/pubs2012/2012001.pdf.

17. U.S. Department of Education, National Center for Education Statistics, Digest of Education Statistics, 2011. Table 369, "Appropriations from state and local governments for public degree-granting institutions, by state or jurisdiction: Selected years, 1990–91 through 2009-10," 523, accessed April 7, 2013, http://nces.ed.gov/pubs2012/2012001.pdf.

18. The official title was *A Test of Leadership: Charting the Future of U.S. Higher Education.* A report of the commission appointed by U.S. Secretary of Education Margaret Spellings, September 2006, accessed February 13, 2013, http://www2.ed.gov/about/bdscomm/list/hiedfuture/reports/pre-pub-report.pdf

19. U.S. Census Bureau, Statistical Abstract of the U.S.: 2012, "Table 301: Degrees and Awards Earned Below Bachelor's by Field: 2009," accessed April 7, 2013, http://www.census.gov/compendia/statab/2012/tables/12s0301.pdf, and, "Table 302: Bachelor's Degrees Earned by Field: 1980 to 2009," accessed April 7, 2013, http://www.census.gov/compendia/statab/2012/tables/12s0301.pdf.

20. These percentages are calculated from data in these two tables: http://nces.ed.gov/das/library/tables_listings/showTable2005.asp?popup=true&tableID=7186&rt=p and http://nces.ed.gov/das/library/tables_listings/showTable2005.asp?popup=true&tableID=7189&rt=p, accessed April 10, 2013.

21. For two superb historical overviews, see Jurgen Herbst, *And Sadly Teach: Teacher Education and Professionalization in American Culture* (Madison, WI: University of Wisconsin Press, 1991), and Gerald Grant and Christine Murray, *Teaching in America: The Slow Revolution* (Cambridge, MA: Harvard University Press, 2002).

22. For a discussion of the challenges of the graduate education of teachers, see Geraldine Clifford and James Guthrie, *Ed School: A Brief for Professional Education* (Chicago: The University of Chicago Press, 1990).

23. Clark Kerr, *The Uses of the University* (Cambridge, MA: Harvard University Press, 1995). Originally offered as the Godkin lectures in 1963 and published later that year, this volume has been published under versions copyrighted in 1972, 1982, and 1995.

24. John R. Thelin, *A History of American Higher Education* (Baltimore: The Johns Hopkins University Press, second edition, 2011).

25. David Ricci, *The Tragedy of Political Science: Politics, Scholarship and Democracy* (New Haven: Yale University Press, 1987).

26. Ricci, *The Tragedy of Political Science*, 36.

27. Ibid., 38.

28. Christopher Newfield, *Ivy and Industry: Business and the Making of the American University, 1880–1980* (Durham: Duke University Press, 2004), 219.

29. Newfield, *Ivy and Industry*, 219.

30. Sheila Slaughter and Gary Rhoades, *Academic Capitalism and the New Economy: Markets, State, and Higher Education* (Baltimore: The Johns Hopkins University Press, 2009), 11.

31. See for example Clayton Christenson, *The Innovative University* (San Francisco: Jossey-Bass, 2011) and Glenn H. Reynolds, *The Higher Education Bubble* (Jackson, TN: Encounter Books, 2012).

BIBLIOGRAPHY

Callen, Patrick. *Measuring Up 2006: The National Report Card on Higher Education*. Accessed by February 1, 2013, http://www.highereducation.org/reports/reports_center_2006.shtml.

Christenson, Clayton. *The Innovative University*. San Francisco: Jossey-Bass, 2011.

Clifford, Geraldine and James Guthrie. *Ed School: A Brief for Professional Education*. Chicago: The University of Chicago Press, 1990.

Grant, Gerald and Christine Murray. *Teaching in America: The Slow Revolution*. Cambridge, MA: Harvard University Press, 2002.

Greenberg, Daniel S. *Science for Sale: The Perils, Rewards, and Delusions of Campus Capitalism*. Chicago: The University of Chicago Press, 2007.

Herbst, Jurgen. *And Sadly Teach: Teacher Education and Professionalization in American Culture*. Madison, WI: University of Wisconsin Press, 1991.

Kerr, Clark. *The Uses of the University*. Cambridge, MA: Harvard University Press, 1995.

Lewin, Tamar. "College Graduates' Debt Burden Grew, Yet Again, in 2010." *New York Times*, November 2, 2011. Accessed February 13, 2013, http://www.nytimes.com/2011/11/03/education/average-student-loan-debt-grew-by-5-percent-in-2010.html?ref=tamar lewin&_r=0.

McAlinden, Sean P., Debra Maranger Menk, and Adam Cooper. "CAR Research Memorandum: The Impact on the U.S. Economy of Successful versus Unsuccessful Automaker Bankruptcies." *Center for Automotive Research*, May 26, 2009.

McMahon, Timothy. "College Tuition and Fees vs. Overall Inflation." Accessed February 13, 2013, http://www.inflationdata.com, 2011.

Newfield, Christopher. *Ivy and Industry: Business and the Making of the American University, 1880–1980*. Durham: Duke University Press, 2004.

Reynolds, Glenn H. *The Higher Education Bubble*. Jackson, TN: Encounter Books, 2012.

Ricci, David. *The Tragedy of Political Science: Politics, Scholarship and Democracy*. New Haven: Yale University Press, 1987.

Slaughter, Shelia and Gary Rhoades. *Academic Capitalism and the New Economy: Markets, State, and Higher Education*. Baltimore: The Johns Hopkins University Press, 2009.

Spellings, Margaret. *A Test of Leadership: Charting the Future of U.S. Higher Education*, September 2006. Accessed February 13, 2013, http://www2.ed.gov/about/bdscomm/list/hiedfuture/reports/pre-pub-report.pdf.

Statistical Abstract, Historical Statistics, U.S. Census Bureau, 2012, Table HS-1 Population 1900 to 2002. Accessed April 10, 2013, http://www.census.gov/statab/hist/HS-01.pdf.

Thelin, John R. *A History of American Higher Education*. Baltimore: The Johns Hopkins University Press, second edition, 2011.

U.S. Census Bureau. Statistical Abstract of the U.S.: 2012. "Table 278—Higher Education: Institutions and Enrollment, 1980–2009." This count does not include students in less-than-two-year institutions. Accessed April 7, 2013, http://www.census.gov/compendia/statab/2012/tables/12s0278.pdf.

——. Statistical Abstract of the U.S.: 2012. "Table 291—Federal Student Financial Assistance: 1995–2011." Accessed April 7, 2013, http://www.census.gov/compendia/statab/2012/tables/12s0291.pdf.

——. Statistical Abstract of the U.S.: 2012. "Table 302: Bachelor's Degrees Earned by Field: 1980 to 2009." Accessed April 7, 2013, http://www.census.gov/compendia/statab/2012/tables/12s0301.pdf.

——. Statistical Abstract of the U.S.: 2012 "Table 301: Degrees and Awards Earned Below Bachelor's by Field: 2009." Accessed April 7, 2013, http://www.census.gov/compendia/statab/2012/tables/12s0301.pdf.

U.S. Department of Education. Institute of Education Sciences. National Center for Education Statistics, 2011. "Table 197." Accessed February 13, 2013, http://nces.ed.gov/programs/digest/2011menu_tables.asp.

——. Institute of Education Sciences. National Center for Education Statistics, 2010. "Table 198." Accessed February 13, 2013, http://nces.ed.gov/programs/digest/2010menu_tables. asp.

——. Institute of Education Sciences. National Center for Education Statistics, 2010. "Enrollment in Degree Granting Institutions, by Age: Fall 1970 through Fall 2019." Accessed April 7, 2013, http://nces.ed.gov/programs/digest/d10/tables/dt10_199.asp.

——. Institute of Education Sciences. National Center for Education Statistics. "Fast Facts: Tuition Costs of Colleges and Universities, chapter 3." Accessed February 13, 2013, http:// nces.ed.gov/programs/digest/d10/ch_3.asp.

——. National Center for Education Statistics. Digest of Education Statistics, Table 382. "Federal on-budget funds for education, by level/educational purpose, agency, and program: Selected fiscal years, 1970-2010," 556. Accessed April 7, 2013, http://nces.ed.gov/ pubs2012/2012001.pdf.

——. National Center for Education Statistics. Digest of Education Statistics, 2010, Table 365. "Appropriations from state and local governments for public degree-granting institutions, by state or jurisdiction: Selected years, 1990–91 through 2008–09." Accessed April 7, 2013, http://nces.ed.gov/programs/digest/d10/tables/dt10_365.asp.

——. National Center for Education Statistics. The Condition of Education, 2011 (NCES 2011-033, Indicator 26). Accessed April 7, 2013, http://www.edpubs.gov/document/ ed005214p.pdf?ck=1.

Washburn, Jennifer. *University Inc.: The Corporate Corruption of American Higher Education.* New York: Basic Books, 2006.

World Development Indicators Database. World Bank, July 1, 2012. Accessed February, 13, 2013, http://data.worldbank.org/indicator/NY.GDP.MKTP.CD.

Chapter Twelve

Institutional Diversity and the Future of American Higher Education

Reconsidering the Vision of David Riesman

Wilfred M. McClay

No one doubts that higher education is in for great changes and much upheaval in the short term. The model of a four-year residential college or university is itself under serious assault, as too expensive, too ineffective, and too inefficient, with dubious relevance to the needs of twenty-first-century students and a twenty-first-century economy. The digital revolution offers the prospect of a far cheaper and far more flexible system of education, one that addresses the most immediate and urgent needs of individuals and communities in a fluid, twenty-first-century economy. Its enthusiasts predict that the old-fashioned residential college is fast on its way to joining the dinosaurs. Those who defend the older model, however, remain convinced of its enduring relevance, and recur, understandably, to an older idea of liberal education as a *formative* influence in the lives of our young people, an idea that requires the physical proximity of teachers, classrooms, and other students to be realized. The frenetic pace of change in the external world may be precisely an argument for stability and permanence in the world of education.

It all depends, in the end, on what one means by "relevance," and how one applies that meaning to the operations of educational institutions. Clearly "relevance" cannot be taken to refer only to the transmission of information and skills that translate into immediate uses. Education is also about a process of enculturation, a preparation and an entrée for students into the larger world of human culture and endeavor. That is in part what we mean by the word "formation." But what kind of culture are we talking about? If we really want to be serious about rededicating ourselves to the proper intellectual and moral formation of our young people, we will need to have the right kind of *ideas* about what it is we are doing in higher education, and why. This change will not likely occur as the result of a happy series of spontaneous events.

What I have just said would seem to be resoundingly obvious. And yet it goes against the grain of our era, an era in which ideas are like pennies— ubiquitous and steeply devalued. We are increasingly drawn to our own version of "muddling through," precisely because we increasingly view reasoning from intellectual or moral principles with grave suspicion, if not outright hostility, as a form of dogmatism or undemocratic confinement.

One sees this with especial clarity in today's institutions of higher education, in which the *formative* dimension of college education has been almost completely abandoned, as unacceptably prescriptive and otherwise unworkable. The American college "experience" is now an extended *Wanderjahre* of social and sexual experimentation, mingled with a program of inculcation into approved tastes and enlightened attitudes—all of it serving little purpose beyond certifying middle-class status at the end of the road. Given the overwhelming force of consumerism in higher education, even the most selective colleges have succumbed to lax standards and grade inflation.

So college has become a middle-class American rite of passage, an enculturation in a very peculiar transitional culture. But it is unclear where the passage is meant to lead. Given the extent to which the lives of sober middle-class American families are focused upon the end of getting their kids into and through the right college, and paying the bills for it all, the incongruity and wasted opportunity of it all is staggering. And the bill is starting to come due, a process that probably will intensify in the years to come, with unprecedented consequences for colleges and universities.

I do not mean to be overly negative. Good things can and do happen to young people in college. But it seems undeniable that we have lost any clear and widely agreed-upon institutional idea of why we are doing all this. Anyone who has sat, as I have, on academic committees deliberating about broad institutional objectives or the formulation of "mission statements" knows that there is no wizard behind the curtain in American higher education. Sometimes it is reasonable to wonder whether there is anyone there at all, only the endless play of vested or prospective interests.

In short, we need to face facts about the indifferent capacity of our colleges and universities to serve as effective shapers of the minds and morals of the young. If we are looking to our present institutions of higher education to do that job, we are, at least at the moment, simply looking in the wrong place. The proper moral formation—or reformation—of undergraduates will not occur by chance, or by unspecific calls for "decency" and "diversity" and "inclusion" and "sensitivity" and "compassion," especially if these are all presented in free-floating form, without being grounded in a normative structure of ideas, including cogent ideas about the institution's reason for being, and its ultimate ends.

And our institutions are currently unable to achieve such groundings: partly because they must seek to please their consumers, partly because they are institutionally unable to marshal their resources, and partly—and perhaps most importantly of all—because our society, and particularly the college-educated portion of it, lacks the intellectual and moral consensus needed to support leaders who are willing to make hard choices.

Consider that most elusive of shibboleths: "diversity." How can one be opposed to "diversity" per se? It is hard even to imagine what that would mean. But one wants to ask: Whose diversity? And for what? To answer that question seriously, one would have to give serious thought to the proper ends of higher education, and the kinds of diversity that would best promote those ends. One would think, for example, that *intellectual* diversity—a wide diversity of ideas and perspectives on contested issues of politics, society, and culture—would be first among these forms of diversity. But that, of course, is almost never what is meant by the term.

Clearly, too, there are other limits to the diversity that academic environments are willing to tolerate. A vivid illustration was the 1997 case of four Orthodox Jewish students who unsuccessfully challenged Yale University's policy of requiring freshmen and sophomores to live in one of Yale's twelve residential colleges.[1] The Jewish students had argued that Yale's policy infringed upon their religiously grounded commitment to sexual modesty, by forcing students to live in a "sexually permissive atmosphere" in which men and women live in close quarters with one another, often even sharing bathrooms. These students argued, bluntly, that the university's policy "makes housing effectively unavailable to Orthodox Jews." The United States Second Circuit Court of Appeals ruled in 1998 against the students, upholding a District Court ruling and fully accepting Yale's contention that the residential college system is "an integral part of a Yale education," and that if the students did not agree with Yale's policy, they could attend college elsewhere.[2] The U.S. Supreme Court tacitly upheld the Second Circuit decision by declining to hear an appeal.

So Yale won and the Orthodox students lost. Possibly that was as it should be, although the negative implications of Yale's actions for the religious liberty of the students are perhaps more clear to us today than they were in the late 1990s. But Yale is a private institution, and as will soon become clear, I am all for the preservation of institutional autonomy in our colleges and universities, and prefer not to have courts mucking about in their affairs. As a private institution, Yale has a right to adopt policies that others may regard as misguided. But it's also important to look at some of the facts here. It should be noted, for example, that the four students in question never did in fact live on campus. Yale requires only that freshmen and sophomores under the age of twenty-one must *pay* for their on-campus housing, not that they actually *live* in the rooms for which they were paying. The latter requirement is one that the university chooses not to enforce or even monitor. So what actually happened, then, was that the four Jewish students lived off campus, but continued to pay the university almost $7,000 a year for their vacant rooms. One can only conclude that the *truly* "integral part of a Yale education" involved here was the willingness to cough up the fees for room and board. This casts a somewhat smokier light on the university's claim to be an institution passionately committed to the formation of its students. Though I daresay that the students learned a lesson of sorts from it all.

So even the loudest partisans of diversity often turn out, on further examination, not to be very diverse at all in certain respects. How surprising! And how strange that a university that would not dream of failing to observe a Jewish holiday, or of failing to enjoin its faculty not to schedule examinations on such days, could not somehow find a way to accommodate four students committed to their ancient faith. What better way to make a genuine contribution to the university's intellectual and moral diversity?

But the students' commitment trumped by the post-1960s commitment to the forced blending of the sexes in residential as well as academic life, with all the consequent commitment to therapeutic dogmas of "openness" and "tolerance" that such impositions necessitate.

That the university's commitment to these ideals is half-hearted and largely unacknowledged is conveyed by its willingness to let the four students stay off campus—though even that choice could be interpreted as an expression of the university's unwillingness to act *in loco parentis*, one of the impermissibles of the post-1960s regime.

But the fact is that even Yale—and by extension, every other residential college or university in the United States—is engaged by default in a kind of moral formation of its students. It simply does not acknowledge it. It is not being candid with its students, their parents, or even itself about the formative effects it seeks. At bottom, that is because it has no serious vision of the good life that it wishes to impart.[3]

Let us concede that this is a diverse country—diverse in almost every imaginable moral, social, religious, and other respect. The transformation of the word "diversity" into an empty and often disingenuous slogan does not change that fact. Let us also concede, as I already have conceded, that Yale has a right to govern itself as it pleases. How then do we deal with the fact that any undergraduate educational institution worth its salt is, by its nature, bound to have a formative effect, without our first reaching some measure of consensus about what formative principles will be applied, and what formative objectives will be sought?

There are only two possible answers. Either we must seek to establish universally applicable standards for higher education. Or we must be willing to foster more genuinely diverse educational institutions. Either we can tailor our institutions in such a way that one size fits all. Or we can allow the free market and the free play of social invention to give rise to a variety of distinctive institutions that are highly diverse in their goals and clientele.

Of course, this is not entirely an either/or. We can and should have both kinds of institutions. That is perhaps the best diversity of all. And there are limits to the amount of diversity that any society can tolerate, which is another way of saying that there have to be some generally agreed-upon principles, however thin and general, that provide the groundwork for pluralism and diversity. But we should not fail to recognize the fact that one of the greatest strengths of American education at all levels is its astounding institutional diversity. No other country comes close to us in this respect. We have schools and colleges that are public, private, Roman Catholic, Jewish, Episcopal and other mainline Protestant, generically evangelical Protestant, sectarian, nonsectarian, single-sex, "historically" black, Native American, colleges specifically tailored for the underprivileged—the list goes on and on.

There is genuine peril that this diversity is being lost in the drive to standardize. *No task facing American education is more important than that of preserving and enriching its already existing institutional diversity.* That means that, for example, religious schools and colleges ought to be especially keen about intensifying their efforts to be distinctive, rather be all things to all people. Such an outcome represents American pluralism at its best, and would be infinitely preferable to the universal adoption of a lowest-common-denominator canon of universalized knowledge. Let the variety of opinions be robustly reflected by a competing variety of *distinctive* institutions— rather than striving to have them be reflected universally, but anemically, by a prescribed "diverse" perspective imposed uniformly upon *all* institutions.

It will be said that we need our schools to help foster a common culture in America. There is some truth to that. One would be more impressed by this claim if there were any evidence that the schools take seriously the old-fashioned idea that they are "educating for citizenship." But a central element in the common culture that we so greatly value is our commitment to freedom of conscience and freedom of association, a commitment that is nowhere more fully embodied than in our varied social institutions. Let there be cultural diversity—but let it be a diversity that encourages institutions to be genuinely different, rather than forcing them all to be "diverse" in precisely the same way.

There are plenty of examples of ways this principle has been violated. Take for example the sad history of the American Catholic colleges in the twentieth century. Burdened for so many years by the perception that they were an anti-intellectual product of the ghetto life, socially and intellectually inferior to the (Protestant) mainstream, Catholic colleges overcompensated, and, falling victim to what might be called "the Hesbergh syndrome," swiftly abandoned almost everything that made them Catholic in the search for mainstream respectability. Now, having achieved some (but not all) of what was sought, they find themselves entirely at sea, without a clear *raison d'être*, and under increasing pressure from Rome to recover their sense of Catholic identity. Such recovery will be exceedingly difficult, so long as these institutions are staffed by faculties who will permit such re-Catholicizing to occur only over their dead bodies. Sadly, many of the Catholic colleges sacrificed their birthright, without even receiving a full mess of pottage in return. It will take very long time, and probably the establishment of entirely new colleges, to reverse the situation—if it is even reversible.

Some the clearest and most prescient thinking on these matters has issued from the pen of David Riesman, the distinguished American sociologist and eminent scholar of American higher education. Riesman was a highly intelligent and consistent defender of academic diversity, long before the cause was a fashionable one; but the defense has always been a subtle one, highly attentive to the need to preserve *institutional* diversity, that is to say, diversity *among* institutions, as well as the diversity existing *within* a given institution. Riesman took up the cause of black colleges, religious colleges, and other educational variants, including boarding schools for inner-city black high-school students, and attempts to revive the Civilian Conservation Corps and other forms of national service. But his most interesting work dealt with the problems and prospects of single-sex educational institutions, especially colleges and universities, in contemporary America. And it is that particular focus of Riesman's work that I should like to focus on in the time that remains.

Throughout his long career, Riesman took a particular interest in the fate of such institutions, and the particular set of issues they must confront. Early in his career he was always a fierce and dogged defender of the then-endangered women's colleges, which were very nearly engulfed by the seemingly inexorable tide of coeducation. In later years, his interest expanded to include the diminishing number of all-male institutions, very much including the formerly all-male Virginia Military Institute and Citadel, for whose losing cause Riesman served as a supporting expert witness. He took a keen interest in tiny Deep Springs College, a highly experimental private school in Nevada which has been on the verge of abandoning of its all-male status, simply out of a growing sense that any school composed of an all-male student body, however small (there are only twenty-five students at Deep Springs) or self-consciously distinctive, must be violating fundamental principles of gender equity. This, despite the fact that Deep Springs is a highly isolated, intimate, extraordinarily demanding, all-consuming "total institution," in which students participate actively in the processes of institutional maintenance and governance—a highly unusual institution in which a single-sex student body would seem eminently justified, if not essential. Such pressures to standardize seemed increasingly objectionable and damaging to Riesman.

Interestingly, Riesman rarely recurred to reasons of institutional or cultural tradition as a sufficient reason for all-male colleges like VMI or Wabash or Hampden-Sydney to continue on as they have been. His arguments were not conservative ones, then, at least not in the usual sense of the word. But one thing his example suggests is that there may be a liberal argument, at least in the classical sense of "liberal," as well as a traditionalist one, for the perpetuation of single-sex institutions. Institutions are multivalent entities, attracting and absorbing many different energies and purposes; because they generally possess multiple constituencies, there are generally multiple reasons for seeking to perpetuate them. For Riesman, the heart of the question relating to single-sex schools is his evolving understanding of diversity in a society, of the value of such diversity, and of the ways one goes about achieving and sustaining it. Riesman's perspective suggests that an institution like Wabash or Hampden-Sydney may be contributing importantly to the healthy diversity of our society, in ways far beyond what it realizes, merely by staying what it is—that is, by staying different.

At the core of Riesman's outlook was the argument that, because we live in a time in which our understanding of the respective characteristics of men and women, and of the best ways to educate them, is in such flux, we need to preserve all the possibilities we can, for every kind of institution is a piece of the puzzle, a piece of evidence bearing upon the larger questions that face us. Standardization therefore is the great enemy of reform, because it closes off the range of possibility. And in an era in which the word "diversity" has become a buzzword of dubious clarity, Riesman's perspective may help us to recover and appreciate its true meaning and value.

Consider Riesman himself more closely for a moment, beginning with his authorship of *The Lonely Crowd*, published in 1950.[4] The work is one of the most famous and most widely read works of sociology ever written; but it is also a deceptively complicated and subtle book. For our purposes, it will be enough to say that it should be understood as part of an extensive literature of social criticism in the postwar era, which focused especially on the perceived problem of growing conformity in American culture. Writer after writer worried that Americans were being socialized within an inch of their lives, and losing the sturdy individuality that had made the national character distinctive. The rapid creation of a sprawling postwar suburbia, which evinced its own tendencies toward homogeneity and uniformity, was another source of anxiety. Books with titles like *White Collar, The Status Seekers, The Affluent*

Society, Growing Up Absurd, The Hidden Persuaders, The Organization Man, The Man in the Grey Flannel Suit, The Crack in the Picture Window— and so on—such books illustrated, in their very titles, some of the era's characteristic concerns. As the United States became a mass society, permeated by mass culture, mass politics, mass consumption, and massive institutions, the problem of homogeneity suddenly loomed very large indeed, as a present danger to the autonomy of the self. As Riesman observed, in the concluding words of *The Lonely Crowd*:

> while I have said many things in this book of which I am unsure, of one thing I am sure: the enormous potentialities for diversity in nature's bounty and men's capacity to differentiate their experience can become valued by the individual himself, so that he will not be tempted and coerced into adjustment. . . . The idea that men are created free and equal is both true and misleading: men are created different; they lose their social freedom and their individual autonomy in seeking to become like each other.[5]

Hence the preeminent importance for *The Lonely Crowd*, and for Riesman, of individual autonomy, one of the chief cornerstones of a liberal social and political order.[6] There was, in fact, very little in *The Lonely Crowd* about the role of institutions, and the prerequisites for social cohesion, in the formation and sustenance of the self. The emphasis went almost entirely the other way. In that sense, the broad interest in *The Lonely Crowd* perhaps drew upon some of the same sentiments that led some postwar thinkers to enthusiastically embrace neoclassical economics and libertarianism—the readers of a book like Friedrich Hayek's antisocialist work *The Road to Serfdom*, the psychological studies of Jung or Erikson, or even the novels and essays of Ayn Rand. Again and again, in a variety of intellectual contexts, one saw the theme of individual autonomy being sounded. It was virtually the leitmotiv of the age.

Yet there were other intellectual influences at work in Riesman's fertile mind. One of the chief of these, which serve in Riesman's case to blunt or counteract his liberal tendencies, was the influence of cultural anthropology. Early in his career, Riesman had come under the personal and intellectual influence of Margaret Mead, who was in turn one of the most distinguished and influential of the students of Franz Boas, the founder of cultural anthropology in the United States. Riesman was intrigued by the possibilities of cultural anthropology, which emphasized the degree to which every distinct culture or society has its own set of normative values and cohesive forces holding it together. By emphasizing the peculiar qualities of each individual culture, and its incommensurability with others, cultural anthropology tended to be antiuniversalistic, even relativistic, in its basic thrust, offering Riesman a perspective on culture that was potentially more radical—and also, in a sense, more conservative—than that of liberalism. Riesman's interest in cultural anthropology, as in other subjects, was in some ways "impure," since he placed its perspectives in competition with other, more normative values. Yet it was a resource he would increasingly fall back upon when moving into the study of higher education. A liberal concern for the preservation of autonomy, for individual self-realization and freedom of inquiry, was balanced by an almost anthropological appreciation for the diverse cultures and microcultures of American higher education.

By the end of the Fifties, Riesman had moved into the study of higher education as his principal "field," a decision from which he did not waver in the ensuing decades. But the interests that had animated his earlier work did not entirely disappear. Indeed, Riesman brought with him into the study of higher education many of those same concerns.[7] He saw higher education as a field of meritocracy, an engine of social mobility, energizing and enabling the liberal pursuit of selfimprovement and selfadvancement. The liberal sociologist in him still valued the ideal of individual autonomy. But the cultural anthropologist in him also brought an awareness that the self is formed in culture, and a growing sense that the strength of American higher education rested not only on its liberal features, as a vehicle of individual selfrealization and advancement, but also on the staggering diversity of kinds of institutions—a feature of American higher education that, as he repeatedly pointed out, made it absolutely unique in the world, and eminently worth preserving.

Linked to this was a growing awareness that, if colleges are to produce diverse individuals sufficiently resilient to withstand the forces of standardization at large in the country, such colleges might need to take a very different view of the formative institutions in that person's life. If a college is a culture, then it has to have certain principles of organization, principles of distinctiveness, in order to remain distinctive, and produce distinctive individuals that, in the larger mix of American society, will add to its diversity. In other words, because different institutions have different organizing principles, the preservation of genuine institutional diversity might entail a high degree of internal homogeneity within each institution—a degree of homogeneity that, in a larger public or political context, might seem undesirable, but which, taken in a strictly educational context, might have salutary results. In other words, to put it in a stronger way—every healthy institution needs to have principles of exclusion, as well as of inclusion. The distinction to be made here, then, is precisely the distinction between diversity of individuals and diversity of institutions; and the study of higher education convinced Riesman that the achievement of the former, of individual diversity, would be enhanced by the preservation of the latter, of institutional diversity.

Hence, Riesman's passionate devotion to the preservation of women's colleges, which became especially pronounced during the 1960s and 70s, when the country moved toward coeducation in a relentless, and to Riesman's way of thinking, mindless way. In retrospect, Riesman's defense of these institutions seems remarkably farsighted, as the virtues of single-sex instruction for women and girls—for *some* women and girls, that is, not all—have been rediscovered and reconfirmed by scores of educational researchers.[8] Yet he was equally devoted to the preservation of historically black colleges, of religious and denominational colleges, whether Catholic, Protestant, Jewish, or Mormon—and of men's colleges, where the research on relative advantages is virtually nonexistent.

Indeed, the lack of interest shown by educational researchers in investigating the potential advantages of single-sex education for men reflects what I have found to be the standard line on single-sex education today: that it is *sometimes* good for women, but *always* bad for men. Is it possible that Riesman will prove equally farsighted on the matter of all-male schools? We may never know, if none are left standing. For once the ones we now have are gone, it will be next to impossible to replace them.

In some respects, Riesman's position suggests a kinship with currently fashionable notions of multiculturalism. But, in fact, his recommendations would take us a good deal further down the road of diversity than does standardissue multiculturalism. For example, he long contended that it might be an interesting experiment to establish an explicitly Afrocentric college, in which young black nationalists would be able to study. Though many mainstream academics would find such a prospect worrisome, Riesman has argued that, given the size of the country, it would represent no great risk; and it might actually produce something highly valuable. It would, in any event, be a useful experiment. What he does not find particularly useful is the notion of setting up Afrocentric theme dorms or residential colleges at mainstream institutions like Cornell or Rutgers. This is the difference between, on the one hand, a freestanding institution with its own raison d'etre, cohesiveness, esprit de corps, and boundaries, and, on the other hand, a strictly oppositional force which sets itself up as an embattled party within a larger, avowedly pluralistic institution.

We are talking about the difference between, on the one hand, being a part of an institution that has a distinctive normative framework, or some particularist principle of selectivity, and whose appeal lies precisely in the presence of such things and on the other hand, an institution without any such framework or guiding principles, aside from certain procedural canons. There is a great difference between the "diversity" of large, inclusive institutions that are designed to be internally diverse, and that of small "exclusive" institutions that are designed to achieve a certain internal homogeneity, in order to better express and occupy a distinct ecological niche.

As the term "ecological niche" implies, Riesman's arguments for diversity drew increasingly upon ecological metaphors, such as notions of niche, habitat, and species, rather than equilibrist ones, such as the notion of countervailing forces. This use of organic metaphors is fraught with significance. For one thing, it implies that the truest source of diversity is the species—which is to say, the institution—rather than the individual. Riesman had been greatly influenced by the work of his Harvard colleague E. O. Wilson, who has championed the cause of biodiversity, praised diversity as a biological end in itself, and urged particular attention to the preservation of vanishing species, since they form an irreplaceable part of the accumulated genetic capital of the organic world.[9] No analogy is perfect, and Riesman would not want to tie individual humans to their institutions quite as rigidly as individual organisms are tied to their species. The point, however, is what best promotes genuine diversity. Individual diversity without institutional diversity becomes merely a prelude to a new uniformity—a "lonely crowd."

Could the same arguments being cited here be used to justify all-white colleges, as a contribution to diversity? And, following along on the same lines, to what extent are differences of gender to be regarded as comparable to differences of race? If the Virginia Military Institute had been permitted to continue its all-male enrollment policies, and to claim the state's Mary Baldwin College program as a "separate but equal" program in military instruction for women, would this be comparable to the restoration of *Plessy v. Ferguson*, the Supreme Court decision of over 100 years ago affirming the legitimacy of "separate but equal" facilities for whites and blacks?[10]

In Riesman's view, the prospect of all-white colleges, while it was a highly undesirable one that should be guarded against, did not represent the threat it did thirty years ago, not even in the South. The real question was to what extent questions of race and questions of gender should be regarded as part of the same continuum. Such questions clearly do not have a simple answer. The bootcamp environment of VMI and the Citadel, where all ascriptive status is removed at the outset, had proved extraordinarily liberating for black males, whose graduate rates at such institutions approach 70 percent—a record that few other institutions can match. Riesman worried that these institutional qualities would be undermined by the introduction of women—thus turning on its head the argument that all-male colleges are like all-white ones.[11]

Riesman also contended that the standard argument against VMI and Citadel, that they produce boorish and incivil pigs who are unable to cope with women, is simply not borne out by the facts, and has not been borne out by his own contact with these institutions and their graduates. Indeed, Riesman has argued that, for some men, an all-male environment is actually a better environment for them to develop the reflective sides of their nature than a coeducational institution, where the presence of the opposite sex—and the prospect of academic competition with the opposite sex—might prove inhibiting, thereby promoting the unreflective boorishness that, alas, one so often sees in coeducational institutions.

If this is true, then the reasons for preserving all-male institutions as an option for some men become exactly analogous to the argument for all-female institutions. Precisely because coeducation is now the universal standard—and this was not yet entirely the case, even as recently as the 1960s— it may be terribly important to preserve other examples, other ways of doing things, not only as a contribution to diversity, but as a hedge against an uncertain future.

We saw something of this happen with women's colleges, which were nearly swept away entirely by the enthusiasm for coeducation. On the verge of being eliminated altogether, they received new life from the second-wave feminism of writers like Carol Gilligan, who pointed out the advantages in educating girls and women separately from boys and men. [12] Such institutions gave girls and women opportunities for leadership they might not otherwise have had, even while showing greater respect for characteristically "feminine" qualities of mind and heart. Such institutions eliminated many of the distractions and dislocations associated with the presence of the opposite sex.

Such institutions are clearly not for everyone. But the proponents of the women's colleges now benefitted from the fact that sex-segregation took on a different meaning when it became optional; and now, the virtues of such institutions are more generally conceded. A genuinely diverse intellectual environment needs to leave room for them.

But there remains the argument that this advantage is entirely asymmetrical, that no such advantage could obtain for men—or, more insidiously, ought to be permitted to men. But now, with the Citadel and VMI cases, the basis for any gender-based schools is also called into question. The argument from affirmative action—that women's colleges are needed as remedies to past discrimination—may not be enough to preserve such schools much longer. With women's enrollment in the most prestigious law schools and medical schools running at roughly 50 percent, it will be increasingly hard for a college like Wellesley to justify itself on the grounds of women's putative exclusion from the academic mainstream. This is why Riesman argued, to no avail, that the advocates of women's colleges should have taken up the Citadel's and VMI's cause as their own, since a strictly legalistic standard of gender equity will hardly leave room for women's colleges either, if strictly enforced.

And indeed, what is at stake may well have deeper ramifications. For what is at stake is the ability of an institution not only to be genuinely *distinctive*, but to be genuinely *formative*—that is, to define itself in a distinctive way, and so organize itself as to sustain its ability to preserve and pass on its distinctiveness, and impart a distinctive stamp to its students. And that, argued Riesman, is the only real basis for diversity in American society—and hence, an indispensable basis for individual freedom. Consider once again the words with which Riesman ended *The Lonely Crowd*:

The idea that men are created free and equal is both true and misleading: men are created different; they lose their social freedom and their individual autonomy in seeking to become like each other.[13]

What is clearer to all of us today, more than a half-century after *The Lonely Crowd*, is the fact that genuine individuality, of the sort Riesman sought to sustain, could not be had without attention to the formative social and cultural contexts that support individuality and make it possible. Some of these contexts are, or can be, colleges and universities. Ultimately, all such contexts are expressions of moral community, shaped by the very principles of inclusion *and* exclusion that are the mark of any society that values the right of free association. Yes, we want diversity, but genuine diversity—institutional diversity—and not merely diversity for its own sake.

To do that, our institutions will need to recover the sense of authority and coherence to be shapers of student's souls. Of course, they *are* shapers in any event. Schoolcraft *is* soulcraft. But much of the shaping that goes on is inadvertent, thoughtless, and counterproductive. We need to be more deliberate and self-conscious about that task. Because we do not have a robust national consensus about the best way to do this, pluralism represents the best possible solution to the problem, since pluralism is content with a thinner national consensus, while it is committed to sustaining and protecting the right of institutions to organize themselves by their own lights. Thus a firm insistence on the preservation of institutional diversity can be seen as the single most valuable contribution to "relevance" that American education can make. That gives educational institutions the ability to pursue, with the greatest freedom and inventiveness, in an incremental and experimental way, their vision of the educational good. Which is precisely why Riesman argued that it is so important to protect and augment the institutional diversity that we already have.

NOTES

1. William Glaberson, "Five Orthodox Jews Spur Moral Debate Over Housing Rules at Yale," *New York Times*, September 7, 1997, accessed February 1, 2013, http://www.nytimes.com/1997/09/07/nyregion/five-orthodox-jews-spur-moral-debate-over-housing-rules-at-yale.html?pagewanted=all&src=pm.

2. *Hack v. President and Fellows of Yale College*, 237 F.3d 81 (2nd Cir. 2000).

3. See Nathan Harden's powerful book, *Sex and God at Yale: Porn, Political Correctness, and a Good Education Gone Bad* (New York: Thomas Dunne Books, 2012).

4. David Riesman, with Nathan Glazer and Reuel Denny, *The Lonely Crowd: A Study of the Changing American Character* (New Haven: Yale University Press, 1950).

5. Riesman, *The Lonely Crowd*, 307.

6. The following account of Riesman's life and work draws heavily on my book *The Masterless: Self and Society in Modern America* (Chapel Hill: University of North Carolina Press, 1994).

7. David Riesman, *Constraint and Variety in American Education* (Lincoln: University of Nebraska Press, 1958).

8. See the fine study by Andrea Hamilton, *A Vision for Girls: Gender, Education, and the Bryn Mawr School* (Baltimore: Johns Hopkins University Press, 2004).

9. Edward O. Wilson, *The Diversity of Life* (Cambridge: Harvard University Press, 2010).

10. Philippa Strum, *Women in the Barracks: The VMI Case and Equal Rights* (Lawrence: University Press of Kansas, 2004).

11. See my interview with Riesman in "The state of American higher education: A conversation with David Riesman," *Academic Questions* 8, Issue 1 (March 1995): 14.

12. Carol Gilligan, *In a Different Voice: Psychological Theory and Women's Development* (Cambridge: Harvard University Press, 1993).

13. Riesman, *The Lonely Crowd*, 307.

BIBLIOGRAPHY

Gilligan, Carol. *In a Different Voice: Psychological Theory and Women's Development.* Cambridge: Harvard University Press, 1993.

Glaberson, William. "Five Orthodox Jews Spur Moral Debate Over Housing Rules at Yale," *New York Times*, September 7, 1997. Accessed February 1, 2013. http://www.nytimes.com/1997/09/07/nyregion/five-orthodox-jews-spur-moral-debate-over-housing-rules-at-yale.html?pagewanted=all&src=pm.

Hack v. President and Fellows of Yale College, 237 F.3d 81 (2nd Cir. 2000).

Hamilton, Andrea. *A Vision for Girls: Gender, Education, and the Bryn Mawr School.* Baltimore: Johns Hopkins University Press, 2004.

Harden, Nathan. *Sex and God at Yale: Porn, Political Correctness, and a Good Education Gone Bad.* New York: Thomas Dunne Books, 2012.

McClay, Wilfred. *The Masterless: Self and Society in Modern America.* Chapel Hill: University of North Carolina Press, 1994.

——. "The state of American higher education: A conversation with David Riesman," *Academic Questions* 8, Issue 1 (March 1995): 14–32.

Riesman, David, Nathan Glazer, and Reuel Denny. *The Lonely Crowd: A Study of the Changing American Character.* New Haven: Yale University Press, 1950.

——. *Constraint and Variety in American Education.* Lincoln: University of Nebraska Press, 1958.

Strum, Philippa. *Women in the Barracks: The VMI Case and Equal Rights.* Lawrence: University Press of Kansas, 2004.

Wilson, Edward O. *The Diversity of Life.* Cambridge: Harvard University Press, 2010.

Index

About the Authors

Stephen Clements is associate professor of political science at Asbury University, where he directs the undergraduate political science program and also serves as Dean of the College of Arts and Sciences. Prior to joining the Asbury faculty in 2008, he served as Director of the University of Kentucky's Institute for Educational Research, Director of UK's EdD program in Community and Technical College Leadership, and as a graduate faculty member in the Department of Educational Policy Studies and Evaluation. Over the course of his career he has served as a Grant Program Manager for Kentucky's Education Professional Standards Board, conducted policy research projects on behalf of numerous organizations, and served as a Staff Assistant in the U.S. Department of Education in Washington, DC. His academic background is in Political Science (MA, PhD, University of Chicago), but he also studied Classical Languages at the graduate level (Vanderbilt University). He received a BA degree from Asbury in 1983, where he majored in history and minored in Greek. He and his wife Markie live just outside of Wilmore and have three grown sons and two daughters-in-law.

Jon M. Fennell is director of teacher education and dean of social sciences at Hillsdale College. He received his BA and MA from the University of California, Davis, before moving to the University of Illinois where he earned a PhD in philosophy of education. Prior to arriving at Hillsdale in 2005, Dr. Fennell spent four years in the Idaho State Department of Education and more than twenty years in the wholesale distribution, computer hardware, and ERP software industries. His teaching and research reflect a deep interest in philosophy, politics, and education and is frequently focused on the domain where the three disciplines overlap. Dr. Fennell has written on educational topics as well as on the thought of seminal thinkers ranging from

Rousseau and Dewey to Allan Bloom, Leo Strauss, Harry Jaffa, and Michael Polanyi. He is currently pursuing the intellectual connections between Polanyi and C. S. Lewis.

Michael Wayne Hail (PhD, Delaware) is professor of government in the School of Public Affairs at Morehead State University where he also serves as assistant dean and Director of the MPA and Government Graduate Programs. Dr. Hail also serves as Director of the Somerset, Kentucky IRAPP Office. He has published in several journals including *Publius: The Journal of Federalism, EURASIP: The Journal of Information Security, P.S. Political Science and Politics, The European Legacy: The Journal of the International Society for the Study of European Ideas*, and contributed to numerous books including the *Encyclopedia of the Constitution, Federalism In America*, and he is the author of "Bush's New Nationalism: The Life and Death of New Federalism." He is the co-editor with John Kincaid of *The Federalism Report* and Dr. Hail serves on the editorial board of *Publius: The Journal of Federalism* and *The Commonwealth Review of Political Science*. Dr. Hail is treasurer of the American Political Science Association, Organized Section One: Federalism and Intergovernmental Relations and Hail serves as treasurer and is past-president of the Kentucky Political Science Association. His research interests include federalism and intergovernmental relations, state and local government, American political thought, and Western political philosophy.

Jason R. Jividen is assistant professor of politics and fellow in civic and constitutional affairs at the Center for Political and Economic Thought, Saint Vincent College. He also serves as director of Saint Vincent's Aurelius Scholars Program in Western Civilization, an undergraduate core curriculum program dedicated to the Western intellectual tradition. He earned an MA in political science at Marshall University and PhD in political science at Northern Illinois University. His teaching and research interests include the history of political philosophy and American political thought and institutions. He is author of *Claiming Lincoln: Progressivism, Equality, and the Battle for Lincoln's Legacy in Presidential Rhetoric*.

James Scott Johnston is associate professor of philosophy and education, Faculty of Education, Queen's University, Kingston, Ontario, Canada. He has published recently in journals such as *Transactions of the Charles S. Pierce Society, Educational Theory, Educational Studies, Studies in Philosophy of Education*, and the *Journal of Philosophy of Education*. He has single-authored three books: *Inquiry and Education: John Dewey and the Quest for Democracy* (2006); *Regaining Consciousness: Self-Consciousness and Self-Cultivation from 1781–Present* (2008); *Deweyan Inquiry: from Educational Theory to Practice* (2009); and co-authored *Democracy and the Intersection* *of Religion and Tradition: the Reading of John Dewey's Understanding of Democracy and Education* (with R. Bruno-Jofre, G. Jover Olmeda, and D. Troehler) (2010).

Mark E. Jonas is associate professor of education at Wheaton College. He holds a PhD in philosophy and education (2009) from Teachers College, Columbia University, a MA in teaching (2002) from the University of Portland, and a BA in philosophy (1999) from the University of Chicago. His research interests are in the educational and political thought of Nietzsche, Plato, Rousseau, and Dewey. Some recent publications include: "Overcoming *Ressentiment*: Nietzsche's Education for an Aesthetic Aristocracy," *History of Political Thought*, (forthcoming); "Appetite, Reason, and Education in Socrates' 'City of Pigs,'" *Phronesis*, vol 57, no. 4 (2012), "Gratitude, *Ressentiment*, and Citizenship Education," *Studies in Philosophy and Education*, vol. 31, no. 1 (2012); "Dewey's Conception of Interest and its Significance for Teacher Education," *Educational Philosophy and Theory*, vol. 43, no. 2 (2011).

Wilfred M. McClay is G. T. and Libby Blankenship Chair in the History of Liberty at the University of Oklahhoma. He has taught at the University of ennessee at Chattanooga, Tulane University, Pepperdine University, the University of Rome, Georgetown University, and the University of Dallas. He is co-director of the Center for Reflective Citizenship at UTC, and also holds positions as a senior scholar at the Woodrow Wilson International Center for Scholars in Washington, DC, Senior Fellow at the Ethics and Public Policy Center in Washington, and Senior Fellow of the Trinity Forum. He served on the National Council on the Humanities, the advisory board for the National Endowment for the Humanities, from 2002 to 2013. His book *The Masterless: Self and Society in Modern America* won the 1995 Merle Curti Award of the Organization of American Historians for the best book in American intellectual history. Among his other books are *The Student's Guide to U.S. History* (ISI Books, 2001), *Religion Returns to the Public Square: Faith and Policy in America* (Woodrow Wilson Center/Johns Hopkins University Press, 2003), *Figures in the Carpet: Finding the Human Person in the American Past* (Eerdmans, 2007), and the forthcoming *Why Place Matters: Geography, Identity, and Public Life in Modern America* (2014).

Michael Schwarz is assistant professor of history at Ashland University, where he teaches in the Department of History and Political Science as well as the Master of Arts in American History and Government Program and also serves as a fellow of the Ashbrook Center for Public Affairs. He has published on Founding-era politics and foreign relations, including essays on Jefferson, Madison, and Hamilton in the *Journal of the Early Republic* and the *Wiley-Blackwell Companion to Madison and Monroe*. A forthcoming essay, "The Origins of Jeffersonian Nationalism," will appear in the *Journal of Southern History*. He recently was named Ashland University's outstanding male faculty member of the year for 2012. He lives in Ashland, Ohio, with his wife and fourteen-year-old beagle.

Timothy L. Simpson is associate professor of education at Morehead State University. He earned his BA in psychology and philosophy from Morehead State University, a MA in philosophy from Miami (OH) University, and a PhD in philosophy of education from the University of Illinois at Urbana/Champaign. He has written on figures such as Socrates and Plato, as well as on such topics as liberal education, political education, social foundations of education, and teacher quality in rural schools. He has published in *Educational Theory*, *Educational Studies*, *Critical Studies in Education*, and *Journal of Thought*. His most recent publications include, "Regional Stewardship and the Redefinition of Higher Education" *Philosophical Studies in Education* 41 (2010), 106–115 and with Jon M. Fennell, "Do No Harm: Leo Strauss and the Limits of Remedial Politics," in *Leo Strauss, Education, and Political Thought* (Madison, NJ: Farleigh Dickinson University Press, 2011).

Lee Trepanier is associate professor of political science at Saginaw Valley State University. He has authored and edited over a dozen books. His most recent publications include: *Political Symbols in Russian History*; *LDS in USA: Mormonism and the Making of American Culture* (with Lynita K. Newswander); *Citizens Without States* (with Khalil Habib); and *Eric Voegelin and the Continental Tradition* (with Steven F. McGuire).

Bryan R. Warnick is associate professor of philosophy of education in the School of Policy and Leadership at Ohio State University. He earned his PhD from the University of Illinois at Urbana-Champaign. His research focuses on questions related to philosophy of education, ethics of education, learning theory, and educational technology. He has published articles in *Harvard Educational Review, Teachers College Record, Educational Theory,* and many other venues. He has published two books: *Imitation and Education* (SUNY, 2008), and *Understanding Student Rights in Schools: Speech, Religion, and Privacy in Educational Settings* (Teachers College Press, 2012).

Bradley C. S. Watson is Professor and Chairman of the Department of Politics at Saint Vincent College, where he holds the Philip M. McKenna Chair in American and Western Political Thought. He is co-director of the college's Center for Political and Economic Thought, a research and public affairs institute dedicated to the scholarly exposition of freedom, Western civilization, and the American experience. He is also Senior Scholar at the

Intercollegiate Studies Institute and a fellow of the Claremont Institute. He has held visiting faculty appointments at Claremont McKenna College and Princeton University, where he was a visiting fellow in the James Madison Program in American Ideals and Institutions. He has authored or edited many books including *Living Constitution, Dying Faith: Progressivism and the New Science of Jurisprudence, Civil Rights and the Paradox of Liberal Democracy, Ourselves and Our Posterity: Essays in Constitutional Originalism, The West at War, Civic Education and Culture, Courts and the Culture Wars*, and *The Idea of the American University*. He has also published articles and essays in a variety of professional and general interest forums, including *Armed Forces and Society, Claremont Review of Books, The Intercollegiate Review, Modern Age, National Review*, and *Perspectives on Political Science*.

Wayne Willis a professor of foundations of education at Morehead State University in Kentucky, where he has served since 1988. He is co-author of two books, *Philosophical and Psychological Foundations of Moral Education and Development* (with Dan Fasko) and *Motivation, Engagement and Educational Performance: International Perspectives on the Context of Learning* (with Julian Elliott et al.) and wrote and illustrated a children's book entitled *This Is How We Became a Family*. He has also written and presented on a variety of topics including ancient philosophy of education, theology and education, and technology and education. He earned his PhD in the historical, philosophical, and social foundations of education at the University of Oklahoma, an MA in Theological Studies/New Testament at Wheaton College, and an MA in studio art at Morehead State. Dr. Willis has served in a variety of administrative positions at Morehead State University, including department chair, assistant dean, and interim dean.